# Consequences of Enlightenment

What is the relationship between contemporary intellectual culture and the European Enlightenment it claims to reject? In *Consequences of Enlightenment*, Anthony J. Cascardi revisits the arguments advanced in Horkheimer and Adorno's seminal work *Dialectic of Enlightenment*. Cascardi argues against the view that postmodern culture has rejected Enlightenment beliefs and explores instead the continuities contemporary theory shares with Kant's theory of judgment. The positive consequences of Kant's failed ambition to bring the project of Enlightenment to completion, he argues, are evident in the aesthetic basis on which subjectivity has survived in the contemporary world. Cascardi explores the link between aesthetics and politics in thinkers as diverse as Habermas, Derrida, Arendt, Nietzsche, Hegel, and Wittgenstein in order to reverse the tendency to see works of art simply in terms of the worldly practices among which they are situated. Works of art, he argues, are themselves capable of disclosing truth. The book explores the post-Enlightenment implications of Kant's claim that feeling, and not only cognition, may provide a ground for knowledge.

ANTHONY J. CASCARDI is Richard and Rhoda Goldman Distinguished Professor in the Humanities at the University of California, Berkeley, where he teaches in the Departments of Comparative Literature, Rhetoric, and Spanish. He is co-editor of the Literature, Culture, Theory series, and author of *The Subject of Modernity*, among numerous other books and articles.

# Literature, Culture, Theory 30

*General editors*

ANTHONY J. CASCARDI, *University of California, Berkeley*

RICHARD MACKSEY, *The Johns Hopkins University*

*Selected series titles*

Theorizing textual subjects: agency and oppression
MEILI STEELE

Chronoschisms: time, narrative, and postmodernism
URSULA HEISE

Cinema, theory, and political responsibility
PATRICK MCGEE

The practice of theory: rhetoric, knowledge, and pedagogy in the Academy
MICHAEL BERNARD-DONALS

Renegotiating ethics in literature, philosophy and theory
*edited by* JANE ADAMSON, RICHARD FREADMAN *and* DAVID PARKER

# Consequences of Enlightenment

ANTHONY J. CASCARDI

CAMBRIDGE
UNIVERSITY PRESS

PUBLISHED BY THE PRESS SYNDICATE OF THE UNIVERSITY OF CAMBRIDGE
The Pitt Building, Trumpington Street, Cambridge CB2 1RP, United Kingdom

CAMBRIDGE UNIVERSITY PRESS
The Edinburgh Building, Cambridge CB2 2RU, United Kingdom
http://www.cup.cam.ac.uk
40 West 20th Street, New York, NY 10011-4211, USA
http://www.cup.org
10 Stamford Road, Oakleigh, Melbourne 3166, Australia

© Cambridge University Press 1999

First published 1999

Printed in the United Kingdom at the University Press, Cambridge

Typeset in Palatino 10/12.5 pt. [VN]

*A catalogue record for this book is available from the British Library*

*Library of Congress cataloguing in publication data*
Cascardi, Anthony J., 1953–
Consequences of Enlightenment / Anthony J. Cascardi.
p.   cm. – (Literature, culture, theory ; 30)
Includes bibliographical references and index.
ISBN 0 521 48149 x. – ISBN 0 521 48490 1 (pbk.)
1. Aesthetics – Political aspects.   2. Aesthetics, Modern – 20th century.
3. Enlightenment.   4. Horkheimer, Max, 1895–1973.
Philosophische Fragmente.   I. Title.   II. Series.
BH301.P64C37   1998
190—dc21        98–21467–CIP

ISBN 0 521 48149 x hardback
ISBN 0 521 48490 1 paperback

# Contents

vii

# Acknowledgments

I am grateful to publishers for permission to include revised versions of material originally published in article form: to the University of Minnesota Press for "Communication and Transformation: Aesthetics and Politics in Habermas and Arendt," parts of which appeared in *Hannah Arendt and the Meaning of Politics*, ed. Craig Calhoun and John McGowan (Minneapolis, 1997); and to Duke University Press for "The Difficulty of Art," an earlier version of which appeared in *Thinking Through Art*, a special issue of *Boundary 2*, ed. Alan Singer (Durham, NC, 1998). To my editor at Cambridge, Ray Ryan, and to my co-editor in the "Literature, Culture, Theory" series, Dick Macksey, go special thanks for their confidence in a project that has been all too long in the making.

The book is dedicated to my family, who have watched it grow along the way: to Elisa, to Matthew, and to Trish.

# 1

❖❖❖❖❖❖❖❖❖❖❖❖❖❖❖❖❖❖❖❖❖❖❖❖❖❖❖❖❖❖❖❖❖❖❖❖❖❖❖❖❖❖❖❖

# The consequences of Enlightenment

❖❖❖❖❖❖❖❖❖❖❖❖❖❖❖❖❖❖❖❖❖❖❖❖❖❖❖❖❖❖❖❖❖❖❖❖❖❖❖❖❖❖❖❖

There has always existed in the world, and there will always continue to
exist, some kind of metaphysics.                          Immanuel Kant [1]

Philosophy, which once seemed obsolete, lives on because the moment to
realize it was missed. The summary judgment that it had merely interpreted the world, that resignation in the face of reality had crippled it in
itself, becomes a defeatism of reason after the attempt to change the
world miscarried . . . Having broken its pledge to be as one with reality or
at the point of realization, philosophy is obliged ruthlessly to criticize
itself.                                                  Theodor Adorno [2]

We have art – lest we perish of the truth.            Friedrich Nietzsche [3]

The present volume represents an attempt to reassess the relationship between certain issues in contemporary critical theory
and the question of Enlightenment. I take my bearings by reference to claims about the self-canceling nature of Enlightenment
rationality as formulated in the opening essay of Max Horkheimer and Theodor Adorno's *Dialectic of Enlightenment* ("The
Concept of Enlightenment"), and move conceptually from there
to address the ways in which their concerns can be reevaluated
in light of an aesthetic critique modeled along lines sketched out

[1] Immanuel Kant, *Critique of Pure Reason*, trans. Norman Kemp Smith (New York:
St. Martin's Press, 1965), B xxxi.
[2] Theodor Adorno, *Negative Dialectics*, trans. E. B. Ashton (New York: Seabury
Press, 1979), p. 3.
[3] Friedrich Nietzsche, *The Will to Power*, ed. Walter Kaufmann, trans. Walter
Kaufmann and R. J. Hollingdale (New York: Vintage, 1968), sec. 435.

in Kant's *Critique of Judgment*. More broadly, I hope to account for the predominantly "aesthetic" forms in which a critical self-consciousness carried forward from the Enlightenment has survived the critique of enlightened reason that seemed to have reached an impasse in Horkheimer and Adorno's essay. I place the term "aesthetics" in quotes so as to indicate its incomplete and problematic association with what we regard as autonomous works of art.[4] When Nietzsche wrote the words cited in the epigraph above, when he claimed even more notoriously that "art is worth more than the truth – for life," and when in *The Birth of Tragedy* and subsequent texts he said that the existence of the world could be justified only aesthetically – it was not only particular artworks that he had in mind, but a project designed to reclaim the world of appearances from what he thought of as the Platonic foundations of the Enlightenment.[5] But so too Kant's theory of aesthetic judgment is independent of the specificity of works of

[4] Theodor Adorno: "The autonomy of art is not something given *a priori*, but is the result of a process that is constitutive of the concept of art." *Aesthetic Theory*, ed. Gretel Adorno and Rolf Tiedemann, trans. C. Lenhardt (New York: Routledge and Kegan Paul, 1984), p. 26 (henceforth cited as *AT*). Cf. Michel Foucault, whose remarks indicate a clear discontent with the restriction of the category of the "aesthetic" to works of art: "What strikes me is the fact that in our society, art has become something which is related only to objects and not to individuals, or to life. But couldn't everyone's life become a work of art? Why should the lamp or the house be an art object, but not our life?" ("On the Genealogy of Ethics: An Overview of Work in Progress," in Hubert Dreyfus and Paul Rabinow, eds., *Michel Foucault: Beyond Structuralism and Hermeneutics* [Chicago: University of Chicago Press, 1983], p. 236). At some level, the source for this discontent is Nietzsche's claim that art is worth more than the truth for life.

[5] What Friedrich Nietzsche called "perspective" was essential to this project. In his view, Platonism (and Christianity) means "standing truth on her head and denying perspective, the basic condition of all life." *Beyond Good and Evil*, trans. Walter Kaufmann (New York: Vintage Books, 1989), p. 2. Martin Heidegger takes up Nietzsche's claim about art in *Nietzsche, 1: The Will to Power as Art*, trans. David Farrell Krell (New York and San Francisco: Harper and Row, 1979), pp. 140–41. Heidegger's remarks on the "new interpretation of sensuousness" (pp. 211–20) are also of help. At the same time, Heidegger insists that Nietzsche had not arrived at a sufficient understanding of the nature of "truth" to warrant the position he holds. For his part, Heidegger argues that the decisive shift in Plato's thought came with the application of the word *eidos* to the world of forms: "We, late born, are no longer in a position to appreciate the significance of Plato's daring to use the word *eidos* for that which in everything and in each particular thing endures as present. For *eidos*, in the common speech, meant the outward aspect [*Ansicht*] that a visible thing offers to the physical eye. Plato exacts of this word, however, something utterly extraordinary: that it name what precisely is not and never will be perceivable with physical eyes." "The Question Concerning Technology," in *The Question Concerning Technology and Other Essays*, trans. William Lovitt (New York: Harper and Row, 1979), p. 20.

fine art.[6] As Jacques Derrida remarks in speaking of Kant,[7] "art" is a misleading title for what lies at stake in the question of aesthetic reflection, which seeks instead to validate the "subjective" moment – the moment of affect, of pleasure or pain – that goes unaccounted by the conceptual frameworks associated with cognition and morality.

In contrast to most contemporary theory, which is interested in subsuming artworks under a series of worldly discourses, my interest is in discovering the ways in which aesthetics is itself the forgotten discourse of the world. It is forgotten, I suggest, to the degree that our confidence in the validity of affective modes of apprehension has been weakened. If I begin with Horkheimer and Adorno, this is because their work is representative of a particularly influential interpretation of the Enlightenment and its consequences as a pervasive disenchantment or world-loss. Although "The Concept of Enlightenment" was originally published in 1947, the principal questions broached in it remain central for critical thinking today.[8] (In an essay entitled "What is Critique?"

---

[6] Kant: "Taste is . . . merely a critical, not a productive faculty; and what conforms to it is not, merely on that account, a work of fine art. It may belong to useful and mechanical art, or even to science, as a product following definite rules which are capable of being learned and which must be closely followed." *Critique of Judgment* (henceforth, *CJ*), trans. James Creed Meredith (Oxford: Clarendon Press, 1986), sec. 48, p. 175. Heidegger remarks that the *Critique of Judgment* has been influential "only on the basis of misunderstandings." *Nietzsche, 1: The Will to Power as Art*, p. 108.

[7] Jacques Derrida writes that "a seminar would treat of art . . . It would thus answer to a program and to one of its great questions. These questions are all taken from a determinate set. Determined according to history and system. The history would be that of the philosophy within which the history of the philosophy of art would be marked off, insofar as it treats of art and the history of art: its models, its concepts, its problems have not fallen from the skies, they have been constituted according to determinate modes at determinate moments." "Parergon," in *The Truth in Painting*, trans. Geoff Bennington and Ian McLeod (Chicago: University of Chicago Press, 1987), p. 18. Behind Derrida's resistance to the objective determination of art stands Heidegger. In the Epilogue to "The Origin of the Work of Art," Heidegger writes that "almost from the time when specialized thinking about art and the artist began, this thought was called aesthetic. Aesthetics takes the work of art as an object, the object of *aisthesis*, of sensuous apprehension in the wide sense. Today we call this apprehension experience . . . Yet perhaps experience is the element in which art dies. The dying occurs so slowly that it takes a few centuries." "The Origin of the Work of Art," in *Poetry, Language, Thought*, trans. Albert Hofstadter (New York: Harper and Row, 1971), p. 79.

[8] For one understanding of the case for Adorno against poststructuralist theory and criticism, see Fredric Jameson, *Late Marxism: Adorno, or, the Persistence of the Dialectic* (London: Verso, 1990), especially pp. 227–52, "Adorno in the Post-

---

3

for instance, Michel Foucault argues that the problem of *Aufklärung* remains the central problem of modern philosophy, the part of our cultural history from which we cannot clear free.[9]) Indeed, it could be said that Horkheimer and Adorno's essay has cast a long shadow over contemporary intellectual debates about the autonomy of the subject as an independent center of feeling and value, as well as about the social and political orders that this notion of subjectivity founds. Horkheimer and Adorno gave a very powerful description of the self-negating tendencies at work in the particular forms of self-reflection that came to dominance during the modern Enlightenment. They suggested that the emancipated society promised by the procedures of Enlightenment – reason's democratic hope – failed to defend the possibility of reciprocal recognition among subject-selves against the ongoing threats of rationalization, reification, and domination. In spite of the Enlightenment's efforts, or on Horkheimer and Adorno's account, because of them, the progressive goals of the Enlightenment remained unrealized: "In the most general sense of progressive thought, the Enlightenment has always aimed at liberating men from fear and establishing their sovereignty. Yet the fully enlightened earth radiates disaster triumphant."[10] For these and related reasons it has been thought, at least since Romanti-

modern." Seyla Benhabib sets the issue against a somewhat broader background: "In their critique of modernity and liberalism, communitarians and postmodernists unwittingly echo many of the themes of the first generation of Frankfurt School thinkers and especially of Adorno and Horkheimer in *Dialectic of Enlightenment*. The uncovering of the darker side of the liberal ideals of economic growth and scientific progress, the memory of non-instrumental human relations, and even the critique of the repressive subjectivity which is always thought to accompany the domination of nature are among the themes, by now well known, of this work." See Benhabib, *Situating the Self: Gender, Community, and Postmodernism in Contemporary Ethics* (New York: Routledge, 1992), pp. 69–70.

9 Michel Foucault writes: "I would like right away to note, in approaching this problem which makes us brothers with the Frankfurt School, that to make *Aufklärung* the central question at once means a number of things." "What Is Critique?" in James Schmidt, ed., *What Is Enlightenment?: Eighteenth-Century Answers and Twentieth-Century Questions* (Berkeley: University of California Press, 1996), p. 391. Foucault's essay was originally given as a lecture at the Sorbonne in 1978. On the hidden importance of aesthetics to Foucault's earlier work, see Peter Bürger, "The Return of Analogy: Aesthetics as Vanishing Point in Michel Foucault's in *The Order of Things*," *The Decline of Modernism*, trans. Nicholas Walker (University Park: Pennsylvania State University Press, 1992), pp. 48–54.

10 "The Concept of Enlightenment," in *Dialectic of Enlightenment* (New York: Continuum, 1972), p. 3.

cism, that any continuation of the ethical and emancipatory goals of the Enlightenment, and certainly any project committed to an ethical praxis grounded in mutual recognition and respect, must overcome Enlightenment rationality.[11]

This volume appeals to Kant's *Critique of Judgment* in order to suggest that we cannot so clearly position ourselves on either side of the debate concerning the Enlightenment and its consequences. As I hope will become clear over the course of what follows, the question of our relationship to the Enlightenment is better understood in terms of the difficulty of locating any position that would be categorically inside or outside the Enlightenment, inside or outside objectivity, inside or outside critical or systematic thought. Our current position is itself a consequence of the non-closure of the Enlightenment. Similarly, this volume represents an effort to challenge the view that the pursuit of constructive social and ethical goals requires an anti-Enlightenment stance. But it proposes to do so without summoning us to return to Enlightenment rationality, either in its orthodox, transcendental versions or in the more recent "communicative" variant endorsed by Jürgen Habermas. These challenges are entered on several grounds, all of which share in their underlying orientations a notion of subjectivity that is based on principles that can broadly be called "aesthetic." The first of these is that many of the concerns of contemporary intellectual culture, including, but by no means limited to, the preoccupations of Frankfurt School critical theory, of Franco-American poststructuralism, and of the neo-pragmatist language philosophies fashioned from elements of Wittgenstein, Dewey, and Heidegger, can themselves be seen as the consequences and continuations of a process of self-criticism that originates within the Enlightenment, rather than as cancellations of Enlightenment

[11] The connections between Romanticism and the critique of the Enlightenment have been made from a variety of different directions in recent criticism. Two of the most fruitful instances are Stanley Cavell, *In Quest of the Ordinary: Lines of Skepticism and Romanticism* (Chicago: University of Chicago Press, 1988), and Jean-Luc Nancy and Philippe Lacoue-Labarthe, *L'absolu littéraire: Théorie de la littérature du romantisme allemand* (Paris: Seuil, 1978), trans. Philip Barnard and Cheryl Lester as *The Literary Absolute: The Theory of Literature in German Romanticism* (New York: State University of New York Press, 1988). Whereas Cavell thinks of Romanticism as a response to Kant, Nancy and Lacoue-Labarthe stress the links between Kant's aesthetic theory and Romanticism, saying that "an entirely new and unforeseeable relation between aesthetics and philosophy" articulated in Kant makes possible the "passage" to Romanticism (*The Literary Absolute*, p. 29).

thought. Calls either for a "return" to the principles of the Enlightenment or for their rejection thus represent significant self-misunderstandings on the part of some of the most critical of the inhabitants of the present age.

In connection with this first claim, my task will be to spell out how the Enlightenment can be understood as having such "consequences," principally by articulating the ways in which the Enlightenment project as formulated by Kant was structurally incomplete. Kant's articulation of the problem of aesthetic judgment, which stems from a reflection upon the separation of the spheres of cognition and morality, represents an effort to reconcile the terms that his own system of critical philosophy had set apart; but in discovering that there was no point beyond the system from which to reflect upon it, this was also the point at which the Kantian critical system encountered the impossibility of achieving closure. Kant's admitted inability to arrive at a proof of the theory of aesthetic reflection, and thereby to complete the system of critical philosophy, can help account for what has remained uninterpreted in the relationship between the fundamental ambitions of Enlightenment rationality and those subsequent modes of thought that claim either to have turned away from Enlightenment rationality altogether or that urge a return to its principles. If we can understand Enlightenment rationality as something whose central ambition to be at once systematic and complete was left unfinished, then it can be argued that the lingering controversy over the Enlightenment itself represents a moment in the ongoing transformation of self-consciousness, but also a continuation of subjectivity even if by other, aesthetic, means. At the very least, this can help us refute what may be left of the idea that we have – for better or worse – reached the "end of philosophy," the "closure of metaphysics," or the "end of history."[12]

To be sure, the rapid succession of "unmaskings" that has characterized critical engagements of Enlightenment thought can tempt us to short-circuit the process of reflection. Consider the fact that each in a line of prominent thinkers – each one prematurely believing himself to be the last – seems to have been

---

[12] These notions originate as consequences of Hegel's thought. They have been explored in, among other places, Francis Fukuyama's *The End of History and the Last Man* (New York: The Free Press, 1992).

complicit with the metaphysical project that each proclaimed to have rejected. Nietzsche, for instance, rejected the Hegelian concept of the rational whole in favor of an aesthetic critique of reason that offered "art" as a way to redeem the world of appearances. But in spite of his commitment to the appearing world (or perhaps because of that commitment), Nietzsche remained a Hegelian, bound also to the idea of the closure of history to the extent that he accepted the principles of his own "eternal return of the same." In fact, Nietzsche's "eternal return" has been seen by Paul de Man as a rearticulation of the figure of prolepsis that de Man finds at work in the Hegelian philosophy of reflection.[13] On Heidegger's account, by contrast, Nietzsche was merely an "inverted Platonist"; Nietzsche's notion of "will to power" still remained within the framework of Western metaphysics. But Derrida has in turn marked Heidegger himself as operating within this framework. Having caught a glimpse of just how ineluctable this problem has been, Richard Rorty has subsequently suggested that we simply circumvent Western metaphysics and dispense with the project of "overcoming" altogether.[14] Rorty addresses the heroic efforts of his predecessors to overcome the past by recommending irony as an alternative to the "sublime" desire for a final overcoming. In Rorty's account, the philosopher of the historical sublime yearns for "a future which has broken all

[13] In "Sign and Symbol in Hegel's *Aesthetics*," Paul de Man reads Hegel's notion of the re-collection of experience through reflection as an instance in which thought projects the hypothesis of its own possibility into a future under the expectation that the process enabling thought will eventually meet up with the projection. *Critical Inquiry*, 8 (1982).

[14] Richard Rorty, "Deconstruction and Circumvention," in *Essays on Heidegger and Others, Philosophical Papers Volume 2* (Cambridge: Cambridge University Press, 1991), pp. 85–106. Cf. Stuart Hampshire, who has written "one cannot pass by a situation; one must pass *through* it in one way or another." "Logic and Appreciation," in William Elton, ed., *Aesthetics and Language* (Oxford: Blackwell, 1954), pp. 162–63. As Michael Fried has nonetheless argued, Hampshire's distinction between "logic" and "appreciation" fails to hold for modernist works of art – which is to say, for precisely the kind of works that I would link with the reflective criticism generated by Kant's third *Critique*. "Once a painter who accepts the basic premises of modernism becomes aware of a particular problem thrown up by the art of the recent past, his action is no longer gratuitous but imposed. He may be mistaken in his assessment of the situation. But as long as he believes such a problem exists and is important, he is confronted by a situation he cannot pass by, but must, in some way or other, pass through; and the result of this forced passage will be his art." Fried, *Three American Painters* (Cambridge, MA: The Fogg Museum of Harvard University, 1965), p. 9.

relations with the past, and therefore can be linked to the philosopher's redescriptions of the past only by negation." As he goes
on to say, "this quest for the historical sublime – for proximity to
some event such as the closing of the gap between subject and
object or the advent of the superman or the end of metaphysics –
leads Hegel, Nietzsche, and Heidegger to fancy themselves in the
role of the 'last philosopher.' The attempt to be in this position is
the attempt to write something which will make it impossible for
one to be redescribed except in one's own terms – make it impossible to become an element in anyone else's beautiful pattern, one
more little thing."[15]

As this passage suggests, Rorty's account of the history of
philosophy is told with an irony that prompts one to ask whether
it can itself be distinguished from cynicism. Already Hegel identified something like cynicism as a possible consequence of the
process by which enlightened thought seeks to correct itself: "To
see that thought in its very nature is dialectical, and that, as
understanding, it must fall into contradiction – the negative of
itself – will form one of the main lessons of logic. When thought
grows hopeless of ever achieving, by its own means, the solution
of the contradiction which it has by its own action brought upon
itself, it turns back to those solutions of the question with which
the mind had learned to pacify itself in some of its other modes
and forms. Unfortunately, however, the retreat of thought has led
it, as Plato noticed even in his time, to a very uncalled-for hatred
of reason (misology)."[16] More recently, the successive unmasking
of theories has impelled some critics to regard cynicism as the
most powerful antidote to the Enlightenment desire for a further
or final unmasking. As Peter Sloterdijk remarked on the occasion
of the 200th anniversary of Kant's *Critique of Pure Reason*, the cynic
attempts to deflect the possibility of any further disenchantment
by claiming that disenchantment is itself the truth of the Enlightenment. The conclusion to be drawn from the history of the
Enlightenment is that "new values have short lives . . . Just bide
your time . . . Our lethargic modernity certainly knows how to
'think historically,' but it has long doubted that it lives in a

---

[15] Rorty, *Contingency, Irony, and Solidarity* (Cambridge: Cambridge University
Press, 1989), pp. 105–06.
[16] *Hegel's Logic*, trans. William Wallace (Oxford: Oxford University Press, 1975),
pp. 15–16.

meaningful history."[17] The unhappiness that accompanies these doubts is thus mollified by the awareness that history can never be brought to an end; the baleful consciousness of reflection is mitigated by the cynic's joyful wisdom. As Sloterdijk argues, the figure of thought best suited to describe these conditions is Nietzsche's "eternal recurrence of the same" (*ibid.*). This is, for the cynic, the principle that can transform unhappiness and even resentment into "joyful knowledge."[18]

But how and why attach the name "aesthetics" to a position that, in its discovery of the non-closure of the Enlightenment, stands in such close proximity to what many would characterize as nihilism?[19] The germ of a response can be identified in Kant's third *Critique*, where Kant describes as "aesthetic" those judgments that take their bearings by the subject's particular pleasure and/or pain and that refuse to yield the knowledge of any "thing." In an effort to find a way of thinking that does not subordinate particulars to

---

[17] Peter Sloterdijk, *Critique of Cynical Reason*, trans. Michael Eldred (Minneapolis: University of Minnesota Press, 1987), p. xxvii. As Sloterdijk also observes (p. 40), the figure of the "eternal return" contains in a nutshell the psychoanalytic insight into the "truth" of the logic of unmasking: what I criticize in others is what I myself am. In Nietzsche's terms, it is the "Romantic" artist who is able to draw creative strength from dissatisfaction with himself. *Will to Power*, sec. 844, p. 445.

[18] Nietzsche's "eternal return" and Slavoj Žižek's analysis of retroactive performativity provide alternatives to the vision according to which the project of critical reflection eventually cancels itself or becomes exhausted when confronted by the apparent endlessness of its task. Rather than see, e.g., Derrida's work as reverting back to the metaphysics from which he attempted to clear free, we can instead read Kant's analysis of reflective judgment as exposing the very difficulties that are essential to deconstruction's understanding of indeterminacy. So seen, the philosophical past can never be "overcome" (much less "circumvented"), if only because the assertive posture demanded by "overcoming" presupposes a self-consistency that can never be assured. But by the same logic of fate we could say that the Enlightenment quest for absolute knowledge is ironically fulfilled by the very failure of that project. As Žižek writes of Hegel, "*the true Absolute is nothing but the logical disposition of its previous failed attempts to conceive the Absolute.*" Žižek, *For They Know Not What They Do: Enjoyment as a Political Factor* (London: Verso, 1991), p. 100. Žižek goes on to say, the *Phenomenology of Spirit* is "the presentation of a series of aborted attempts by the subject to define the Absolute and thus arrive at the longed-for synchronism of subject and object. This is why its final outcome ('absolute knowledge') does not bring a finally founded harmony but rather entails a kind of reflective inversion" (p. 99).

[19] While Kant is often regarded as standing at the origin of modern aesthetic theory, it should be recognized that he has important predecessors in these matters, including Baumgarten, Wolff, Hume, and even Gracián.

universal categories, Kant's theory of reflective judgment begins from the affects. Aesthetic reflection originates in "pleasure" and "pain," which are not so much positively constructed experiences as ways in which the subject responds to the contingency of the world.[20] Indeed, the description of affect as something other than a positively constructed and determinable experience that the subject "has" suggests that pleasure and pain are moments of passion, something the subject undergoes. Recall Horkheimer and Adorno's analysis of pleasure as originating in the separation of individuals, which is to say, in loss. Pleasure, they suggest, begins in sacrifice to another.[21] The point is not that "pleasure" and "pain" need to be situated within a network of overlapping frameworks – social, cultural, and historical – but rather that there always remains something that these frameworks cannot adequately determine. As we shall see in connection with Kant, this is a "something" that may be described in terms of the qualitative dimension of our relationship to the representations formed in making cognitive and moral judgments.[22]

To think of affect in this way allows us to see a closer link between Kant's theory of aesthetic reflection and postmodern positions that are often thought of as standing in opposition to Kant. For Jean-Luc Nancy (whose links to Kant are mediated by Heidegger) for instance, the "something" that cannot be captured by the determinative reasoning of cognitive and moral judgments points to the subject's openness to whatever may happen to it from outside. Affect indicates a form of passivity, a mode in which the subject is capable of being affected from without: "Pass-

[20] Heidegger offers a succinct account of the genealogy of "experience" in "The Origin of the Work of Art," beginning with a clarification of the relationship between beauty and form: "The beautiful does not lie in form, but only because the *forma* once took its light from Being as the isness of what is. Being at that time made its advent as *eidos*. The *idea* fits itself into the *morphe*. The *sunolon*, the unitary whole of *morphe* and *hule*, namely the *ergon*, is in the manner of *energeia*. This mode of presence becomes the *actualitas* of the *ens activa*. The *actualitas* becomes reality. Reality becomes objectivity. Objectivity becomes experience" (p. 81). On Adorno's engagement with the issue of "experience" in *Aesthetic Theory*, see Jameson, *Late Marxism*, pp. 127 ff.

[21] As such, pleasure is distinctively non-natural: "Nature does not feature enjoyment as such; natural pleasure does not go beyond the appeasement of need. All pleasure is social – in unsublimated no less than in sublimated emotions. It originates in alienation." *Dialectic of Enlightenment*, p. 105.

[22] The best discussion of qualities remains that of Charles Altieri in *Act and Quality* (Amherst: University of Massachusetts Press, 1981).

ivity 'is' in fact only that: the fact that something happens to it, from somewhere else, from the other. The fact that some difference happens to it. Passivity is not the property of being passive – of, for example, letting such or such a mark be given or imprinted. Passivity does nothing, not even in the mode of 'doing' that would be letting something be done. More 'passive' than what is called passivity, the soul is itself only in that it is affected from outside. Its 'passivity' is given to it with the affection. Its passivity does not come first, like a property of soft wax. The soul *is* affected . . . "[23] As for Derrida, the affects of "pleasure" and "pain" indicate the openness, vulnerability, or dislocation of the subject by pointing to the "*constitutive* outside" on which any structure depends. The indeterminacy of the domain that Kant couches in affect thus becomes the basis for a conception of the subject as a site of loss or dispossession rather than for the recuperation of a positive relationship to the world. The affects are not subjective analogues of the lost order of nature, as is the case in certain versions of Romanticism (to which Kant's *Critique of Judgment* has itself been linked). Rather, as for thinkers like Derrida and Nancy, the affects provide an opening for an ethical determination of the subject – ethical because determined by a responsibility to the other: "Almost nothing remains (to me): neither the thing, nor its existence, nor mine, neither the pure object nor the pure subject, no interest of anything that is in anything that is . . . I do not like, but I take pleasure in what does not interest me, in something of which it is at least a matter of indifference whether I like it or not . . . And yet *there is* pleasure, some still remains; *there is, es gibt, it gives* the pleasure is what *it gives*; to nobody but some remains and it's the best, the purest" (Derrida, "Parergon," p. 48). [24]

My second set of claims is related to the first and argues that in responding to the Enlightenment many critics have tended to homogenize and flatten the object of their critical attention, thus only magnifying the monster of abstraction they are seeking to tame. Thinkers notably less subtle than Horkheimer and Adorno

---

[23] Nancy, *The Birth to Presence* (Stanford, CA: Stanford University Press, 1993), p. 29.
[24] Once again anticipating the concerns of postmodern critical theory, Adorno takes the procedures of negative dialectics as having as their goal a turn toward non-identity whose ethical aim is a "total self-relinquishment" that yields an almost Levinasian openness toward the other. *Negative Dialectics*, p. 13.

have been especially prone to imagine that the cultural paradigm they are attempting to address is a monolithic formation, homogeneously constituted, and devoid of any significant internal differentiations. To be sure, the great conceptual leaps of "The Concept of Enlightenment," which link everything from thinking with numbers in Plato's last writings to the "repressive equality" of modern democratic culture lend themselves to this interpretation. But I would challenge any such reductive reading of the central thesis of "The Concept of Enlightenment" first, by arguing that such an interpretation is not sufficiently sensitive to what Horkheimer and Adorno meant in their analysis of the entwinement of Enlightenment and myth and, second, by arguing that such a thesis at best represents a truncated interpretation of the dialectic of self-consciousness at stake in the question of Enlightenment.

So that my own invocation of the term "Enlightenment" will not have this effect, I propose to mark the principle of differentiation as an integral moment of the critical Enlightenment project, and to recognize that such a principle is itself constitutive of the Enlightenment understanding of reason, not merely congruous with it.[25] As is best exemplified in the work of Kant, Enlightenment rationality stakes its claims to truth on the basis of the *systematic* limitation of reason's different powers with respect to the various spheres or domains of knowledge.[26] As a paradigmatic example of systematic thought, I refer to the Kantian effort to distinguish and delimit the cognitive and moral spheres over which reason has jurisdiction, in order to establish "fact" as separate from "value" and to preserve a realm of absolute value or moral freedom not constrained by the contingencies of any fact. First, Kant wishes to secure the validity of cognitive claims by establishing their independence from desire and the will. This

[25] In Sloterdijk's view, differentiation eventually breaks down: "Critique does not have a unified bearer but rather is splintered into a multitude of schools, factions, currents, avant-gardes. Basically, there is no unified and unambiguous enlightenment 'movement.' One feature of the dialectic of enlightenment is that it was never able to build a massive front; rather, early on, it developed, so to speak, into its own opponent" (*Critique of Cynical Reason*, pp. 76–77).

[26] In "The Age of the World Picture" Heidegger explains "system" in terms of the essential standing-together characteristic of the picture-thinking of the modern age; Heidegger locates systematic thought in opposition to an interest in the particularities of experience (*empeiria*). Heidegger, "The Age of the World Picture," p. 141.

means that what we claim to know (as fact) should be independent of what we might want or desire to be true. Second, Kant wishes to preserve a realm of moral freedom that would not be constrained by the contingencies of fact: we should, for instance, credit an action as moral only when it is done out of a sense of obligation to the moral law (duty), and not when it comes about by merely fortuitous means. In this same regard, I would note Kant's philosophical adjudication of the "contest of the faculties" of the University proposed in the *Streit der Facultäten*, where Kant justifies the systematic division of teaching faculties on the basis of its resemblance to the rational Idea and not according to any internal principle.

Not surprisingly, the Kantian notion that knowledge claims can be legitimized only insofar as they are articulated within a duly constituted object-sphere drives a contemporary thinker like Habermas to suspect that an aesthetic critique of reason may result in the "de-differentiation" of these autonomous spheres and, consequently, in a collapse of the powers of reason. Horkheimer and Adorno themselves recognized that differentiation is a way to reduce fear: "Everything unknown and alien is primary and undifferentiated: that which transcends the confines of experience; whatever in things is more than their previously known reality" ("The Concept of Enlightenment," p. 15). But, as we shall see over the course of what follows, the Habermassian attempt to defeat the specter of "de-differentiation" through a theory of communicative action is based upon a fundamental misreading of Kant's third *Critique*. Specifically, Habermas treats Kant's notion of the *sensus communis aestheticus* as if it were the *sensus communis logicus*, thus presupposing that the conflict of the faculties can be adjudicated by reference to an order of "reason" rather than an order of "sense."

Rather than accept Kant's (or any other) systematic division of the rational faculties as self-contained or self-justifying, as something that can be verified as categorically valid or *a priori* true, I would call attention to the legislative force that must divide reason into these separate domains. In Kant, this legislative force attempts to isolate our cognitive understanding of nature (as theorized in the first *Critique*) from the work of practical reason or morality (theorized in the second *Critique*). Aesthetic judgment is called into play as Kant attempts to reflect upon and thereby justify the principle of differentiation that divides the two in the third *Critique* when Kant discovers that pleasure and pain cannot be accommodated within it.[27] (It is in the project to re- mark this difference that Kant's *Critique of Judgment* stands closest to Hegel's philosophical expressivism.[28]) In the "Preface" to the first edition of the *Critique of Judgment* Kant speaks of a critique "which sifts these faculties one and all, so as to try the possible claims of each of the other faculties to share in the clear possession of knowledge from roots of its own" (*CJ*, p. 3). And in the "Introduction" he claims that "in the division of a rational science the difference between objects that require different principles for their cognition is the difference on which everything turns" (*CJ*, p. 9).[29]

---

[27] The detailed argument is contained in the first section of the "Introduction" to the *Critique of Judgment*, entitled "Division of Philosophy" (pp. 8–10). There Kant speaks of the distinction between the "concept of nature" and the "concept of freedom." In technical terms, the issue is whether the concept of the will (which, Kant argues, acts as one among the many causes in the world) gets its rule by a concept of nature or a concept of freedom. In other words, Kant needs to know whether the principles of the will are "technically practical" or "morally practical."

[28] For a recent commentary on the logic of the "re-mark," see Žižek, *For They Know Not What They Do*, pp. 72–84.

[29] Thus Jürgen Habermas dutifully records the fact that "Kant's *Critique of Judgment*... provided an entry for a speculative Idealism that could not rest content with the Kantian differentiations between understanding and sense, freedom and necessity, mind and nature." *The Philosophical Discourse of Modernity*, trans. Frederick Lawrence (Cambridge, MA: MIT Press, 1987), p. 48. But in saying that Kant "perceived in precisely these distinctions expressions of the dichotomies inherent in modern life-conditions" Habermas unwittingly attributes to Kant a view that is more accurately Schiller's in the "Letters on the Aesthetic Education of Man." When Habermas writes that "the mediating power of reflective judgment served Schelling and Hegel as the bridge to an intellectual intuition that was to assure itself of absolute identity" (*ibid.*), he correctly notices that the Hegelian dialectic may be seen as a carrying forward of some of the central problems outlined in Kant's third *Critique*; but he misses the central point of Hegel's own critique of "absolute identity," which is emphatic in the *Phenomenology of Spirit*. Hegel writes that "Dealing with something from the perspective of the Absolute (for which we may now read 'Being') consists merely in declaring that, although one has been speaking of it just now as something definite, yet in the Absolute, the A = A, there is nothing of the kind, for there all is one. To pit this single insight, that in the Absolute everything is the same, against the full body of articulated cognition, which at least seeks and demands such fulfillment, is to palm off its Absolute as the night in which, as the saying goes, all cows are black – this is cognition naively reduced to vacuity. The formalism which recent philosophy denounces and despises, only to see it reappear in its midst, will not vanish from Science, however much its inadequacy may be recognized and felt, till the cognizing of absolute actuality has become entirely clear as to its own nature." *Phenomenology of Spirit*, trans. A. V. Miller (Oxford: Oxford University Press, 1981), par. 16, p. 9.

14

In the arguments that have been advanced by a range of thinkers from Schiller to Weber and Habermas, the discourse of aesthetics and the problem of reflective judgment could only come to light in an environment that embeds these differentiations socially and materially. The best-known consequence of this differentiation is the autonomization of art as a purely aesthetic phenomenon. In Heidegger's essay on "The Age of the World Picture," the aestheticization of art is marked as a definitive feature of the differentiated landscape of enlightened modernity. As we shall see later, it is the phenomenon of differentiation that ties the theory of aesthetic judgment to that of intersubjective communication, whose aim is to reestablish the links among the various spheres that Enlightenment reason sets apart. In the Romantic tradition, which Habermas, following Hegel, identifies with Schiller's "Letters on the Aesthetic Education of Man," it is the more ambitious task of aesthetics to reinscribe value within fact and thereby to endow a disenchanted empirical world with the powers of self-animating spirit. To be sure, there is a (re)conciliatory desire traceable directly to Kant's third *Critique*, as evidenced in his commitment to the communicability of aesthetic judgment and to the unity of experience. As Adorno takes pains to argue in the posthumous *Aesthetic Theory*, each of the spheres that Kant needs to recognize as separate and distinct preserves a trace of its significant relation to the others from which it is cut off, if only as a way of recalling (or, perhaps, in the Kantian sense, imaginatively reconstructing) the unity of experience that has been carved up into separate realms. But even for Kant the unity of experience can only be felt in pleasure, or its loss registered in pain, never proved to the satisfaction of reason or the understanding. Indeed, the failure of the Kantian effort to offer a rational proof of the unity of cognition (nature) and morality (freedom) is a driving force in the third *Critique*, where the specific difficulty involved in the exposition of the theory of reflective aesthetic judgment serves as evidence of the final impossibility of a rational apprehension of the integration of cognition and morality. In spite of Kant's wish to identify the role of reflective aesthetic judgment with the functions of recuperation and repair with respect to the Enlightenment division of fact (nature) and value (freedom) articulated in the first two *Critiques*, and in spite also of Kant's effort to position aesthetics in such a way as to seal the integrity of the critical system as a whole, thus reuniting our understanding of nature as a "disenchanted" realm of cause and effect with the demand to acknowledge others as ends in themselves, existing in a "kingdom of ends," the problem of the aesthetic or reflective judgment as formulated in the third *Critique* is more accurately seen as the frustration of Kant's reintegrative project, and Kant's position is best understood in accordance with the claims articulated in the "Preface" cited above, which promises a clear statement of the "difficulty" of the aesthetic judgment, rather than a resolution of it.[30] For Kant, the "difficulty" of aesthetic judgment is meant to excuse the absence of a suitably clear proof of the principles on which it rests:[31] "to supply a determinate objective principle of taste in accordance with which its judgments might be derived, tested, and proved, is an absolute impossibility," Kant writes, "for then it would not be a judgment of taste. The subjective principle – that is to say, the indeterminate idea of the supersensible within us – can only be indicated as the unique key to the riddle of this faculty, itself concealed from us in its sources; and there is no means of making it any more intelligible" (*CJ*, sec. 57, pp. 208–09). The subjective principle of "reflective judgment" is the "unhappy consciousness" of the Enlightenment, however, only insofar as reason expects to apprehend the world by means of "determinate concepts."

In connection with my reevaluation of the Horkheimer–Adorno theorem, my third and perhaps most difficult task will be to determine how the process of subjective self-reflection has con-

[30] This is the thesis of Howard Caygill's *Art of Judgment* (Oxford: Blackwell, 1989). As Caygill has argued, however, the aporia of aesthetic judgment is the point of departure for Kant's third *Critique*, not its solution, as contemporary critical theory has tended to presuppose. See also Caygill, "Post-modernism and Judgement," *Economy and Society*, 17 (February 1988), 1–20.

[31] As Kant says, his hope is that "the difficulty of unraveling a problem so involved in its nature may serve as an excuse for a certain amount of hardly avoidable obscurity in its solution, provided that the accuracy of our statement of the principle is proved with all requisite clearness" (*CJ*, Introduction, pp. 6–7). I take up this issue in greater detail in chapter 2. In the *Anthropology*, Kant admits that some readers may admire a certain degree of mystery, but even there it remains clear that reason's inclination is for the kind of clarity and distinctness that Descartes associated with the truth. See Kant, *Anthropology from a Pragmatic Point of View*, trans. Victor Lyle Dowdell (Carbondale: Southern Illinois University Press, 1978), p. 21.

tinued beyond the logical point at which Horkheimer and Adorno believed it was destined to cease. As we will see in detail beginning in chapter 2, the principle of reflective judgment models a form of reason that, strictly speaking, does not proceed according to concepts. Instead, it begins from a process of reflection on those relations that resist, escape, or are otherwise lost to conceptual thought, including the so-called "primary" aesthetic experiences of pleasure and pain. For Kant, pleasure and pain are what our conceptual cognitive and moral structures fail to accommodate. Specifically, the *Critique of Judgment* takes its point of departure in the specific element in subjectivity that is "incapable of becoming an element of cognition," which Kant describes as the feeling that accompanies and qualifies our relationship to cognitive and moral representations. To argue that the experiences of pleasure and pain escape conceptual thinking is not to suggest that one cannot have thoughts about or make statements about pleasurable or painful experiences (although, particularly in the case of pain, such thoughts are notoriously difficult to put into words).[32] Rather it suggests that the immediacy of pleasure and pain is lost with any attempt to represent them discursively. For Derrida in *The Truth in Painting*, what Kant describes as pleasure is not an "experience" at all. It is more like the residue (*reste*) of our attempt to conceptualize experience, and it is its residual or remaindered quality that, in Derrida's interpretation of Kant, incites us to discourse on the beautiful: "it is this remainder which causes talk, since it is, once again, primarily a question of *discourse* on the beautiful, of discursivity *in* the structure of the beautiful and not only of a discourse supposed to happen accidentally *to* the beautiful."[33] Similarly, it is a particular configuration of pain, very closely associated with the loss of our proximity to nature, that incites us to discourse on the sublime. In Kant, the pleasure and the pain that escape cognition provide special access to human purposiveness. Pleasure and pain lie at the basis of everything that is potentially ethical about the beautiful and the sublime – even if what Kant thinks of as the corporeal basis of ethics must

---

[32] Elaine Scarry gives a remarkable account of the resistance of pain to discourse in *The Body in Pain* (New York: Oxford University Press, 1985).

[33] Regarding the "immediacy" of pleasure, it is true that Kant says that "the beautiful pleases immediately" *Critique of Judgment*, sec. 59, p. 224; but he qualifies that claim to say that this occurs "only in reflective intuition."

ultimately be placed under judgment and transformed in order for its ethical force to be revealed.[34]

Consistent with what I think are the concerns at play in Kant's third *Critique*, I take the question of aesthetic reflection to originate not in any inherent disposition of the subject but rather in an awareness of our vexed relationship to all that is invoked in the name of "nature," or in social terms, the "natural praxis of life," the specifically problematical nature of which was formulated for philosophy by the skeptical tradition to which Kant's attempt at a critical philosophy was already a response. And I take Kant's response in turn to have been decisively shaped by his prior notion of the sovereignty of critical reason, which organizes the separation of fact (epistemology) from value (ethics), and both of these from reflective aesthetic judgment, which we bring to bear in the claims we make about the beautiful and the sublime. But at the same time I would argue that the contemporary critical response to the question of Enlightenment points in the direction of a reflective or "aesthetic" critique of reason as a way of acknowledging the survival of the subject beyond the point at which Horkheimer and Adorno envisioned its demise.

These claims are substantially less puzzling than it might at first seem because even in Kant the aesthetic is not just one sphere among others equal to it. When Habermas speaks of aesthetics as equivalent to the sphere of "symbolic" reason, he misses the fundamental point about the indeterminacy of the aesthetic in Kant. Indeed, Kant's own discussion of the "symbolic" relationship between beauty and morality in section 59 of the third *Critique* emphasizes the difficulty of grounding that link in any direct intuition of a concept. Misled perhaps by Schiller's "Letters on the Aesthetic Education of Man" and by Weber's thesis of the "separation of the spheres" of modern culture, Habermas takes the term "aesthetics" as coextensive with the socially constituted field of autonomous art. Better, I would argue, to insist with Kant upon aesthetics as the place in which a process of reflection on what is lost or divided by the operations of the first two critiques is begun. To be sure, it may well be Kant's *wish* for aesthetics to reconcile the separate realms of nature and ethical freedom. Similarly, the

[34] Regarding "transformation" as the work of ethics, see Geoff Harpham, *Getting it Right* (Chicago: University of Chicago Press, 1992), especially ch. 3, "From Conversion to Analysis."

desire of reflective judgment may be to advance a "higher" critique of reason by deducing the principle according to which the various faculties are divided from one another and their proper territories secured. But what Kant in fact concludes is that the derivation of this "higher" principle of judgment remains opaque: we know it must exist, we may remember or presuppose it to exist, but we cannot demonstrate to the satisfaction of reason that it does in fact exist. Kant thus admits that aesthetics offers a sign of the *impossibility* of conjoining the worlds of nature and of ethical freedom and explicitly states that "it is not possible to throw a bridge from the one realm to the other" (*CJ*, Introduction, p. 37). Beauty remains a "symbol" of morality, which is to say that morality is something that beauty can at best figure.

For Derrida, the failure of aesthetics to bridge the gulf separating Kant's two worlds is also its success in revealing the abyss that is created by any effort to delimit a position that is stably inside or outside a given structure. It is in terms of this "parergonal" form that Derrida refashions the Kantian notion of a "critique." But as I shall argue in chapters 4 and 5, the "failure" of aesthetics to bridge fact and value has social and political implications beyond what any of these thinkers may have recognized. For it is in terms of the particular "difficulty" of aesthetic judgment that we can see how artworks call forth claims of taste that refer to the ideal of a *sensus communis*, the underlying principle of which cannot be derived in theoretical terms, but must be either remembered or presupposed as a condition of judgment. The difficulty inherent in deriving the principle of aesthetic judgment suggests that we are challenged to make binding claims that would preserve and validate the particularity of subjective experience over against the universal categories to which reason in its cognitive operations would otherwise subsume such experience, all the while recognizing that the validity of those claims would have to count on the existence of a community which it is also their purpose to (re)create.

In these and other ways, the determinations we make when confronted with examples of the beautiful and the sublime can provide a model for the kind of critique that goes beyond the aims of cognition or practical reason in order to focus on the subject's affective response to its non-necessary, purely contingent relation to the natural world. Following Adorno's analysis in *Aesthetic Theory*, these claims can be reconciled with the role of certain artworks in modern society because (great) art alone among the socially differentiated spheres of Enlightened modernity – the cognitive, the practical, and the aesthetic – suffers the effects of that differentiation and invites us to reflect upon it as an objective and irrefutable fact. In what may be regarded as Derrida's complementary stance on this point, this is because art is the place in which we discover an "uneconomic" loss, in which what is lost is never fully amortized: if art involves work, this is because art is the place in which the work of mourning never ends.[35] Adorno's argument is that while "rational cognition can subsume suffering under concepts" nonetheless "it can never express suffering in the medium of experience, for to do so would be irrational by reason's own standards. Therefore, even when it is understood, suffering remains mute and inconsequential . . . What recommends itself, then, is the idea that art may be the only remaining medium of truth in an age of incomprehensible terror and suffering."[36] It may accordingly be argued that any attempt to disown our inheritance of that suffering – either by the purely subjective aestheticization of art, as Adorno sees happening in the privileging of aesthetic "immediacy" by figure "A" of Kierkegaard's *Either/Or*,[37] or by subordinating art to the structures of the more "worldly" discourses of history, society, ethics, or politics (as so often occurs in literary applications of critical theory today)[38] – suppresses the awareness of that suffering and avoids the very problem that gives rise to it. In *Negative Dialectics*, for instance, Adorno argues that suffering is the condition of truth. This claim must be interpreted in light of the assertion later made in the *Aesthetic Theory*, that "the enigma of works of art is their having been broken off" (p. 184). In Adorno's view, it is the fate of artworks in the modern age to have to refuse the conditions of wholeness whose ethical ideals they would also like us to remember, and which we must

[35] For instance, Derrida writes in "Economimesis": "It is in poetry that the work of mourning, transforming hetero-affection into auto-affection, produces the maximum of disinterested pleasure," *Diacritics*, 2, 2 (1981), 18. Similar remarks can be found in *The Truth in Painting*.    [36] *AT*, p. 27.

[37] See Adorno, *Kierkegaard: Construction of the Aesthetic*, trans. Robert Hullot-Kentor (Minneapolis: University of Minnesota Press, 1989). See also Heidegger's struggle to break free from Romanticism in "The Origin of the Work of Art."

[38] Cf. J. Hillis Miller, *The Ethics of Reading* (New York: Columbia University Press, 1987). See also Derrida's comment in *The Truth in Painting* regarding art criticism as a struggle between history and philosophy, in which history seems naturally superior but is not necessarily so.

also presuppose. Artworks transmit the memory of what it was like to be whole while at the same time resisting the knowledge of what they remember to be true. Artworks bear the trace of aura, the sensuous "this," the presence of the past, the whole embodied in the particular. And, on Adorno's account, their burden is to convey that memory in a tangible form.

## What is Enlightenment?

Before proceeding further to develop the notion of an aesthetic critique, some clarification is in order regarding the status of the potentially vague and troubling term "Enlightenment," noting at the outset the peculiar status of this term (*Aufklärung*) in the title of Horkheimer and Adorno's essay as both the designation of an historical epoch and as the description of a conceptual paradigm. While the issues I am concerned with are specific to the modern European Enlightenment and its aftermath, Horkheimer and Adorno's critique of the instrumentalization of reason says nothing about whether what lies at stake in the question of Enlightenment is itself historical or theoretical. Is the critical project outlined by Horkheimer and Adorno in the opening essay of *Dialectic of Enlightenment* to be understood as part of an historical analysis of the modern world, or is the critique they initiate meant to address something fundamental in the nature of reason itself? In methodological terms, is "The Concept of Enlightenment" to be regarded as a work of speculative philosophy or is it a work of historical sociology? Is it to be thought of as the statement of a theory valid always and everywhere, true for all human consciousness, or is it to be taken as an analysis of social formations specific to a certain culture at a determinate time and place? What status – historical or theoretical, contingent and context-specific or universal – is to be attributed to the concept of "Enlightenment"?

On the one hand, Horkheimer and Adorno recognize that the self-conscious subject stands for something more qualitative and specific than any conceptual position or construct can articulate normatively or in the abstract. Moreover, the problems of reification and rationalization demand accounting in historical terms. But Horkheimer and Adorno also see that any analysis of the structure of self-consciousness in terms of an empiricist understanding of history would constitute a negation of the possibility of self-reflection by relegating consciousness to one of Kant's two worlds at the expense of the other. Insofar as the subject is self-conscious, it amounts to something more than an historical positivity to be explained in purely causal terms; as critical theory from Kant and Hegel to Habermas has recognized, the self-conscious subject seeks a stance beyond history from which to reflect upon experience. But at the same time, and with equal force, Horkheimer and Adorno see that a critique of subjectivity that makes no reference to the historical processes through which subjects are constituted can itself only be abstract. This is the dilemma revealed in their seemingly anomalous use of the term "enlightenment": no position for such historico-theoretical reflection can be found, yet such a position must be found.

In the work of Horkheimer and Adorno the concept of "Enlightenment" betrays a struggle both to describe a fundamental structure of reason and to characterize the historical practices that, in modernity, have led to rationalization and reification. But the essay can only negotiate these demands dissonantly and ironically rather than categorically or synthetically. "Enlightenment" is a term that in their hands works consistently against itself, routinely dislocating its own historical and theoretical powers to the point where it becomes less a concept in its own right than the mechanism for unseating the conceptual relations such a term conventionally calls into play. Because of a resistance to theory that would urge an understanding of "Enlightenment" in historical terms, and because of a resistance to a positivist account of history that would embrace a conceptual paradigm they cannot accept, the concept of "Enlightenment" at work in Horkheimer and Adorno's essay marks the site of an impasse at this stage in the development of critical theory.

The antinomy of history and theory can be dealt with, if not resolved, through the resources of reflective judgment that Kant develops in the third *Critique*. Not surprisingly, though, "The Concept of Enlightenment" does not itself articulate a way around this impasse. The essay takes only a glancing look at the emergence of autonomous art in relation to the rise to dominance of cognition-only knowledge, which it theorizes in terms of what C. P. Snow called the problem of the "two cultures."[39] It pauses

[39] C. P. Snow, *The Two Cultures and the Scientific Revolution* (Cambridge: Cambridge University Press, 1959).

only briefly to take up Walter Benjamin's analysis of art in the rationalized world in terms of the loss of art's originary quality or "aura." Moreover, the essay makes no explicit reference to the problem of reflective judgment outlined in Kant's third *Critique*. Rather, Horkheimer and Adorno's essay shuttles back and forth between the historical and the theoretical meanings of the term "Enlightenment." The desire to sustain a critique of the Enlightenment requires Horkheimer and Adorno to think simultaneously on two levels: not only socially and historically, but categorically and "transcendentally" as well. It compels them to find a way of addressing the nature of enlightened reason that would respect the specificity of the modern Enlightenment as an historical phenomenon, while simultaneously advancing a critical comprehension of the history in question.[40] Accordingly, the essay must be read on two distinct levels in order to be understood.

On the historical level, their notion of "Enlightenment" eschews the Weberian analysis of social differentiation in favor of Marx's critique of "equivalence," which finds its most important articulation in the first chapter of *Capital*.[41] Horkheimer and Adorno argue that what Marx identifies as the logic of equivalence began with the substitution of signs and tokens for things, within the context of myth; this process of substitution gradually produced the much larger problems of abstraction and universal mediation characteristic of modern, capitalist cultures. Under the conditions of commodity capitalism a set of formal equivalences

[40] Jay M. Bernstein explains this demand in the following terms: "If history matters to philosophy then philosophical forms are also historical forms and events bound up with other historical events; but they are not just historical forms and events since, if they are of philosophical significance in some sense continuous with what philosophy has been, then they 'inform' the events surrounding them in a categorical way. In brief, we appear to require a philosophy of history, where the (teleological) movement of that history takes up the burden of the work previously accomplished through transcendental legislation by providing categorial orientation for the concrete items under review. Yet, finally, such a philosophy of history would not be the full response to the analysis of Kant since on its own it would repeat, and make worse, the suppression of judgment the analysis sought to demonstrate . . . and further, it would contravene the concluding thesis that the transcendental conditions for the possibility of knowing are not fully exponible." *The Fate of Art* (University Park: Pennsylvania State University Press, 1992), p. 67. What Bernstein does not sufficiently explain is that, especially for Adorno, art came to indicate the possibility of a position that is both internal to and critical of social production.

[41] See Jameson, *Late Marxism*, pp. 148–49, on this issue in relation to Horkheimer and Adorno.

came to stand in place of the qualitative relationships of particular subjects to one another and to the products of their labor. Similarly, Horkheimer and Adorno suggest that the Enlightenment's understanding of subjective self-consciousness as standing in opposition to a world of objects defines subjectivity in terms of a system of formal equivalences. In a more contemporary idiom, one might say that the process of modern subject-formation involves subjection, the submission to compulsory norms.

On the theoretical level, by contrast, "The Concept of Enlightenment" can and must be read as an analysis and critique of the structure or *logos* of "Enlightenment" as such. On this plane, the essay aspires to what has since come to be known as a critique of "Western metaphysics," except that Horkheimer and Adorno recognize no particular need to limit their claims to the cultures of the West. At the theoretical level, they argue not just that the Enlightenment is an embodiment of the self-canceling ideals of bourgeois, democratic culture. Indeed, the essay's own lingering and somewhat desperate emancipatory hopes might even be seen as the sign of an affinity with those relatively naive elements in bourgeois culture that regard change as possible on the basis of thought alone.[42] More devastatingly, perhaps, the essay suggests that enlightened reason is subject to the fundamental form of dialectical contradiction that had been posited by Hegel as inherent to all forms of consciousness – according to which reason is both itself and something other than, opposed to, itself. But whereas Hegel's understanding of the nature of subjective self-consciousness hinges on the transformation of every prior moment of consciousness into some higher or more complex form, Horkheimer and Adorno suggest that self-consciousness is finally canceled by the return of whatever was left behind in the process of its gradual emergence from nature. The later essays in *Dialectic of Enlightenment* argue that the freedom of self-consciousness is negated by the return of the fundamentally brutal passions and instincts of an internal nature that is unable to hide its constitutive fear or to conceal its interest in self-preservation.[43] The negativity

---

[42] See *ibid.* and Stanley Fish's critique of Roberto Unger in "Unger and Milton," in *Doing What Comes Naturally: Change, Rhetoric, and the Practice of Theory in Literary and Legal Studies* (Durham, NC: Duke University Press, 1989), pp. 399–435.

[43] For Habermas, this process extends to encompass Horkheimer and Adorno's critical reflections themselves. See Habermas, *The Philosophical Discourse of Modernity*.

of desire that fuels Hegel's dialectic – but which in Hegel moves considerably beyond self-preservation – is thus set to work against all that is purified in the Hegelian march toward Wisdom. Hence Horkheimer and Adorno describe a process of reflection that uncovers the image of domination in freedom, that finds reification in every act of reason, and that reveals the Enlightenment's hidden complicity with "myth." They argue that "myth is already enlightenment; and enlightenment reverts to mythology" (Introduction to *Dialectic of Enlightenment*, p. xvi). Since Horkheimer and Adorno regard Enlightenment rationality as reluctant to recognize its implication in a dialectical process of any sort whatsoever, they find themselves obliged to point out that reason is subject throughout history to a process wherein it appears to assume an absolute and omnipotent stance over and against its objects, only to collapse into new forms of the very conditions it had set out to overcome:[44] "mythology itself set off the unending process of enlightenment in which ever and again, with the inevitability of necessity, every specific theoretic view succumbs to the destructive criticism that it is only a belief" ("Concept of Enlightenment," p. 11). Hence the essay's affinities with cynical reason.

But this critique of "Enlightenment" is not a dead end. At the very least it calls into question the ways in which the historical Enlightenment has represented itself. Often it has been remarked that the modern Enlightenment was committed to understanding itself as having overcome history, as having achieved a definitive distance from all constraints inherited from the past. In the view of thinkers like Descartes and Kant, the modern Enlightenment was not the *expression* of anything at all – and certainly not the expression of anything fundamentally contingent, particular, or historical – but was the necessary result of reason's self-authorizing acts. As Kant claims in the essay "What Is Enlightenment?" the basis of the Enlightenment – its prerequisite – is the freedom of rational self-assertion; its only obstacles are cowardice, laziness, or the public limitation of this freedom. So seen, the Enlightenment is a consequence not just of reason but of the rational will. Indeed, well before Kant, Descartes had argued that the freedom of the will reveals a fundamental likeness between human beings and God:

[44] See the very apt formulation of this question by James Bradley in his essay "Frankfurt Views," *Radical Philosophy*, 13 (Spring 1975), 39–40.

"It is only the will, or freedom of choice, which I experience within me to be so great that the idea of any greater faculty is beyond my grasp; so much that it is above all in virtue of the will that I understand myself to bear in some way the image and likeness of God. For although God's will is incomparably greater than mine . . . nevertheless it does not seem any greater than mine when considered as will in the essential and strict sense."[45]

As Hans Blumenberg and other intellectual historians have pointed out, the Enlightenment effort to overcome history was not without substantial contradiction. First, the characterization of that which precedes the Enlightenment as a period of darkness or ignorance marked by superstitions and uncritical beliefs (the "dogmatism," "skepticism," and "intolerance" that Kant describes in the Preface to the first edition of the *Critique of Pure Reason*) fails to acknowledge the historical validity of the beliefs and practices of the "pre-Enlightenment" world.[46] But insofar as the Enlightenment recognizes that it cannot overcome history, it has recourse to the notion of progress, in which reason's "new beginning" is referred to as the originating point of a continuously ascending line. In the second edition of the *Critique of Pure Reason*, for instance, Kant maps the progress of enlightened self-consciousness in the form of the unbroken course of "logic": "That logic has, from the earliest times, proceeded upon this sure path is evidenced by the fact that since Aristotle it has not required to retrace a single step" (B, viii). (Oddly enough, Kant also says that "it is remarkable also that to the present day this logic has not been able to advance a single step," *ibid*.) But the Enlightenment notion of progress cannot defend itself against the charge that it may be the product of a distorted reading of the past. The figure of the continuously ascending line does not necessarily afford us a critical comprehension of the history it represents. (In addressing a related issue, the early Kant himself speaks of the "bias of reason"; he invokes the concept of method as the way in which judgment can escape its own bias; but as the discussion of genius in the third *Critique* goes to show, method proves to be an insuffi-

---

[45] René Descartes, *Meditations*, IV, in *The Philosophical Writings of Descartes*, vol. II, trans. John Cottingham, Robert Stoothoff, and Dugald Murdoch (Cambridge: Cambridge University Press, 1984), p. 40.
[46] In this context, one needs to acknowledge the prejudicial nature of the phrase "pre-Enlightenment."

cient guide for judgment's most difficult tasks.[47]) The interpretation of the Enlightenment's progressive stance as an ideological "distortion" is reinforced by the fact that it produces only self-serving explanations of what motivates its rejection of the past. Autonomous reason – reason which is authorized to constitute itself independently – presents itself as both the product and the cause of progress in history. It points to its own success as evidence of the fact that progress has in fact been achieved. Indeed, the historical necessity that Enlightenment rationality invokes for itself might best be seen as a consequence of what Hans Blumenberg has called "rational self-assertion." As Blumenberg says, "reason's interpretation of itself as the faculty of an absolute beginning excludes the possibility that there could be even so much as indications of a situation that calls for reason's application now, no sooner and no later. Reason, as the ultimate authority, has no need of a legitimation for setting itself in motion; but it also denies itself any reply to the question why it was ever out of operation and in need of a beginning. What God did before the Creation and why He decided on it . . . these are questions that cannot be asked in the context of the system constituted by their basic concepts."[48] Thus while it might be said that the modern Enlightenment understood its claim to having "overcome" the contingencies of history to be a guarantee and safeguard against the potential collapse of enlightened self-consciousness into the imagined "darkness" of its historical antecedents, the narrative of progress appears to be as sharply inflected as the narrative of regression or the return to origins.

"The Concept of Enlightenment" challenges the self-judgment implicit in this stance by contesting the unreflective form in which its self-judgment is rendered. One implication of Horkheimer and Adorno's work is to question the Enlightenment narrative of progress by representing the process of Enlightenment as incomplete, not in the sense in which Habermas intends this phrase (i.e., in order to call for its completion), but rather as a structure that was never fully formed in the separation of reason from myth.

---

[47] Kant, *Dreams of a Visionary Elucidated through the Dreams of Metaphysics* (1766), cited in Caygill, *Art of Judgment*, p. 194.

[48] Hans Blumenberg, *Legitimacy of the Modern Age*, trans. Robert M. Wallace (Cambridge, MA: MIT Press, 1983), p. 145. I discuss the problem of self-assertion at greater length in *The Subject of Modernity* (Cambridge: Cambridge University Press, 1992).

Not only is the Enlightenment's "overcoming" of myth incomplete; myth's "beginning" was not itself originary. As Slavoj Žižek suggests with respect to Schelling, there is something that precedes the Beginning itself – in Schelling's case "a rotary motion whose vicious cycle is broken, in a gesture analogous to the cutting of the Gordian knot, by the Beginning proper, that is, the primordial act of decision . . . 'eternity' is not a nondescript mass – a lot of things take place in it. Prior to the Word there is the chaotic-psychotic universe of blind drives, their rotary motion, their undifferentiated pulsating; and the Beginning occurs when the Word is pronounced which 'represses,' rejects into the eternal Past, this self-enclosed circuit of drives."[49] For Horkheimer and Adorno, by contrast, the opacity[50] of the Enlightenment with respect to the insights of history and theory anchors a critical posture that rejects the recuperative gestures that, since Schiller, hoped to find in art a mirror of the finality of nature aligned with human purposiveness; it rejects these in favor of a double vision that sustains the antagonism of mutually opposing terms, exposing each to the pressure of the other within an open-ended, contestatory space. The "dissonant thinking" of their essay represents both the limit and the trace of the Kantian aesthetic of unreconciled reflection in their work – a trace that, in resisting a vision of the subject as synthesis, involves a resistance to Hegel as well as to Kant. According to the Adorno of *Negative Dialectics*, "contradiction is nonidentity under the aspect of identity; the dialectical primacy of the principle of contradiction makes the thought of unity the measure of heterogeneity . . . What we differentiate will appear divergent, dissonant, negative for just as long as the structure of our consciousness obliges it to strive for unity, as long as its demand for totality will be its measure for whatever is not identical with it."[51] The "dissonant thinking" of

---

49 Slavoj Žižek, *The Indivisible Remainder: An Essay on Schelling and Related Matters* (London: Verso, 1996), p. 13.
50 As an examination of Kant's third *Critique* will help make clear, "enlightenment" can be described in this regard as a "dislocated" or "opaque" structure. The term "dislocation" derives from Ernesto Laclau. See *New Reflections on the Revolution of Our Time* (New York: Verso, 1990).
51 *Negative Dialectics*, pp. 5–6. The term "dissonant thinking" is suggested by Adorno's *Dissonanzen: Musik in der verwalteten Welt* (Göttingen: Vanderhoeck & Ruprecht, 1958). An alternative would be the "logic of disintegration" suggested in *Negative Dialectics*, pp. 144–46. See also Jacques Attali, *Bruits: Essai sur l'économie politique de la musique* (Paris: Presses Universitaires de France, 1977).

this essay is the result of a resistance to the separation *and* the synthesis of history and theory carried out in the interest of the subject, whose position likewise resists any categorical separation of these terms.[52]

To say this much is to suggest that the problems posed by "The Concept of Enlightenment" cannot be resolved either by situating subjectivity historically or by theorizing about our historical situation.[53] The following questions nonetheless remain. Where can Horkheimer and Adorno's practice of "dissonant thinking" lead except to a restatement of the antinomies of Enlightenment in a more densely opaque form? If history and theory as they structure and inform self-consciousness are neither absolutely reconcilable nor entirely unreconcilable, what can issue from the effort to express their dissonance?[54] My ambition in later chapters is to suggest that such matters can be addressed in terms of the logic of reflective judgment that follows from Kant's aesthetic critique. In "The Concept of Enlightenment," however, the dissonance of history and theory is never resolved or reduced.[55] For this reason, the essay's critical power may appear muted or obscure. And although Adorno eventually moved to the formulation of an explicitly aesthetic critique wherein art is regarded as the domain

[52] Cf. *CJ*, sec. 59. p. 224. This is to say that there is indeed an interest in aesthetic disinterestedness.

[53] For the Adorno of *Negative Dialectics*, this was impossible for another reason. Citing Benjamin's *Origin of German Tragic Drama*, Adorno describes the process whereby metaphysics was transformed into history as a process of irreversible secularization: "The transmutation of metaphysics into history . . . secularizes metaphysics in the secular category pure and simple, the category of decay" (*Negative Dialectics*, p. 360).

[54] These questions might also be asked of the method more properly called "negative dialectics." For example: "However varied, the anticipation of moving in contradictions throughout seems to teach a mental totality – the very identity thesis we have just rendered inoperative. The mind which ceaselessly reflects on contradiction in the thing itself, we hear, must be the thing itself if it is to be organized in the form of contradiction; the truth which in idealistic dialectics drives beyond every particular, as onesided and wrong, is the truth of the whole, and if that were not preconceived, the dialectical steps would lack motivation and direction. We have to answer that the object of a mental experience is an antagonistic system in itself – antagonistic in reality, not just in its conveyance to the knowing subject that rediscovers itself therein." *Negative Dialectics*, p. 10.

[55] On the contrary, their analysis of a text like the *Odyssey* from the perspective of technical-instrumental reason is meant to produce a sense of the absurd that, on Žižek's analysis, in turn opens actual historical distance to us. Žižek, *For They Know Not What They Do*, p. 103.

in which the particular is preserved in the guise of its irreducibility or "non-identity," in this earlier work the problem of Enlightenment is only heightened by the thesis of the entanglement
of Enlightenment with myth, a term of quite foreboding power
that appears at first blush to be the nemesis and shadow of all
possible Enlightenment.

In its simplest formulation, their argument is that what we
recognize as "Enlightenment" begins with the shift from the
practices of "specific representation" found in myth and magic to
"nonspecific" modes of representation. In an example of specific
representation, the lightning bolt was taken as Zeus himself; in
"nonspecific" representations the same "$x$" can stand in innumer-
able equations for the particular value that might complete each
one. We can surmise that the aesthetic symbol or figure occupies a
place in between these two: it recalls the quality of a determinate
relationship to the world, while it also reveals that relationship as
open to contingency, change, and chance. More broadly, their
argument rests on the claim that all symbolization, and likewise
all conceptualization, involves operations that are general and
abstract, and so cannot be anything other than a negation of
human experience, the particularity of which resists representation and remains fundamentally unmasterable by concepts.[56]

At the same time, the introduction of the term "myth" and the
revelation of its role in the process of Enlightenment involves a
direct challenge to the progressive view of history. Consistent
with a stance that questions the linear, ascending form in which
"progress" has been represented, Horkheimer and Adorno
would lead us to conclude that myth was preserved within Enlightenment not just as a vestige or a trace, but as an example of a
prior mode of cognition that continues to inhabit enlightened

[56] This notion is anticipated by, among other thinkers, Hegel, whose *Phenomenology* turns on the idea that, prior to the moment of the Absolute, where thinking
and actuality coincide, thought and experience are never one. Indeed, the
*Phenomenology* can be read as a systematic account of the ways in which all
thinking betrays experience. It is recirculated in Nietzsche, whose barbed style
represents an attempt to communicate aesthetically what we would otherwise
negate by merely grasping conceptually – that thought negates experience. Cf.
Nietzsche's Zarathustra, who claims that the desire to "*make* all being conceiv-
able" means that "it must become smooth and subject to the mind as the mind's
mirror reflection," and who in turn identifies conceptual thought with the "will
to power." Nietzsche, "Of Self-Overcoming," in *Thus Spoke Zarathustra*, trans. R.
J. Hollingdale (Harmondsworth: Penguin, 1961), p. 136.

reason. "Myth" stands for an ordering of the world that works by cunning, mimesis, and analogy, rather than by "concept." And as Horkheimer and Adorno make abundantly clear, everything relegated by the process of Enlightenment to "mythical thinking," which reason attempts to suppress – ranging from superstition and madness to religion, genius, and art – was at best repressed. This is also to say that myth – or, more deeply perhaps, the fear to which myth was a first response – was never fully eliminated by the process of Enlightenment, but was instead preserved and enveloped; as the driving force behind hegemonic forms of power, myth has revealed itself to be one of the "consequences" of the Enlightenment itself.

To be sure, the Enlightenment sought the "disenchantment" of the world in an effort to uproot "prejudice" and "superstition" and thereby to bring the sources of fear under control. With "disenchantment" came the elimination of purposiveness from nature, the sources of which were subsequently attributed to "animistic thinking" or to "primitive thought." In the ambit of "enlightened" thinking, to model human purposes on the purposiveness of the natural world, even if by a process of imitation or analogy, is to threaten the distinction between nature and culture, or, as Habermas says, to confuse the purposes of agents with the world of nature.[57] Habermas's views would seem to have a firm foundation in Horkheimer and Adorno's essay. They write that "Enlightenment has always taken the basic principle of myth to be anthropomorphism, the projection onto nature of the subjective . . . the supernatural, spirits and demons, are mirror images of men who allow themselves to be frightened by natural phenomena" ("Concept of Enlightenment," p. 6).

Horkheimer and Adorno nonetheless go on to suggest that myth is *already* Enlightenment. Myth, it would seem, represents an attempt to provide an ordering of particular phenomena and submit them to "universal" rules in order to reduce the fearsome externality of nature to consciousness. Myth on their account

---

[57] As Habermas goes on to argue, "myth" invites a fundamental confusion between nature and culture that can only be rectified by a process of critical thinking and additional efforts at disenchantment: "only demythologization dispels this enchantment." Habermas remains faithful enough to his Frankfurt School roots to add that "the process of enlightenment leads to the desocialization of nature and the denaturalization of the human world." See *The Philosophical Discourse of Modernity*, p. 115.

31

embraces both of what we recognize as science and morality: "Myth intended report, naming, the narration of a Beginning; but also presentation, confirmation, explanation: a tendency that grew stronger with the recording and collection of myths. Narrative became didactic at an early age" (p. 8).[58] In this respect, Horkheimer and Adorno suggest that Enlightenment is itself a carrying-forward, *Aufhebung*, or sublation of myth. Both represent an attempt to conceal the inconsistency of the symbolic order in which we live. "Just as the myths already realize enlightenment, so enlightenment with every step becomes more deeply engulfed in mythology. It receives all its matter from the myths, in order to destroy them; and even as a judge it comes under the mythic curse . . . The principle of immanence, the explanation of every event as repetition, that the Enlightenment upholds against mythic imagination, is the principle of myth itself" (pp. 11–12).

In sum, Horkheimer and Adorno argue that Enlightenment is not just the result of a process of disenchantment that was left incomplete, but that the Enlightenment's vaunted notion of progress is in fact undermined by the hidden identity of Enlightenment and myth: "Enlightenment *returns to* mythology, which it never really knew how to elude" (p. 27). For instance, Horkheimer and Adorno claim that mathematics is an example of "ritual thought" in which the underlying principles of repetition and equivalence function as fetishes (p. 20). Similarly, they argue that the systematicity of the Enlightenment operates on the same basis as a "universal taboo"; its obligatory inclusiveness demands that "nothing at all may remain outside, because the mere idea of outsideness is the very source of fear" (p. 16). And just as the idea of a categorical difference between Enlightenment and myth is challenged by their claim, so too they suggest that this "identity" is subtended by a difference that could only make sense from an "enlightened" point of view. The existence of myth "prior" to reason serves to prove that human experience is "always already" structured in some rational form, while the consequences of rationalization go to "prove" that Enlightenment is a continuation

---

[58] Horkheimer and Adorno's work raises the difficult question of the relative priority of language and social practice (which a thinker like Wittgenstein would resolve by seeing language *as* social practice). According to Lacanian psychoanalysis, it is the entry into the symbol-system of language that marks the fundamental difference between what is human and what is not.

of the work of myth.[59] Given this analysis, it would seem that the escape from myth and the movement toward autonomy promised by the Enlightenment's attempt at a rational critique of all universal claims through a differentiation of its own powers represents a false and unsustainable hope.

As Habermas reads Horkheimer and Adorno, the problem of the identity and difference of Enlightenment and myth results in an impasse rather than an opening for critical theory, and especially for any theory with commitments to the Enlightenment's progressive social goals. On the Habermassian account, the thesis of the Enlightenment's entwinement with myth leads us into a *cul de sac*. It would seem to mark the movement from one omnipotence to another and to indicate the untransformability of the world by any purposive human action. History would at best be a process of repetition or, as suggested above, a manifestation of cynical reason. Thus, Habermas marks the work of Horkheimer and Adorno in *Dialectic of Enlightenment* as the dead end of Enlightenment thought.[60] Habermas summarizes the consequences of this work as follows: "The suspicion of ideology becomes *total* . . . It is turned not only against the irrational function of bourgeois ideals, but against the rational potential of bourgeois culture itself, and thus it reaches into the foundations of any ideology critique that proceeds immanently. But the goal remains that of producing an effect of unmasking. The thought-figure, into which a scepticism regarding reason is now worked, remains unchanged: Now reason itself is suspected of the baneful confusion of power and validity claims, but still with the intent of enlightening."[61]

In part as a response to Horkheimer and Adorno, Habermas has proposed that a new form of rationality, grounded in the theory of communicative action, can sustain all the practical concerns of myth, which he identifies with its integrative role in the "lifeworld," while resisting any tendency to approach the world and others in it as objects simply to be manipulated or controlled. Habermas puts forward the theory of communicative action as a

[59] On the continuation of myth, see Blumenberg, *Work on Myth*, trans. Robert M. Wallace (Cambridge, MA: MIT Press, 1985).
[60] See the alliance made in *The Philosophical Discourse of Modernity*, pp. 106–30, "The Entwinement of Myth and Enlightenment."
[61] Habermas, *The Philosophical Discourse of Modernity*, p. 119.

way in which the subject can successfully coordinate the goals of rationality and purposiveness. Specifically, Habermas advances the theory of communicative action as an antidote to conditions in which "the disenchantment of the religious-metaphysical world view robs rationality, along with the contents of tradition, of all substantive connotations and thereby strips it of its power to have a structure-forming influence on the lifeworld beyond the purposive-rational organization of means." As opposed to this, the communicative-action account of rationality is said to be "directly implicated in social life-processes insofar as acts of mutual understanding take on the role of a mechanism for coordinating action. The network of communicative actions is nourished by resources of the lifeworld and is at the same time the *medium* by which concrete forms of life are reproduced."[62] But we shall have ample occasion to see that the Habermassian judgment of Horkheimer and Adorno's work is, at the very least, premature. First and foremost, it would have to be recognized that "The Concept of Enlightenment" renders suspect Habermas's own position within the Enlightenment progression from *mythos* to *logos*. For, if nothing else, Horkheimer and Adorno showed that the Enlightenment's self-conception of "reason" as standing in clear opposition to "myth" is false: no matter which way one chooses to look, myth is already a species of reason and what is offered as "reason" is sustained by a form of myth.[63]

Suffice it here to say that my own understanding of the consequences of the Enlightenment is substantially different from Habermas's in part because Habermas's theory of "communicative reason" serves mainly to recast and neutralize what Kant identified as the specific difficulty of aesthetic judgment by the invocation of a free and spontaneous act of the will, through which a community of peaceable speakers is bound together. And insofar as Habermas simply invites us to derive consensus from the

---

[62] *Ibid.*, pp. 315–16.
[63] This relationship has direct implications for our concept of the presentness of the present, understood historically. As Jameson notes: "In this sense, the present – the most up-to-date form of the dialectic of enlightenment – produces the past, and more specifically that immediate past of its own present which is now stigmatized as archaic, old-fashioned, mythic, superstitious, obsolete or simply 'natural'; but this is true as far back into the past as we can see or imagine, and indeed the temporal dialectic proposed here might better be analogized in terms of optics, where with every shift in visual attention a new lateral field establishes itself, forever out of reach." Jameson, *Late Marxism*, p. 99.

disposition toward understanding said to be implicit in speech his position remains dangerously close to the "dark" Enlightenment thinkers, among whom he includes Machiavelli and Hobbes, whose pessimism he is ostensibly seeking to correct.[64] One of those writers, Hobbes, had already recommended a political version of something like Habermassian communication (Hobbes's "civil society") as a response to the problem of a radical disgregation among the members of society, which produces a mutual, constitutive fear. For Kant, the response to fear was to be derived from the courage of reason itself. *Sapere aude,* "dare to know," the maxim adopted in 1736 by the Society of the Friends of Truth, was roundly embraced by Kant as the Enlightenment's motto and standard of virtue in his 1784 essay "Answer to the Question: What Is Enlightenment?" In the *Critique of Judgment* Kant refers to courage as "the maxim of a never-*passive* reason." He argues that "to be given to such passivity, consequently to heteronomy of reason, is called *prejudice,*" and elaborates that "the greatest of all prejudices is that of fancying nature not to be subject to rules which the understanding by virtue of its own essential laws lays at its basis, i.e. *superstition*" (*CJ,* sec. 40, p. 152).[65]

If Kant's response to the question "What is Enlightenment?" is "man's emergence from his self-incurred immaturity," or his release from "tutelage" (where "tutelage" indicates "man's inability to make use of his understanding without direction from another"[66]) then ignorance must be the result not of a failure of knowledge but of a weakness of the will, or the inability to overcome fear. In *Dialectic of Enlightenment* Horkheimer and Adorno revise Kant to say that such weakness derives from a

---

[64] See *The Philosophical Discourse of Modernity,* especially p. 106.

[65] Horkheimer echoes Kant when, at what seemed to be the desperate "end" of the Enlightenment tradition in *The Eclipse of Reason,* he wrote that "faith in philosophy means the refusal to permit fear to stunt in any way one's capacity to think." Horkheimer, "On The Concept of Philosophy," in *The Eclipse of Reason* (1947; rpt. New York: Seabury Press, 1974), p. 162. Horkheimer goes on to argue that, because the only obstacle to Enlightenment is fear, human beings can change their circumstances just as soon as they recognize they are themselves the source of their own oppression: "Until recently in Western history, society lacked sufficient cultural and technological resources for forging an understanding between individuals, groups, and nations. Today the material conditions exist. What is lacking are men who understand that they themselves are the subjects or the functionaries of their own oppression" (pp. 162–63).

[66] Kant, "What is Enlightenment?" in *Kant on History,* ed. Lewis White Beck (Indianapolis, IN: Bobbs-Merrill, 1963), p. 3.

failure of the instincts of self-preservation, and jeopardizes our ability to survive. And yet it would seem that even for Kant thinking autonomously and independently is not in itself enough to secure the goals of Enlightenment. Thus in the *Critique of Judgment* Kant describes the ethical transformation of fear in the form of a requirement to "think from the standpoint of every one else." This fundamentally analogical principle of "enlarged mentality" (*erweiterte Denkungsart*), fully endorsed by Hannah Arendt in "The Crisis in Culture" and in her 1970 lectures on the third *Critique*, is for Kant the aesthetic complement to the need to think autonomously and consistently (*CJ*, sec. 40, p. 152).[67] As for Hume and Rousseau, Kant's enlarged mentality requires a mutuality of affect, a "thinking with" that is every bit as much a form of "feeling with."

Humean and Rousseauian "sympathy" aside, the intractability of the fear that underlies rational self-assertion is one of the lessons that Horkheimer and Adorno taught in "The Concept of Enlightenment," where myth in one of its principal functions, as an ordering of the natural world and an imitation or *mimesis* of its powers, is seen as an organized response to fear that serves to bind together the members of a community in a common life-world: it is a systematic remembering and preservation of the practices that are instituted as the antidote to a fear that can never be entirely overcome. The question of fear returns both in Kant's account of the sublime[68] and in Adorno's posthumous *Aesthetic Theory*, where art is not just an expression of any sort, but something closer to a recollection or remembering of the archaic experi-

---

[67] Hannah Arendt, "The Crisis in Culture," in *Between Past and Future: Eight Exercises in Political Thought* (Harmondsworth: Penguin Books, 1968), pp. 197–226 (see especially pp. 220–24), and *Lectures on Kant's Political Philosophy*, ed. Ronald Beiner (Chicago: University of Chicago Press, 1982), pp. 42–44, 73–74.

[68] It is clear nonetheless that the fear Kant speaks of in relation to the sublime is a *faux* fear, and that its main purpose is to prove the power of subjectivity over nature: "The *astonishment* amounting almost to terror, the awe and thrill of devout feeling, that takes hold of one when gazing upon the prospect of mountains ascending to heaven, deep ravines and torrents raging there, deep-shadowed solitudes that invite to brooding melancholy, and the like – all this, when we are assured of our own safety, is not actual fear. Rather, it is an attempt to gain access to it through imagination, for the purpose of feeling the might of this faculty in combining the movement of the mind thereby aroused with its serenity, and of thus being superior to internal and, therefore, to external, nature, so far as the latter can have any bearing upon our feeling of well-being." *CJ*, "General Remark," pp. 120–21. See Chapter 7 below.

ences that give rise to fear. Art, Adorno says, registers fear "like a seismograph" (*Aesthetic Theory*, p. 185).[69]

In his work beginning with *The Philosophical Discourse of Modernity*, Habermas has sought through what I would regard as an act of unnecessary and misguided heroism to rescue the constructive dimension of the project of Enlightenment from the "pessimistic" implications of Horkheimer and Adorno's views by recourse to the notion of community as modeled on the ideal speech situation. But whereas Habermas believes that he can complete the constructive process of Enlightenment and solve the problem of rationalization by theorizing "communicative reason" as a non-coercive form of exchange among free and willing subjects, I would suggest that the Habermassian project represents an impoverishing reduction of the dialectic of Enlightenment. This reduction occurs at the very moment the Habermassian project thinks that it can correct reason's understanding of itself by representing rationality as a closed circuit of communication.[70] Habermas claims that an ethics based on the principles of communicative action ("discourse ethics") relies on no *a priori* structures other than the universals of language.[71] But these remain universals nonetheless, and language, when seen as the fund of such universals, is apt to become nothing more than a substitute for what Horkheimer and Adorno designated in terms of abstract "concepts." As we shall see in chapter 2, Kant's insistence that claims of taste make reference to a pleasure that is *sui generis* suggests the need to theorize communication outside of the presuppositions regarding language universals that govern the Habermassian theory. Indeed, even the notion of a universal "pragmatics" would seem suspect in light of Kant's understanding of communication, since the pleasure at stake in Kant's third *Critique* assumes no interest, hence is divorced from praxis. Similarly, the third *Critique* theorizes a purposiveness whose principal interest lies in its refusal of all practical interests.[72]

[69] Cf. *ibid.*, p. 121.
[70] See Derrida's "Economimesis," and also Jean-François Lyotard, *Dérive à partir de Marx et Freud* (Paris: Union Générale d'Editions, 1973) and *Discours, Figure* (Paris: Klincksieck, 1971). The question of economy bears directly on the analysis of pleasure and pain in Kant's third *Critique*.
[71] Habermas, *Moral Consciousness and Communicative Action*, trans. Christian Lenhardt and Shierry Weber Nicholson (Cambridge, MA: MIT Press, 1990), p. 203.
[72] Derrida has, of course, challenged Kant's claim on this matter in his essay "Economimesis."

In order to be successful on its own terms, Habermas's theory of intersubjective communication would need to show that neither the self nor the other takes precedence in a given exchange, indeed, that what Emmanuel Levinas has called the "dissymmetry of intersubjective space"[73] does not exist, that self and the other are bound together by a (pre-ethical) desire to speak. But in this case one would be hard pressed to imagine what subjects might desire to say, much less account for something as complex as the desire for recognition, which in its classical Hegelian form takes the self and other as divided and unequal parts of consciousness.

As I hope will become clear, my analysis of the problem of Enlightenment is different from Habermas's in a further way, for Habermas claims that the theory of communicative action allows him to "complete" the project of Enlightenment by shifting the basis of rationality away from the field of subject-centered reason. As we have already begun to glimpse, however, the theory of reflective judgment developed in Kant's third *Critique* leads to a concept of the Enlightenment as having no possible completion. Rather, the theory of aesthetic reflection marks affect (pleasure, pain) as evidence that the process of Enlightenment as a mode of systematic critical reflection is necessarily *in*complete. By contrast, Habermas's attempt to circumvent the logic of reflection by means of an appeal to the image of communication as itself both rational and good[74] fails to reflect on the way in which the subject affectively apprehends the differences that must exist if one is to risk a conversation in the first place. The same can be said about Rorty's appeal to "shared conversations" as a way to circumvent metaphysics insofar as Rorty wishes to distinguish the role of the (private) imagination from the constitution of the collective (public) sphere. Habermas turns away from the Kantian idea that claims of taste represent a way in which we may apprehend the ethical ideals of purposive action and of reciprocal recognition through the pleasure of the beautiful and the pain of the sublime. In a very tangible way, both Habermas and Rorty leave the problem of the affective basis of the subject, as well as its relationship

---

[73] See, for example, Emmanuel Levinas's essay on Buber in *Outside the Subject*, trans. Michael B. Smith (Stanford, CA: Stanford University Press, 1994), pp. 40–48.
[74] See Rorty, "Deconstruction and Circumvention," pp. 85–106.

to others and to the world at large, unanalyzed.[75] In so doing, they forget to ask about the means through which the punctual "I," whose experiences originate in the discursive and, therefore, historical transformation of pleasure and pain, undergoes a splitting into an "I" that is also a "me," how this split subject in turn can be shaped by the desire to become part of the "we," and finally how the "we" is not just the "I" made plural or multiple but is in fact the "I" "ethicized" in response to the desire for recognition by the "you." For Rorty, there is no significant need for recognition (nor any possibility of achieving it) because the subject is assumed to be split along public/private lines. For Habermas, the social identity of the participants in the ideal conversation (if not in actual, practical conversations) is not just constructed and contingent, it is also presupposed to be an extension of the "I." But if this is the case, then what is the purpose of Kant's claim in section 44 of the *Critique of Judgment*, according to which fine art has the effect of "advancing the culture of the mental powers *in the interests of social communication*" (*CJ*, p. 166, emphasis added)? What would communicative subjects have to talk about?[76]

The Habermassian theory of communicative action and the Rortian program of edifying conversations represent only one set of possible alternatives that might be offered to the notion of a self-canceling "dialectic of Enlightenment." A second potential set of objections to the notion of an "aesthetic critique" arises from

[75] Laclau has identified this as one of the central issues raised by the problem of structural dislocation: "to the very extent that dislocations increasingly dominate the terrain of an absent structural determination, the problem of *who* articulates comes to occupy a more central position. It is this problem of who the subjects of historical transformations are – or, more fundamentally, what being a subject entails – that we must now consider" (Laclou, *New Reflections on the Revolution of Our Time*, p. 59).

[76] As far as Habermas is concerned, "art" is the source of a utopian longing that rests on a foundation of uncontrollable excitations. In a typical passage Habermas writes that "since early Romanticism, limit experiences of an aesthetic and mystical kind have always been claimed for the purpose of a rapturous transcendence of the subject . . . In this constellation, which persists from Nietzsche to Heidegger and Foucault, there arises a readiness for excitement without any proper object; in its wake, subcultures are formed which simultaneously allay and keep alive their excitement in the face of future truths [of which they have been notified in an unspecified way] by means of cultic actions without any cultic object." See *The Philosophical Discourse of Modernity*, pp. 309–10. While renouncing the "aesthetic" basis of contemporary critical theory Habermas fails to appreciate the ways in which the subject presupposed by his own theory of communicative action has its origins in the very aesthetic project he rejects.

classically oriented critics of the Enlightenment, who envision a return to the wisdom of the Ancients as offering the most desirable solution to the problems posed by the Enlightenment. The effort to return to the Ancients may initially be understood as a sophisticated attempt to deny the fact that Enlightenment has consequences for us at all. In its baldest form, the neoclassical argument shares Horkheimer's and Adorno's belief that the consequences of the Enlightenment project are ultimately regressive rather than progressive, suggesting that since reason does not refine and perfect itself over the course of history, then the opposite must be the case – that autonomous, Enlightened reason represents a degeneration or falling way from some earlier moment of fullness, social harmony, or transparent relationship to others in the form of ethical praxis. To adopt this view is to see the Enlightenment as nothing more than a mask for decadence; it is to respond with a radically unhistorical prescription to Hegel's diagnosis of the "peculiar restlessness and dispersion of modern consciousness" offered in the preface to the second edition of the *Science of Logic*.[77] Motivated strongly by a desire to reclaim what Hegel imagined to be the ethical life of the Greek polis, this critique represents an effort to step back to a moment before the actions of social subjects were differentiated into separate spheres, in order to recover what is imagined as the unitary and binding moment in which cognition and morality were one.[78] But as I argue in chapter 4, these efforts constitute a failed attempt to reverse the process of Enlightenment if only because they attempt to ignore the process of self-reflection by which their own critical consciousness was produced. They may be able to suggest an alternative to the Enlightenment, but that alternative represents a diminution of the possibilities of self-consciousness precisely because it rejects rather than transforms the dissatisfactions that drive it.

Among contemporary philosopher-critics, both Alasdair MacIntyre and Stanley Rosen have advanced sophisticated versions of the neoclassical critique that go well beyond the mere rejection of

[77] *Wissenschaft der Logik* (Leipzig: Felix Meiner Verlag, 1951), vol. I, *p.20*. Cited in Stanley Rosen, *The Ancients and the Moderns: Rethinking Modernity* (New Haven, CT: Yale University Press, 1989), p. vii. Cf. Hegel's comments on the "new age" in the *Phenomenology of Spirit*, par. 11, pp. 6–7.

[78] In psychoanalytic terms, the same critique may be leveled at those who propose a return to the mother as a solution to the problems of domination that have been brought about by the imposition of the father's law.

the Enlightenment. MacIntyre has for instance argued that the vocabulary of modern moral theory is funded by concepts that originally were designed to make sense of the relations implicit in societies that understood themselves through myth. He suggests that Enlightened modernity is the result of an invisible trauma or "catastrophe" in the history of culture by virtue of which the "original content" of ethics (virtuous action) was forgotten or suppressed. On his account, the dilemma that follows from this catastrophic loss manifests itself in the form of an emotivism that has a decisively aestheticist cast. Specifically, MacIntyre identifies the aesthete as living a form of moral perspectivism. The rich Europeans of Henry James's novels, Kierkegaard's "A," and Diderot's Rameau all exemplify "a tradition in which the social world is nothing but a meeting place for individual wills, each with its own set of attitudes and preferences and who understand the world solely as an arena for the achievement of their own satisfaction, who interpret reality as a series of opportunities for their enjoyment and for whom the last enemy is boredom."[79] MacIntyre nonetheless believes that we can grasp a clear enough understanding of the meaning of the Ancient philosophy of praxis in order to make the possibility of a return to the ethics of virtue possible. More forcefully, MacIntyre posits Aristotelian ethics as the only viable alternative to the Nietzschean perspectivism that underlies modern aestheticism. But since MacIntyre cannot defend the naturalistic teleology that supports Aristotle's ethics, he stakes his hopes for a renewed ethics of the virtues on a reconstruction of the purposiveness of practical reason in narrative form. In the process he nonetheless overlooks the fact that the purposiveness of narrative – and, indeed, narrative's own relationship to ethics – is dependent upon "aesthetic" principles; specifically, the purposiveness of narrative provides an analogue of natural teleology whose form must be apprehended affectively. Moreover, it remains to be seen just what relationship obtains between the narratives of heroism and virtue that MacIntyre has in mind and the novelistic narratives that came to dominance in the Enlightenment world.[80]

---

[79] Alasdair MacIntyre, *After Virtue* (Notre Dame, IN: University of Notre Dame Press, 1980), p. 24.

[80] Throughout, Georg Lukács's *Theory of the Novel* provides a more subtle account of the transformations of narrative in relation to the fate of heroism and virtue in the modern world.

A rather different critique of the Enlightenment has been offered by Stanley Rosen in a variety of works including *Hermeneutics as Politics* (1987), *The Ancients and The Moderns* (1989), and *The Mask of Enlightenment: Nietzsche's Zarathustra* (1995). Rosen describes a series of "consequences of the Enlightenment" not unlike those predicted by Horkheimer and Adorno. For both, the most devastating effect of the modern establishment of mathematics as the paradigm of rationality is a divorce of truth from goodness that renders reason incapable of establishing its own worth. So seen, mathematics becomes one perspective among many, or another form of myth.[81] The crucial difference is that Rosen believes that an alternative can be found through a Platonic "leap beyond" the internal contradictions of the modern Enlightenment and a recovery of the inherent goodness of reason. For Rosen, a common malady of the Enlightenment and of contemporary critiques of it lies in the attempt to deprive the subject of the pre-discursive forms of intuition necessary to make and implement determinate judgments. (Aesthetic reflection would then become a central symptom of modernity and postmodernism.) On this account, philosophy beginning with the Enlightenment represents a turning away from nature and from the "natural praxis of life." Enlightenment thinking, as instigated by skepticism, denies the givenness or accessibility of ordinary experience, and so amounts to a loss of our *sensus communis* or "common sense." The Enlightenment dream to transform the world into a concept fails not, as in Kant, because pleasures and pains cannot be apprehended by the concepts of cognition or morality, but because such a project requires, but cannot admit, the grounding of reason in the natural praxis of life.

Rosen's critical reassessment of the Enlightenment and its aftermath is one of the most thoroughgoing we have to date, but I would dispute some of the conclusions he draws on the basis that their underlying presuppositions require an alliance between reason and nature that has potentially dangerous political consequences. At the very least, it forces us to sacrifice the commitment to contingency that lies at the heart of modernity and gives undue advantage to those in whom power has come to rest. (Its capacity for resistance against hegemonic power is virtually nil.) Rosen

[81] Rosen, *The Mask of Enlightenment: Nietzsche's Zarathustra* (Cambridge: Cambridge University Press, 1995), p. 249.

nonetheless argues that if we refuse to let reason be guided by and responsive to nature, we will be condemned to inhabit a world of conflicting interpretations and antagonistic perspectives, where judgment is not just difficult but impossible.[82] As a corollary, he suggests that every program of interpretation must be regarded as a political manifesto or the corollary of one; the loss of true political theory, he contends, is the fate of the postmodern attack upon the Enlightenment and a confirmation of the decadence of the modern age.[83]

Given the problematic nature of our relationship to the "natural praxis of life" since at least the skeptics to whom Kant was responding, I would argue that the notion of reflective aesthetic judgment provides a more complex and accurate account of the fact that we inhabit a world in which reason and goodness are not connected in any obvious way. Especially in its analysis of "common sense," the third *Critique* portrays the alliance of reason and goodness not just as presupposed, but as something that is yet to be created. According to the third *Critique*, reflective judgment represents an effort to coordinate the purposiveness of human action with the causality of the natural world while nonetheless recognizing the fact that both "purposiveness" and "causality" imply action in accordance with a concept or end that we can know only in hypothetical or fictional terms. The pleasure and the pain felt in response to the beautiful and the sublime provide the subject with only the *semblance* that human actions are conducted in accordance with the purposiveness of nature itself. Not surprisingly, then, the twin affects of pleasure and pain are unlocatable in

[82] Thus it may not be too surprising to learn that a thinker like Edmund Husserl, whose work was crucial for determining the course of post-Enlightenment thought, produced an account in which judgment was not just difficult but impossible unless we gain access to a stratum of experience that neither logic nor psychology can successfully postulate. In *Experience and Judgment*, Husserl concludes that to reveal the true foundations of predicative evidence would require a return to self-evident experience, which is to say, a recovery of the pre-theoretical ground of experience in the original lifeworld. *Experience and Judgment: Investigations in a Genealogy of Logic*, trans. James S. Churchill and Karl Ameriks (Evanston, IL: Northwestern University Press, 1973).

[83] See especially the essays "Theory and Interpretation" and "Hermeneutics as Politics" in the volume *Hermeneutics as Politics* (New York: Oxford University Press, 1987). The issue of "common sense" of course has a long philosophical history in continental thought. See, for instance, Hegel's discussion in the "Introduction" to the *Phenomenology of Spirit* and Heidegger, *Hegel's Concept of Experience* (New York: Harper and Row, 1970).

terms of the teleology of cause and effect; they are effects for which there is no determinate "cause"; as Kant freely admits, beauty can be aligned with morality only in symbolic terms.

## Deep-structure theory or aesthetic critique?

Kant's formulation of the problem of aesthetic reflective judgment, which concentrates on the ways in which the division of cognition and morality (and the desire for their reintegration) is affectively apprehended by the subject can shed some light on the relationship between the world of appearances on the one hand and the "deep-structures" that are thought to constitute or explain it on the other. Indeed, Kant's formulation prompts us to question the usefulness of "deep structure" theory in prevailing approaches to the problem of subject-formation. Here a word of clarification is in order, in part because deep-structure theory has itself been eclipsed by more recent accounts of social action originating in thinkers as diverse as Althusser, Foucault, Lacan, and Wittgenstein. (I would hope to add the aesthetic reflection that originates in Kant to this list.) What may nonetheless be referred to as deep-structure theory is a form of causal or structural expressivism which suggests that subjectivity can be explained in terms of the effects that some deeply underlying or otherwise concealed "base" has upon phenomena at some other "higher" level, sometimes called a "superstructure." (The orthodox Marxist notion of "expressive causality" as involving a base and superstructure constitutes a prominent example of deep-structure logic.) Deep-structure theory is an example of the ways in which social and historical phenomena can be interpreted by a logic that subsumes the particularities of experience under some general pattern that is assumed to exist independently of them. Deep-structure theory has three principal functions, all of which can be taken to represent examples of the logic of subsumption at work in determinate judgments. To paraphrase Roberto Mangabeira Unger, who has been one of the most articulate critics of deep-structure theory, the notion of a deep-structure serves, first, to organize the social actions of subjects around the differences between conventions, routines, or effects, and underlying causal frameworks. Second, the notion of a deep-structure underpins an effort to represent the interests at work in particular situations as producing a repeatable and indivisible set of phenomena (e.g., industrial society, the Oedipal complex). Third, it substantiates the appeal to entrenched constraints and to laws that generate a circumscribed range of effects by describing these as somehow constituting the "directed" or "driven" consequences of underlying conditions.[84]

Insofar as deep-structures are thought to play a truly organizing and shaping role in the process of subject-formation, they also lead us falsely to think of society as fully constituted and formed. Unger argues that a strong commitment to deep-structure thought means accepting the belief that the structures so organized are untransformable by any human effort and, indeed, that they cannot coherently be described in relation to any form of human striving at all. Deep-structure theory may be able to explain how the subject is constituted in terms of cause and effect, but it understands little about the affects as pure (i.e., irreducible) effects and can say relatively little about how this same subject can play a role in constituting its world. Deep-structure theory thus tends to reinforce a set of unfounded, naturalistic premises about the untransformable nature of society and the self. As Unger states,

[The naturalistic thesis] takes a particular form of social life as the context of all contexts – the true and undistorted form of social existence . . . The natural context of social life may pass through decay or renascence, but it cannot be remade. Nor is there, in this view, any sense in which the defining context of social life can become less contextual – less arbitrary and confining. It is already the real thing . . . This authentic pattern of social life can undergo corruption and regeneration. But it can never be rearranged.[85]

The naturalistic thesis is no doubt a product of the desire for the wholeness and transparency of a rational society. But it also fuels the fears articulated in Kant's third *Critique* – that the world we know might be unalterable by any effort of the will, hence that the purposiveness of moral action might have no bearing whatsoever upon the world.

Given such concerns, it is understandable how the rejection of

---

[84] Roberto Unger, *Social Theory: its Situation and its Task* (Cambridge: Cambridge University Press, 1987). See especially pp. 88–91. Also relevant are the companion volumes to this work, *Plasticity into Power* (Cambridge: Cambridge University Press, 1987), and *False Necessity: Anti-Necessitarian Social Theory in the Service of Radical Democracy* (Cambridge: Cambridge University Press, 1987).

[85] Unger, *Social Theory*, pp. 23–24.

deep-structure theory might itself be seen as a sufficient basis for a critique of the Enlightenment. Especially in its neo-pragmatist orientations, the rejection of deep-structure theory can be seen as part of a noble attempt to alert us to Wittgenstein's insight that although praxis may give expression to human purposiveness, there is nothing that should in itself be thought of as the "natural praxis of life." But we do well to recall that it was a suspicion about our relationship to the "natural praxis of life" that motivated the Enlightenment critique of neo-Scholastic essentialism and its skepticism of inherited institutions in the first instance. For Unger, the alliances that are forged between deep-structure theory and the naturalistic thesis are both the intellectual legacy of the Enlightenment's critique of essentialism and the thing that inhibits the transformations the Enlightenment had hoped to achieve. And because Unger holds that deep-structure theory represents the clearest example of the ways in which Enlightenment thinking was crippled by the explanatory paradigms it advanced, he recommends that it be cast aside. Only in this way, he suggests, can the possibility of radical social change originally promised by the Enlightenment be fulfilled. In the case at hand, social subjects would be freed from the difficulty of reflective judgment and readied for true progress. Once "theory" or the drive for reflection is set aside, the tensions between Kant's two worlds – between the causality of nature and the freedom of the will, as between fact and value, epistemology and ethics, "is" and "ought" – would simply wither away. Reflective judgment would become not just difficult but unnecessary, and we would be empowered to transform ourselves by nothing more than an exertion of the will. The Enlightenment dream would be achieved not through the schematization of the world as a concept, but rather through what might be described as *Wunschdenken* (wishful thinking).[86]

Unger's critique of the naturalistic thesis has resonances, albeit in different registers, with a series of neo-pragmatist positions that have been articulated by thinkers like Richard Rorty and Stanley Fish. Insofar as such positions remain indebted to Kant's aesthetic critique, it is largely on account of their insistence upon the primacy of particulars over universals, or as Kant puts it in

---

[86] Cf. Drucilla Cornell's remarks on Schopenhauer in *The Philosophy of the Limit* (New York: Routledge, 1992), pp. 26 ff.

section 10 of the *Critique of Judgment*, the primacy of effect over cause in determining ends.[87] To invoke one of Rorty's quasi-aesthetic criteria, these are some of the most "interesting" responses to the Enlightenment that have been invented to date. And yet Rorty himself provides no further account of what this "interest" might involve, and even denies that it might warrant a further account. In this, Rorty relies on a postmodern version of the "aestheticism" that MacIntyre so harshly criticizes in *After Virtue*; as MacIntyre avers, aestheticism risks nothing so much as boredom.[88]

As Horkheimer and Adorno remind us, the dialectic of Enlightenment cannot be brought to a halt merely by wishing it away. History cannot be put to an end simply by claiming that the chains of historical necessity are false. Nor can the problems of self-reflective subjectivity be resolved, as Rorty would seem to suggest, simply by declaring that metaphysics was a bad philosophical idea. As Kant and Adorno both understand, the difficulty that subtends the position of the subject cannot be resolved just by granting the wish to be clarified. Even if the social and historical structures in which subjectivity is set, and which have been in some measure produced by subjects themselves, offered no resistance to modification and change, we could not so easily re-enchant ourselves. Passion and affect, which bear traces of world-division and world-loss, remain a part of the subject and incite reflection even in the case of those strategies that claim to have abandoned all theorizing about subjectivity, or (as in the case of Rorty and some others) that have turned to literature and art as a more ironic substitute for systematic thought.[89] As I argue below, such strategies need better to understand their own indebtedness to the project of aesthetic reflection outlined by Kant; at the same time they need to appreciate the complications involved in marshaling art or aesthetic reason as an alternative to metaphysical thought.

[87] Kant: "The representation of the effect is here the determining ground of its cause and takes the lead of it," *CJ*, sec. 10, p. 61.

[88] Rorty's separation of the public and the private spheres also revokes the fundamental Kantian idea that aesthetic judgments might allow for a transformation of "private feeling" into "public sense." See Kant, *CJ*, sec. 22, p. 84.

[89] The contrast between Heidegger's understanding of world-decay in "The Origin of the Work of Art" and Rorty's complacency about world-loss in "The World Well Lost" in *Consequences of Pragmatism* (Minneapolis: University of Minnesota Press, 1982) is a striking reinforcement of this point.

My goal in the chapters to follow is thus to suggest that the resistance to a deep-structure mapping of the dialectic of Enlightenment can more profitably be replaced by an aesthetic critique that would recognize subjectivity as an expression or effect of conditions that can be traced to no underlying set of causes but that must ultimately be referred back to the subject itself, or perhaps more accurately, to the subjectivity of the subject as an irreducibly particular center of affectivity. According to Kant's *Critique of Judgment*, the task of an aesthetic critique is to establish the validity of claims that originate in the purely subjective, affective realm of pleasure and pain. Phrased somewhat more constructively, it could be said that the task of an aesthetic critique is to arrive at an account of subjectivity that might satisfy the explanatory needs that various forms of deep-structure theory attempted to meet while at the same time saving the contingency of appearances that deep-structure theory found it necessary to suppress. And I would further suggest that affect is, in the realm of the subject, a trace of the contingency of the world itself. In the hope of making these claims more explicit, I turn first to a more detailed discussion of the theory of aesthetic judgment as formulated by Kant in the third *Critique*, and proceed from there to a further account of its implications for contemporary thought.

# 2

## Aesthetics as critique

Heimit endige ich also mein ganzes kritisches Geschäft.
(With this, then, I bring my entire critical undertaking to a close.)

Immanuel Kant[1]

To summarize a central claim of the preceding chapter, it is my
contention that the contemporary critique of the Enlightenment
originates from within the Enlightenment itself and must be
understood as a consequence or continuation of the Enlightenment, and not as a rejection of its critical program. More specifically, recent critiques of the Enlightenment – many of which
profess to have "overcome" the Enlightenment model of reason –
represent protracted developments of the problem that Kant
broached in the theory of reflective aesthetic judgment, in which
the separation of fact and value deemed necessary for the Enlightenment program fails to account for the "free particulars" of
pleasure and pain, which escape the control of cognition and
morality. Not at all surprisingly, then, post-Enlightenment
thought as manifested in an impressively wide range of figures,
from Nietzsche to Barthes and Žižek, has found substantial energy in the power of pleasure to trouble our existing frameworks
and routines. When faced with the problem of the non-closure of
the system of critical philosophy, Kant reasoned that there must
be a form of knowledge, modeled in the judgments we make
about the beautiful and the sublime, that remain rational while

[1] Immanuel Kant, *Critique of Judgment*, trans. James Creed Meredith (Oxford:
Clarendon Press, 1986), p. 7. (Henceforth cited as *CJ*.)

refusing to subsume particulars under pre-existing categories or rules. The rationality of Enlightenment philosophy modeled in Kant's critical system is thus upset by the discoveries of the third *Critique*, in which Kant finds it manifestly difficult to prove the validity of aesthetic judgment. Kant's theory of reflective judgment can be established, if at all, by reference to a "community sense" (the *sensus communis aestheticus*); but, as we shall see, it is also the paradoxical task of reflective aesthetic judgments to create the very community to which the notion of "common sense" refers.

To recognize the problem of aesthetic judgment articulated in Kant's third *Critique* as a form of the Enlightenment's self-criticism can help shape a critical response to canonical interpretations of Horkheimer and Adorno's *Dialectic of Enlightenment*. It can do so, first, in ways that are generally consistent with postmodern readings of Kant, i.e., by identifying the ways in which the Enlightenment desire to be both systematic and complete proved impossible to achieve. But its broader purpose is to locate an affective mode of subjectivity that does not depend upon the subsumption of the free or contingent particulars exemplified in pleasure and pain under the rule of universal concepts. Indeed, the critical potential of aesthetic judgment is most forcefully registered in critical response to a world in which claims of truth are grounded in the empirically determinable, sense-perceptible properties of objects, which in acts of cognition are subordinated to universal laws.[2] As Heidegger argues in "The Origin of the Work of Art," "truth means today and has long meant the agreement or conformity of knowledge with fact . . . The critical concepts of truth which, since Descartes, start out from truth as certainty, are merely variations of this definition of truth as correctness. This nature of truth which is familiar to us – correctness in representation – stands and falls with truth as unconcealedness of beings."[3] Feeling nonetheless remains cognitive in a deeper

---

[2] Cf. Jay M. Bernstein, *The Fate of Art* (University Park: Pennsylvania State University Press, 1992), pp. 59–60.

[3] Martin Heidegger, "The Origin of the Work of Art" in *Poetry, Language, Thought*, trans. Albert Hofstadter (New York: Harper and Row, 1971), pp. 51–52. In "The Age of the World Picture" Heidegger speaks of mathematics as the paradigm for what in Kant are determinate judgments: *Ta mathēmata* indicates that which is known already (always already), in advance; the ground plan according to which things can be known. *The Question Concerning Technology and Other Essays*, trans. William Lovitt (New York: Harper and Row, 1979), pp. 118–19. For

sense; affect possesses what Heidegger would describe in "The Origin of the Work of Art" as "world-disclosive" power.

As far as Horkheimer and Adorno are concerned, the Enlightenment project to gain a conceptual grasp of the world is bound to run aground on account of its universalizing ambitions. If it is true, as Horkheimer and Adorno seem to be saying, that the roots of domination lie in conceptual thought, then the Enlightenment labors against its own ambitions insofar as it continues to labor conceptually. The work of the concept inaugurates a self-canceling dialectic in which the ethical and emancipatory goals of the Enlightenment are undermined by the demands of a conceptual framework that exacts an oppressive conformity as the price of existence in the world. The consequences of the Enlightenment so seen involve the transformation of purposive action into instrumental behavior, the elimination of judgments of quality, and the reduction of all questions of value to the principles of fact, with which positivist science is best equipped to deal. Indeed, Horkheimer and Adorno clearly say that though the Enlightenment model of emancipation begins with the emergence of free, subjective, self-consciousness from what Kant called the "leading-strings of nature" it results in the domination of the natural world and, in a final twist of fate, in the cancelation of the subject's ability to establish a sphere of purposive action of its own.

Following this interpretation, there would seem to be no alternative to the dead-end of Enlightenment thought, in part because the historical Enlightenment is but a manifestation of the essential nature of Western rationality. But if the essays in *Dialectic of Enlightenment* simply amount to an account of the degeneration of reason, if the logic of reason's undoing is both systematic and irreversible, and if their history tells of a reversal of the Enlightenment's optimistic narrative in such a way as to plot the course of Western culture as regressive, then truly we reflect and reason in the dark.[4] Our situation with respect to the Enlightenment would

modern science, experiment means to represent or conceive the conditions under which a specific series of motions can be made susceptible of being followed. The ground plan furnishes a criterion and constrains the anticipatory representing of the conditions (p. 121). This is vastly different from the Aristotelian concept of experiment, which was "the observation of things in themselves, their qualities and modifications under changing conditions" (*ibid.*).

[4] Cf. Hannah Arendt's *Lectures on Kant's Political Philosophy*, ed. Ronald Beiner (Chicago: University of Chicago Press, 1982), p. 10; Bernstein, *The Fate of Art*, p. 65, who makes this claim about Kant's third *Critique*.

not be just perspectival, parergonal, or indeterminate, but altogether unintelligible.

In part as an attempt to avoid this fate, Habermas has sought to elaborate a paradigm of reason that would avoid what he saw as the self-canceling tendencies of Enlightenment rationality. His theory draws heavily on a notion of communicative action that is grounded in the concerns that all speaking subjects share by virtue of their pragmatic investment in the lifeworld. In Habermas's view, all speaking subjects are linked by the desire to understand what is said; this desire in turn presupposes that what is communicated in speech has a structure that is intelligible and can be shared. I will discuss the Habermassian theory at greater length in connection with the issue of communication in Kant's third *Critique* in chapter 4. There I hope to clarify that the Habermassian understanding of communication is based upon an "intersubjective" reading of Kant that mistakes Kant's *sensus communis aestheticus* for the *sensus communis logicus*. Not surprisingly, perhaps, Habermas does not regard affect as offering a legitimate basis for validity-claims. For the moment, however, I wish only to comment on Habermas's reading of the essays of *Dialectic of Enlightenment*, for it suggests a pressing need to rethink the relationship between the critical Enlightenment project and the contemporary "critiques" of the Enlightenment that Habermas there rejects.

According to Habermas in *The Philosophical Discourse of Modernity*, Horkheimer and Adorno find themselves in a position that duplicates Nietzsche's attempt to think critically after having recognized the impossibility or exhaustion of the Enlightenment model of systematic and complete critical thought. Habermas clearly recognizes that the cynicism which may follow upon the collapse of rational structures may undermine whatever purposive or pragmatic orientation we might bring to bear upon the world.[5] For Habermas, the possibility of avoiding cynicism requires that we identify at least one rational criterion that remains unscathed by the corrosive dialectic of Enlightenment: "If [Horkheimer and Adorno] do not want to renounce the effect of a final

[5] As Habermas elsewhere charges, "Horkheimer and Adorno . . . surrender themselves to an uninhibited scepticism regarding reason, instead of weighing the grounds that cast doubt on this scepticism itself." *The Philosophical Discourse of Modernity*, trans. Frederick Lawrence (Cambridge, MA: MIT Press, 1987), p. 12.

unmasking and still want to *continue with critique*, they will have to leave at least one rational criterion intact for their explanation of the corruption of *all* rational criteria. In the face of this paradox, self-referential critique loses its orientation."[6] According to Habermas, there are only two options that remain available after the strategy of "unmasking" has been exhausted, and they prove equally untenable. The first is Nietzsche's recourse to the "theory of power," though precisely why or how the notion of will-to-power is a "theory" is something that Habermas fails to explain. To be sure, Nietzsche makes a distinction between active and reactive forces, but as Habermas himself recognizes, Nietzsche refuses to think of the will to power as a "theory" open to verification or falsification in any conventional sense.[7] Rather, "will to power" describes purposes of the kind that artworks demonstrate – purposes that can best be evaluated in terms of qualities like intensity, subtlety, or strength. But it is precisely here that Habermas sees the Nietzschean recourse to power as vulnerable to co-optation by an irrational aestheticism. Indeed, Habermas describes Nietzsche's stance as consistent with Horkheimer and Adorno's position in *Dialectic of Enlightenment* insofar as neither provides an objective basis for judgment. On Habermas's account, Nietzsche confirms the truth of what Horkheimer and Adorno have to say – that we cannot finally distinguish reason from myth: "the fusion of reason and power revealed by critique abandons the world to the irreconcilable struggle between powers, as if it *were* the mythic world" (*The Philosophical Discourse of Modernity*, p. 127). More extensively, Habermas argues that the Nietzschean position implicitly taken up in *Dialectic of Enlightenment* amounts to an "aesthetic" critique of reason whose reliance on the notion of power severs all ties with the rational, universal elements in judgments of taste and renders these unavailable for all progressive social and ethical projects. In Nietzsche, he argues, the aesthetic notion of "taste" becomes nothing more than an expression of the irrationality of the will identifiable in the "yes and no of the palate":

Nietzsche detaches that moment of reason, which comes into its own in the logic proper to the aesthetic-expressive sphere of value, and especially in avant-garde art and art criticism, from its connection with theoreti-

---

[6] *Ibid.*, pp. 126–27.     [7] *Ibid.*, p. 125.

cal and practical reason . . . he stylizes aesthetic judgment, on the model of a "value appraisal" exiled to irrationality, into a capacity for discrimination beyond good and evil, truth and falsehood. In this way, Nietzsche gains criteria for a critique of culture that unmasks science and morality as being in similar ways ideological expressions of a perverted will to power, just as *Dialectic of Enlightenment* denounces these structures as embodiments of instrumental reason . . . The architectonics of Adorno's later philosophy, in which his *Negative Dialectics* and *Aesthetic Theory* mutually support one another, are also evidence of this – the one, which develops the paradoxical concept of the nonidentical, points to the other, which deciphers the mimetic content hidden in avant-garde works of art.

(*The Philosophical Discourse of Modernity*, pp. 128–29)

The second option that Habermas claims is available for critical thinking that has recognized the exhaustion of the process of "unmasking" is said to lie latent in Horkheimer and Adorno's own work, which Habermas describes as dramatizing its own contradictions aesthetically, rather than resolving them theoretically, or as he puts it, "stirring up, holding open, and no longer wanting to overcome theoretically the performative contradiction inherent in an ideology critique that outstrips itself" (p. 127). As Habermas makes clear, however, his own belief is that the performance of a contradiction does nothing to immunize the performer against the charge of irrationality. On his account, the performance of irrationality leaves open no room for reflection on the contradictions that this performance may express. Rather, he argues that a performative contradiction negates any effort at clear or systematic thinking and can lead only to *ad hoc* judgments of affirmation or dissent. This is his opinion of what aesthetic reflection involves, and on his account of Horkheimer and Adorno's position "any attempt to develop a theory at this [aesthetic] level of reflection would have to slide off into the groundless; they therefore eschew theory and practice determinate negation on an ad hoc basis, thus standing firm against that fusion of reason and power that plugs all crevices . . . A practiced spirit of contradiction is all that remains of the 'spirit of . . . unrelenting theory.' And this practice is like an incantation seeking 'to turn . . . to its end' the negative spirit of restless progress."[8] In response, Habermas summons us to exercise what Kant describes as the power of judgment (*Urteilskraft*); but as we shall have occasion

---

[8] *Ibid.*, pp. 127–28. The passage from *Dialectic of Enlightenment* is on p. 42.

further to see, the Habermassian notion of judgment veers sharply away from the aesthetic orientation of Kant's third *Critique*. Habermassian communicative action is based upon the principles of what Kant would call "determinant" judgment, whereas Kant's notion of aesthetic reflection is closer to Wittgenstein's interest in modes of knowledge that proceed in the absence of criteria.[9]

Following the lead of Kant's third *Critique*, I believe that it may indeed be possible to locate a critical value in a form of judgment that takes its bearings by the affects and whose procedures are fundamentally reflective. This project bears certain affinities with poststructuralist thinking insofar as it recognizes the incommensurability of the aesthetic domain with respect to the realms of cognition and morality; but it proposes to go beyond the poststructuralist reading of Kant by reassessing what Kant seeks in arguing for the universal validity of subjectively grounded claims: a reappraisal of the role of the passions in revealing how human purposes fit in relation to the contingency of the world. At the same time, a reassessment of Kant's theory of reflective judgment can allow us to save the project of aesthetic critique from the "performative contradiction" that Habermas finds in Horkheimer and Adorno's work, to dissociate it from the utopian longings of Romantic poetry, and to buffer it against the sheer "iconoclasm" Habermas sees in modern art. Rather than think of aesthetics as a manifestation of what Habermas describes as a Romantic "excitation" of the spirit, and rather than suppose that aesthetics designates a range of properties that mark autonomous works of art (thereby presupposing that we know what it is that sets "art" apart from everything that is non-art), the Kantian theory of aesthetic judgment leaves the identity of artworks largely unspecified and concentrates instead on the claims we make when confronted with instances of beauty (pleasure) and sublimity (pleasure/pain). The indeterminacy that is characteristic of the aesthetic domain in the third *Critique* stems from the fact that Kant is unwilling to accept what a thinker like Hegel later takes for granted: the existence of a determinate and autonomous class of

---

[9] On judgment without criteria in Wittgenstein, see Stanley Cavell, *The Claim of Reason* (Oxford: Oxford University Press, 1979). Likewise, Habermas's critique of Horkheimer and Adorno provides no defense against what Slavoj Žižek has recently described in psychoanalytic terms as "retroactive performativity." See Žižek, *For They Know Not What They Do: Enjoyment as a Political Factor* (London: Verso, 1991).

objects called "works of art." The indeterminacy of the aesthetic in Kant is nonetheless consistent with the fact that the central preoccupation of the third *Critique* lies in grappling with what goes unaccounted for by the categorical operations of cognition and morality.

This is to say that the third *Critique* is mistakenly seen as inaugurating a theory of art. On the contrary, the third *Critique* can help us appreciate what Adorno means in his posthumous *Aesthetic Theory* when he says that what is accepted in academic discourse as the normative "theory of art" constitutes a systematic betrayal of the critical potential of the aesthetic domain.[10] What lies at stake in the third *Critique* is not any quality that inheres in "works of art" *qua* objects, but how the subject feels the divisions between fact ("is") and value ("ought"), between pure theoretical reason (cognition) and pure practical reason (morality), the phenomenal and the noumenal realms. If any basis for relating these domains is to be found – if the subject is to feel the world as a whole – Kant thinks it must take as its point of departure the particular pleasures or pains that remain unaccounted for when all pragmatic and economic interests have been subtracted, and likewise when all desire for or interest in the existence of objects has been removed.[11]

But if aesthetic reflection in Kant does not subtend an autonomous object-domain, if aesthetic judgment is not a theory about objects or experience, and if Kant leaves the relationship between reflective judgment and those forms of praxis manifested in works of art necessarily undetermined, then we are pressed even

[10] Adorno's reaction in *Aesthetic Theory* represents an indictment of academic philosophy's refusal to respect the indeterminacy of art: "academic philosophy has assigned aesthetics a place in the division of philosophical labor. True aesthetics reacts to this debasement by demanding that phenomena be lifted of their mere existence and made to reflect on themselves . . . aesthetics must try to articulate what its object in its immediacy is driving at." Theodor Adorno, *Aesthetic Theory*, ed. Gretel Adorno and Rolf Tiedemann, trans. C. Lenhardt (New York: Routledge and Kegan Paul, 1984), Appendix A-1, p. 370. Lambert Zuidervaart expresses this problem well when he adds that traditional aesthetics "assumes that there are individual perceivers seeking unique experiences toward discrete objects." *Adorno's Aesthetic Theory: The Redemption of Illusion* (Cambridge, MA: MIT Press, 1991), p. 235.

[11] As Jacques Derrida writes, "[the third *Critique*] cuts out its field only by cutting itself off from the interests in desire, by losing interest in desire." "Parergon," in *The Truth in Painting*, trans. Geoff Bennington and Ian McLeod (Chicago: University of Chicago Press, 1987), p. 37.

more strongly to say what such judgment reveals and to pursue the problem of defining its powers with respect to the domains of cognition and morality. What are the claims that beauty and sublimity make, and how can they be seen as the basis for claims that do not conform to the theories of cognitive or moral judgment? By way of responding to these questions, my aim in the pages that follow is to explore the specific indeterminacy that attaches to aesthetic reflection in Kant. Then I can identify the ways in which a notion of judgment modeled on elements at work in the third *Critique* can move us beyond Horkheimer and Adorno's response to the Enlightenment by establishing the role of feeling in the subject's relationship to the world.

In proceeding, I want to recall the place of the third *Critique* with respect to Kant's philosophical system as a whole, recognizing all the while that Kant had no intention of advancing a theory of aesthetic experience and made no effort to limit his claims to what we have come to recognize as autonomous works of art. As we shall see, it is the very fragility of Kant's notion of reflective aesthetic judgment that is a key to its critical power with respect to the Enlightenment distinction of value and fact. In the process, I hope to draw out the further implications of Kant's critique by identifying in the problem of judgment the impossibility of sustaining the division of experience according to the distinct articulations of theory (cognition) and practice (morality), hence the contingency of that distinction. Specifically, I want to argue that the self-criticism of the Enlightenment that originates in Kant's third *Critique* takes as its point of departure reflection on what is otherwise lost or sacrificed by the need to maintain a distinction between a cognitive understanding of the causal relations of nature and the unconditioned freedom of the will, which affords the subject a pure legislative autonomy: what is lost is feeling – which is to suggest that the price of Enlightenment was indeed a certain "disenchantment" of the world.

The third *Critique* was designed to seal Kant's philosophical system with a closure and a finality that otherwise it would have lacked by addressing the formation of a principle that would justify, determine, but also comprehend the difference between the fact-world of theoretical reason and the moral world of pure practical reason, as elaborated in the first and second

*Critiques*.[12] The proud and conclusive statement that punctuates the end of the Preface to the *Critique of Judgment*, cited in the epigraph above, suggests nothing less: "With this, then, I bring my entire critical undertaking to a close" (Heimit endige ich also mein ganzes kritisches Geschäft) (*CJ*, Preface, p. 7). At the same time, and for many of the same reasons, Kant hoped that the theory of reflective judgment would be able to repair the appearance of a fissure or gap between the natural world, where the laws of causality reign, and the moral world, where the will is free and autonomous and empowered to legislate for itself, thus securing the claim that it is in principle a single world – the world of "experience" – that we inhabit.[13] In so doing, the third *Critique* was meant to show how the powers of subjective freedom and autonomy can be realized within the world of nature, principally by realigning the causal understanding of nature at work in the first *Critique* with the moral conception of praxis grounded in the freedom of the will rooted in the second. In Kant's terms, the purpose of the third *Critique* was to show that "the concept of freedom is meant to *actualize* in the sensible world the end proposed by its laws" (my emphasis) *and* that "nature must consequently also be capable of being regarded in such a way that in the conformity to law of its form it at least harmonizes with the possibility of the ends to be effectuated in it according to the laws of freedom" (*CJ*, Preface, p. 14). For Kant, there must be some basis on which to think that nature (or, at any rate, the "supersensible realm" that he posits as the basis of nature's lawfulness) is consistent with the concept of unconditioned and autonomous human freedom. The world of nature must be recognized as lawful, but it must also be amenable to transformation by the human will.

---

[12] Specifically, Kant asks about the nature of the concept by which the causality of the will gets its rule. Is it a concept of nature or a concept of freedom? Is it "technically-practical" or "morally-practical"? *Critique of Judgment*, p. 9. Kant argues that this principle cannot be either technical or moral, for then it would be located within one of the spheres whose boundaries he is attempting to adjudicate.

[13] Cf. "Parergon," in *The Truth in Painting*, p. 17. In uncovering an abyss that is formed by a hollowing out of the "ground" of philosophy – a hollowing out that is produced as a consequence of the search for a principle, foundation, or ground – the problem of reflective judgment addressed by the third *Critique* already contains much of the machinery of postmodern "difference." Indeed, it could be said that the philosophy of difference was "discovered" by Kant, who intended the third *Critique* to demonstrate the impossibility of building a bridge across the fictional abyss separating nature and freedom.

Likewise, we must be able to recognize one another as the potential citizens of a "kingdom of ends," but we also wish to know that the lawfulness we ascribe to nature does not contravene the principles of moral freedom. Yet it seems that our knowledge of the ground that could unify experience in such ways is remarkably difficult to locate and even more difficult to prove, in part because it is itself neither theoretical nor practical. As Kant explicitly states, "the concept of this ground neither theoretically nor practically attains to a knowledge of it, and so *has no peculiar realm of its own*" (*ibid.*; my emphasis). It is precisely a domain of knowledge that is without grounds or, as Wittgenstein would say, without criteria, that the theory of reflective judgment is meant to establish.[14]

In its insistence on the object-less nature of the pleasures and pains that form the ground for judgments of taste, the *Critique of Judgment* represents an attempt to pursue the process of self-reflection begun in the first two *Critiques* by means of a more radical thinking-through of the principle that divides the world of "experience" into two domains. But, as Kant himself admits, the third *Critique* fails in its attempt to achieve a clear conceptual justification for these divisions. According to Kant's own account, a critique of reflective judgment rests on principles that cannot themselves be justified within the framework of critical thought. Thus, the theory of aesthetic reflection does not provide a firm or final unifying "ground" for experience, as Kant hoped it might. It is not a critique-to-end-all-critiques. Rather, aesthetic reflection discovers in feeling the non-closure of the philosophical project of critique.

In conjunction with the desire to recover the unity of experience, the third *Critique* took it as its task to respond to the aesthetic theories of Alexander Baumgarten and Christian Wolff, who had begun to give definition to aesthetics as a separate and independent realm of philosophy, but who had also accepted the belief that the knowledge associated with things beautiful and sublime was inherently "confused" or "mixed."[15] The notion that aesthetics is a

---

[14] It is precisely in the discovery of the circularity or groundlessness of its claims that any theory of interpretation (and, likewise, any theory of the limits of interpretation) must recognize the ways in which taste can fulfill the desire to regard those qualities that are associated with the subject's affective life as revealing something true and valid about the world that cognition and morality could not.

[15] See *CJ*, sec. 15, pp. 69–71. Kant wishes to purify aesthetic judgments as part of the project to distinguish the role of the philosopher in separating the culture of modern Enlighteners from that of the untutored masses.

hybrid form of knowledge stems at least from Descartes, who described hunger, thirst, pain, and other similar intentional states based upon sensation as "nothing but confused modes of thinking which arise from the union and, as it were, intermingling of mind with the body."[16] What Descartes specifically wants the "imagination" to explain is how we can move from the knowledge of facts to the more complex states we customarily attribute to self-conscious beings. As thinkers as diverse as Terry Eagleton, Paul Guyer, Howard Caygill, and Luc Ferry have all pointed out, the term "confusion" in Baumgarten's *Aesthetica* of 1750 and 1758 indicates a similar "fusion" or "mixture" of sense and reason, and not a muddle of knowledge. Eagleton is particularly clear on this point: "in their organic interpenetration, the elements of aesthetic representation resist that discrimination into discrete units which is characteristic of conceptual thought. But this does not mean that such representations are obscure: on the contrary, the more 'confused' they are – the more unity-in-variety they attain – the more clear, perfect and determinate they become."[17]

Kant's response to Baumgarten and Wolff – who most likely

---

16 René Descartes, *Meditation* VI, in *The Philosophical Writings of Descartes*, vol. II, trans. John Cottingham, Robert Stoothoff, and Dugald Murdoch (Cambridge: Cambridge University Press, 1984), p. 56. Descartes also speaks of the imagination as a form of "confused representation," as in *Meditation* VI, where he describes the imagination of a chiliagon in these terms. For Descartes, imagination is an apprehension by the "inward vision" of the mind.

17 Terry Eagleton, *The Ideology of the Aesthetic* (Oxford: Blackwell, 1990), p. 15. He goes on to say that, according to this pre-Kantian thinking, "A poem is in this sense a perfected form of sensate discourse. Aesthetic unities are thus open to rational analysis, though they demand a specialized form or idiom of reason, and this is aesthetics. Aesthetics, Baumgarten writes, is the 'sister' of logic, a kind of *ratio inferior* or feminine analogue of reason at the lower level of sensational life. Its task is to order this domain into clear or perfectly determinate representations, in a manner akin to (if relatively autonomous of) the operations of reason proper. Aesthetics is born of the recognition that the world of perception and experience cannot simply be derived from abstract universal laws, but demands its own appropriate discourse and displays its own inner, if inferior, logic. As a kind of concrete thought or sensuous analogue of the concept, the aesthetic partakes at once of the rational and the real, suspended between the two somewhat in the manner of the Lévi-Straussian myth" (pp. 15–16). Cf. Wittgenstein's rejection of psychologistic attempts to explain aesthetic judgment: "People still have the idea that psychology is one day going to explain all our aesthetic judgments, and they mean experimental psychology. This is very funny – very funny indeed. There doesn't seem to be any connection between what psychologists do and any judgment about a work of art. We might examine what sort of thing we would call an explanation of an aesthetic judgment." *Lectures and Conversations on Aesthetics, Psychology and Religious Belief* (Berkeley: University of California Press, n.d.), pp. 19–20.

count among the "philosophers of reputation" referred to in section 15 of the "Analytic of the Beautiful" – is stunning, and turns out to be indicative of the place that Kant ascribes to aesthetics with respect to his critical system as a whole. This response is not to clarify the problem of aesthetic judgment or to fix the position of aesthetics with respect to cognition and morality, but rather to argue that aesthetic judgments do not represent knowledge in the customary (cognitive or moral) sense at all! In comparison with cognition and morality, which give us knowledge, respectively, of fact and of value, aesthetic judgment stands on no ground other than that of the subject:

I have already stated that an aesthetic judgment is quite unique, and affords absolutely no, (not even a confused,) knowledge of the Object. It is only through a logical judgment that we get knowledge. The aesthetic judgment, on the other hand, refers the representation, by which an Object is given, solely to the Subject, and brings to our notice no quality of the object, but only the final form in the determination of the powers of representation engaged upon it. The judgment is called aesthetic for the very reason that its determining ground cannot be a concept, but is rather the feeling (of the internal sense) of the concept in the play of the mental powers as a thing only capable of being felt. (*CJ*, sec. 15, p. 71)

In making claims of taste, Kant says, we invoke concepts "from which nothing can be cognized in respect of the Object, and nothing proved, because it is in itself indeterminable and useless for knowledge" (*CJ*, sec. 57, p. 208). Similarly, Kant insists that although the principle of reflective judgment rests on an underlying *a priori* concept, this is a concept "from which, properly speaking, we get *no cognition of a thing*" (*CJ*, Preface, p. 5; emphasis added). So too Kant claims in section 2 of the "Analytic of the Beautiful" that aesthetic pleasure concerns itself not at all with the "real existence of the thing, but rather [with] what estimate we form of it on mere contemplation" (*CJ*, sec. 2, p. 43).[18] It is in part as a response to the subjectivism that seems to govern Kant's claims that Adorno later attempts to reclaim the objectivity of art, in part by theorizing art as that which cannot be appropriated by

---

[18] Section 9 provides a somewhat more intricate formulation of this claim. There, Kant argues that when we call something beautiful, beauty is to be regarded as "a quality of the object forming part of its inherent determination according to concepts; although beauty is for itself, apart from any reference to the feeling of the Subject, nothing" (*CJ*, p. 59).

the subject's consuming passion to make the world respond to its desires or needs. And yet Kant goes on to suggest that the power of beauty is to show that cognition may not be all of knowledge, thus holding out the possibility that there may indeed be something valid in the way of knowledge that we communicate in making aesthetic judgments. As Kant says, although claims of taste "do not of themselves contribute a whit to the knowledge of things, *they still belong wholly to the faculty of knowledge*" (*CJ*, Preface, pp. 5–6; emphasis added).

How is this possible? What is it that we claim to know in aesthetic judgments that is not the knowledge of any "thing"? How can there be a kind of judgment that operates without either concepts or categories?[19] In section 8 of the "Analytic of the Beautiful," Kant specifies that the universality of the pleasure informing judgments of taste is a "subjective universal validity" (*CJ*, p. 55). To say that "subjective universal validity" is based upon feeling may be right, but it leaves open the question of how something that is "subjective" (like feeling) can also be categorically and universally true. Kant reasons that if claims of taste represent any kind of knowledge at all, this must be a knowledge that does not subsume the particularities of sensuous experience under the laws associated with categories and concepts, in part because the particularities in question – the feelings of pleasure or pain that arise in instances of the beautiful and the sublime – do not bear a necessary relationship to any objects.[20] It has long been thought of as a "fallacy" of the pathetic or projective imagination (or, in Horkheimer and Adorno's language, a relapse into myth) to ascribe subjective feelings to artefactual creations or to the things of the natural world. This is not to say that we may not wish to make such ascriptions, or that we do not in fact make them, even or especially in what Adorno calls the "disenchanted" world. Indeed, the history of our engagement with Romanticism could be understood as the ongoing negotiation of this wish; Kant

---

[19] The first *Critique* clearly states that "All synthesis . . . is subject to the categories; and since experience is knowledge by means of connected perceptions, the categories are conditions of the possibility of experience, and are therefore valid a priori for all objects of experience." Kant, *Critique of Pure Reason*, trans. Norman Kemp Smith (New York: St. Martin's Press, 1965), B 161.

[20] I note here that the first problem is not, as Eagleton and others have suggested, that these particulars cannot be subsumed under laws, but rather than they are not readily associable with objects.

himself refers to something like it in his account of the sublime, which is said to involve "a certain . . . substitution of a respect for the Object in place of one for the idea of humanity in our own self – the Subject."[21] Indeed, even Adorno acknowledges the desire to make a mute nature speak.[22] Kant is nonetheless emphatic that affect is an irreducible quality of the *subject*.

The point most directly at issue is that claims of taste, grounded in subjective feelings of pleasure and pain, constitute what Kant calls "reflective" as opposed to "determinant" (*bestimmend*) judgments. Whereas determinant judgments *subsume* or *subordinate* particulars to universal laws that are given in advance, in reflective judgments only the particular is given. But insofar as claims of taste are indeed valid judgments and not merely statements of preferences or pronouncements about what one happens to find agreeable, a universal term must somehow be found to govern them. Jean-François Lyotard suggests that this requires the power of what in Kant's *Anthropology* is called *Witz* or *Ingenium*.[23] Hannah Arendt says at one point that in reflective judgments we "derive" the rule from the particular, but this seems wrong because the relationship is not exactly one of derivation,[24] at least not in the logical sense. Kant's account is as follows: "if the universal (the rule, principle, or law) is given, then the judgment which subsumes the particular under it is *determinant*. This is so even where such a judgment is transcendental and, as such, provides the conditions *a priori* in conformity with which alone subsumption under that universal can be effected. If, however, only the particular is given and the universal has to be found for it, then the judgment is simply *reflective* . . . The reflective judgment which is compelled to ascend from the particular in nature to the universal, stands, therefore, in need of a principle" (*CJ*, Introduction, p. 18). To help establish the contrast between determinant and reflective judgments, Gilles Deleuze offers the example of a doctor who knows what "typhoid" means conceptually, but who is incapable of diagnosing it in individual cases. "We might be inclined to see in the diagnosis (which implies a gift or an art) an

---

21 *CJ*, sec. 27, p. 106.    22 See *Aesthetic Theory*, p. 115.
23 Kant, *Anthropology from a Pragmatic Point of View*, ed. and trans. Mary J. Gregor (The Hague: Martinus Nijhoff, 1974), sec. 44. p. 96.
24 Arendt, "Imagination" (Seminar on Kant's *Critique of Judgment* given at the New School for Social Research, Fall, 1970), in *Lectures on Kant's Political Philosophy*, p. 83.

example of determining [*sic*] judgment, since the concept is supposed to be known. But in relation to an individual case the concept itself is not given: it is problematic, or altogether indeterminate. In fact the diagnosis is an example of reflective judgment. If we look to medicine for an example of determining judgment, we must turn to a therapeutic decision: there the concept is given in relation to an individual case, but what is difficult is its application."[25] The problem of reflective aesthetic judgment is equally difficult, for it requires judgments for which there are no prior rules. It is as if in instances of reflective aesthetic judgment the universal concept must each time be invented anew.[26]

As this discussion may suggest, reflective judgments, which labor in search of universal concepts, hope to accomplish something more than the validation of the free, sensuous particulars associated with pure subjective experience (*my* pleasure, *my* pain). By the same token, a Kantian account of the critical potential of aesthetic judgment must involve something more than a revolt by particulars against the tyranny of universal concepts, if only because the aesthetic judgments lodged in claims about beauty and sublimity are communicable and so place us in the position of presupposing a common ground. The specific difficulty of judgment discovered in the third *Critique* leads neither to a "performative contradiction" nor to the practice of "ad hoc determinate negation," as Habermas might suspect. Rather, what is articulated in the third *Critique* is something like the process in which "free particulars" refuse the governance of those universal laws that stand waiting for them in advance in the hope of (re)creating a community of sense. Not surprisingly, thinkers like Habermas and Arendt have wished to extract a communitarian politics and a rationalist ethics from the principle of communicability advanced in the third *Critique*. But what is in fact discovered in the third *Critique* is the difficulty of invoking community as the pre-existing ground of ethical or political relations. For while it seems that a community must be presupposed to exist in the same way and for the same reasons that a "common sense" must be presupposed to exist for the purpose of aesthetic judgment, its

25 Gilles Deleuze, *Kant's Critical Philosophy*, trans. Hugh Tomlinson and Barbara Habberjam (Minneapolis: University of Minnesota Press, 1984), pp. 59–60.
26 On certain accounts of aesthetics, this is the further burden of the modernist arts: the reinvention of the *institution* of art with each particular case.

existence cannot be proved; it must also be created by the exercise of judgment in making claims of taste.

These observations may help shed further light on the issue of the difference between reflective aesthetic judgments on the one hand and cognitive and moral judgments on the other. Clearly, aesthetic judgments do not have the status of epistemological claims, which operate by subsuming the particulars of experience under laws that are given in advance. But neither are they moral assertions, for they are said to originate in and continue to make reference to the world of sense. And yet precisely because they do not fall into a province of their own, there is a constant temptation to assimilate reflective aesthetic judgments to these other categories.[27] Jay M. Bernstein provides an insightful account of this issue:

Kant's vocabulary and argument move so as to sustain, precisely, the autonomy of judgment from the interests of knowledge and morality. To attempt, as all Kant's interpreters have, to force Kant's argument into either an epistemological or a moral mode necessarily does violence to the overall strategy governing the argument. To subsume judgments of taste wholly under either the goals of understanding or the demands of reason necessarily violates the free delight specific to judgments concerning the beautiful. Conversely, however, if aesthetic reflection were wholly separated from questions about the true and the good, it is difficult to see what sense or point could be attributed to it beyond simple pleasure (which would reduce the question of beauty to mere agreeableness, and hence accede to aesthetic scepticism). It is this that explains Kant's own temptations to assimilate aesthetic judgment to either morality or understanding: they are to provide the "hidden" interest behind aesthetic disinterestedness.[28]

---

[27] Lawrence Cahoone offers quite a different view of the matter when, from a post-Nietzschean perspective, he reasons that "goodness and truth are types of aesthetic values. This is not to aestheticize truth or morality in the sense of making truth and goodness resemble other aesthetic qualities, like beauty; nor does it collapse the other functions of judgment into the exhibitive. Beauty is one among many different aesthetic values, and its vicissitudes are not those of truth or moral goodness. The distinction between truth and all other values is not diminished by the recognition that aesthetic valuing is the valuing of something in and for itself." *The Ends of Philosophy* (Albany: State University of New York Press, 1995), p. 352.

[28] *The Fate of Art*, p. 27. Where I disagree with Bernstein is in his claim that "then the category of disinterestedness loses its grip; it becomes a mask or façade for the 'hidden' interest. Kant's difficulty is that he has no other instruments available, at least in the first instance, with which to prise open the domain of taste, other than those provided by understanding (the faculty of knowledge) and reason (the faculty of freedom)" (pp. 27–28), in part because this explanation leads us to believe that aesthetics is in fact a region of its own, that it constitutes something more than the prime example of the problem of reflective judgment Kant chooses to discuss.

Indeed, Kant's description of the "subjective necessity" attributed to claims of taste in section 19 of the "Analytic of the Beautiful" says nothing about the force of aesthetic claims other than to indicate that their imperative force remains "conditional": "The judgment of taste exacts agreement from every one; and a person who describes something as beautiful insists that every one *ought* to give the object in question his approval and follow suit in describing it as beautiful. The *ought* in aesthetic judgments, therefore, despite an accordance with all the requisite data for passing judgment, is *still only pronounced conditionally*" (*CJ*, sec. 19, p. 82).[29]

On Kant's account, claims of taste describing merely pleasurable or unpleasant experiences would stand in need of no particular constitutive or regulative principle. Such claims would be understood as judgments of the "taste of sense" (*CJ*, sec. 8, p. 54). They might reflect delight in what we find contingently "agreeable" and would at best constitute elements in the "formation or culture of taste" (*CJ*, Preface, p. 6). Kant found all of this of interest in the pre-critical *Observations on the Feeling of the Beautiful and the Sublime*, published in 1764.[30] In the *Critique of Judgment* (1790), however, the question of taste as a mode of discrimination, or as a "finer feeling," is found to be in equal measures unproblematic and uninteresting. The history and culture of taste are, for Kant, irrelevant to reflective judgments of taste, which are meant to be categorically valid and not merely true in some *ad hoc* sense. What is difficult and therefore interesting for Kant is to demonstrate the *principle* by which claims of beauty and sublimity, which are said to have subjective pleasure at their base, can be asserted as *necessarily* true and valid. No use to wait, Kant says, for universal assent to be verified empirically, in practice, over the course of historical time. Indeed, an inductive or empirical proof of the principle of taste would at best lead us to envision the non-closure of the Enlightenment project in the form of a "bad infinity" in which the possibility of truth is dependent solely upon the open-endedness of time. (Kant means something very different in the Preface to the second edition of the *Critique of Pure Reason*, where he says that

---

[29] Last emphasis mine. In *The Fate of Art*, Bernstein takes this imperative categorically, not conditionally. See especially pp. 23–29.

[30] In the *Observations*, Kant follows in the tradition of Cicero and Gracián, which understands taste as an art of discrimination whose basis and whose ends are in society.

"some kind of metaphysics" will always be with us.) Moreover, to conceive of the notion of agreement as being hopeful because deferred indefinitely into the future could not overcome Kierkegaard's critique of Hegel, which said that every defining statement that might be binding for human existence could be postponed until the system was completed.[31] At the very least, the categorical claims of aesthetic reflective judgment must be retained if the notion of judgment modeled according to the principles of an aesthetic critique is not to expose itself to the possibility of dissolution by the bad infinity of its own temporal openendedness or to self-deception by the sheer seductiveness of *Wunschdenken*.

Kant's point is that the principle of taste seeks agreement on the basis of what it claims to be true *categorically* about the subjective experiences of pleasure and pain: "How is a judgment possible which, going merely upon the individual's *own* feeling of pleasure in an object independent of the concept of it, estimates this as a pleasure attached to the representation of the same Object *in every other individual*, and does so *a priori*, i.e. without being allowed to wait and see if other people will be of the same mind?" (*CJ*, sec. 36, p. 145).[32] This is what the *Critique of Judgment* seeks to establish, and in an account like Arendt's this is the basis for both its political import and its ethical claims. In reflective judgment, she says, one adopts the "community sense": "This *sensus communis* is what judgment appeals to in everyone, and it is this possible appeal that gives judgments their special validity" (*Lectures on Kant's Political Theory*, p. 72). And yet this account leaves two important matters unresolved. First, it does not adequately explain the way in which the subjective experiences of pleasure and pain inform the operations of the *sensus communis*. And second, it does not explain how the notion of "common sense" can be invoked in order to *ground* reflective judgments when it is only in the absence of this "common sense" that the problem of reflective

[31] As Adorno said, such a criticism could just as well be leveled back against Kierkegaard himself: "through such a deferment of the whole, the particular present – and even more the past – gains a concrete fullness that Kierkegaard's repetitions seek in vain to procure." Adorno, *Kierkegaard, Construction of the Aesthetic*, trans. Robert Hullot-Kentor (Minneapolis: University of Minnesota Press, 1989), p. 106.

[32] As Kant goes on to say, "this problem of the Critique of Judgement, therefore, is part of the general problem of transcendental philosophy: How are synthetic *a priori* judgements possible?" *CJ*, sec. 36, p. 145.

judgment comes to light. In other words, this account either ignores or pretends to have resolved what Kant himself recognized as the "difficulty" of aesthetic judgment.[33]

While demanding a form of universal assent or acknowledgment, judgments of taste are meant to preserve their grounding in the purely subjective experiences of pleasure and pain. In Kant's own estimation, there is no doubt that claims of taste have such a basis, and also no doubt that they must rely on a transcendental principle. Indeed, he takes these to be quite uncontroversial facts, "obvious to the most commonplace criticism" (*CJ*, Preface, p. 5). What remains nonetheless difficult for Kant is the issue of what he describes as a proof, deduction, or "derivation" of the transcendental, *a priori* principle of taste; what proves impossible for him to achieve is a derivation of what taste wants to claim in its *prima facie* assertions of beauty and sublimity: that the pleasure or pain taken in a given object should be held categorically true, valid for everyone, assertable by all, and likewise that the experiences of this "I" should have a share in and a claim upon whatever is to count as "experience as a whole." Kant admits that the "subjective" principle of reflective judgment "can only be indicated as the unique key to the riddle of this faculty, itself concealed from us in its sources; and there is no means of making it any more intelligible" (*CJ*, sec. 57, pp. 208–09).

The difficulty of providing a deduction of reflective aesthetic judgments leaves claims of taste radically underdetermined. Here again the distinction between aesthetic judgments, claims of fact, and moral commands is relevant. Taken as a psychological claim, an aesthetic judgment could not possibly explain *why* we must all respond aesthetically to specific objects in the same way. Nor, taken as a moral command, could it explain why one might wish to assert that *my* particular claims should command the assent of *everyone*.[34] Pure practical reason attempts to do this on the basis of a formalization of the "I," but this is precisely what Kant wishes to

---

[33] The notion of "difficulty" itself has an important and interesting history in modernism. The subject is taken up at various points by Stanley Cavell in *Must We Mean What We Say?* (Cambridge: Cambridge University Press, 1969), and especially in the essay "The Availability of Wittgenstein's Later Philosophy" (pp. 44–72).
[34] The formulation offered in section 9 is nonetheless categorical: "In a judgment of taste the pleasure felt by us is exacted from every one else as necessary" (*CJ*, p. 59).

reject in turning to pleasure and pain as the bases for judgment in the third *Critique*. In the absence of any such explanations, however, Kant risks reducing the normativity of claims of taste to the status of a prediction about factual matters that might or might not possibly be verified in time. Clearly, judgments of taste must be understood as distinct from claims of fact. By the same token, the moral interpretation of the judgment of taste overdetermines it by converting the claim of taste into an *a priori* obligation or command of the will. The result would be a tyranny inimical to the Enlightenment spirit of tolerance and to Kant's respect for the laws of causality that reign in the natural world. To propose that we respond directly to commands from the "kingdom of ends" in assimilating claims of taste to the realm of morality would moreover be to disregard its grounding in sense experience.[35]

Kant's proposed "resolution" of the antinomy of taste, which is not unlike his resolution of other antinomies elsewhere, is itself neither epistemological nor moral. Rather, it relies on a fictional or figurative expansion of the ground on which the antinomic terms are situated so that both may be accommodated. The argument takes the following form: while judgments of taste apply to objects of sense (and, as such represent "only a private judgment") they are also said to contain an "enlarged reference" which "lays the foundation of an extension of judgments of this kind to necessity for every one" (*CJ* sec. 57, p. 207). Thus in consideration of the "antinomy of taste," Kant asks us to imagine the (common / universal) position from which subjective feelings could be judged as valid for all and, likewise, to imagine such feelings as containing within them the elements of a truly common and universal sense. Kant's imaginative reconstruction of the principle of aesthetic reflection proceeds thus:

There is no possibility of removing the conflict of the above principles, which underlie every judgment of taste . . . except by showing that the concept to which the Object is made to refer in a judgment of this kind is not taken in the same sense in both maxims of the aesthetic judgment; that *this double sense, or point of view,* in our estimate, is necessary for our power of transcendental judgment; and that nevertheless *the false appearance arising from the confusion of one with the other is a natural illusion, and so unavoidable.*　　　　　　　(*CJ*, sec. 57, p. 206; emphasis added)

---

[35]　See Bernstein, *The Fate of Art*, pp. 29–30.

It is roughly on this basis that Hannah Arendt suggested that the force of Kant's *Critique of Judgment* is political, in part by arguing that the "enlargement" of one's mentality required for making claims of taste involves seeing things from the perspective of everyone else. This might happen roughly as explained in section 40 of the third *Critique*, where Kant says that the "enlargement" of our mentality is accomplished by "comparing our judgment with the possible rather than the actual judgments of others, and by putting ourselves in the place of any other man." For Arendt, "enlarged thinking" (*erweiterte Denkungsart*) is the result of over-coming the limitations that contingently attach to our judgments, of disregarding its purely subjective and private conditions, there-by defeating self-interest. And yet Arendt goes on to admit that the task of judging from the perspective of an enlarged mentality (which is to say, from the perspective of the community sense), is possible only by means of the imagination: "by the force of the imagination [critical thinking] makes the others present and thus moves in a space that is potentially public, open to all sides . . . To think with an enlarged mentality means that one trains one's imagination to go visiting" (*Lectures on Kant's Political Philosophy*, p. 43). The "enlarged mentality" necessary for making claims of taste requires the work of the imagination, which functions as the middle term between sense and understanding. But to invoke the imagination as the basis for the "enlarged mentality" is to fix something that in Kant is neither public nor private, but indetermi-nate with respect to both of these insofar as it is simply subjective. It is to beg the very question of the nature of reflective judgments rather than to isolate the specific difficulty of that question.[36]

[36] In an illustrative remark, Žižek recalls Freud's reference to a joke about a newly married husband, who responds to his friend's questions about his wife with the answer: "'I personally don't like her, but that's a matter of taste.' The paradox of this answer does not point towards an attitude of selfish calculation ('True, I don't like her, but I married her for other reasons – her wealth, her parents' social influence . . .'). Its crucial feature is that the subject, in providing this answer, pretends to assume the standpoint of universality from which 'to be likeable' appears as an idiosyncrasy, as a contingent 'pathological' feature which, as such, is not to be taken into consideration. The joke therefore relies on the impossible/untenable position of enunciation of the new husband: from this position, marriage appears as an act which belongs to the domain of universal symbolic determination and should, as such, be independent of personal idio-syncrasies – as if the very notion of marriage did not involve precisely the 'pathological' fact of liking a particular person for no particular rational rea-son." Slavoj Žižek, *The Indivisible Remainder: An Essay on Schelling and Related Matters* (London: Verso, 1996), pp. 198–99.

As we shall see further in chapter 4, Arendt's desire to secure the validity of reflective judgments by associating them with the imagination and by locating them in the public sphere does not sufficiently stress the fact that the role of the imagination in Kant is to facilitate the schematism that makes judgments of any sort possible. If the first *Critique* is to be believed, it seems that even the operations of determinant judgment require the imagination for the subsumption of particulars under general rules. Likewise in the case of determinant judgments Kant is hard pressed to say just how a particular is actually subsumed under a universal. In the "Transcendental Doctrine of Judgment" in the *Critique of Pure Reason*, for instance, Kant asks: "How, then, is the *subsumption* of intuitions under pure concepts, the *application* of a category to appearances, possible?" (A 138, B 177, p. 180). His initial answer is as follows: "obviously there must be some third thing, which is homogeneous on the one hand with the category, and on the other hand with the appearance, and which thus makes the application of the former to the latter possible. This mediating representation must be pure, that is, void of all empirical content, and yet at the same time, while it must in one respect be *intellectual*, it must in another be *sensible*. Such a representation is the *transcendental schema*" (p. 181). But Kant goes on to say that this mechanism is inscrutable and that the precise nature of this process is opaque: "This schematism of our understanding, in its application to appearances and their mere form, is an art concealed in the depths of the human soul, whose real modes of activity nature is hardly likely ever to allow us to discover" (B 181, p. 183). The appeal to "imagination" as a solution to the problem of aesthetic reflective judgment thus serves only to trade one set of opacities for another, not to resolve the difficulties at hand.

The status of the imagination as anomalous and in-between is representative of the indeterminacy of the aesthetic domain in Kant. For a philosophy so strongly oriented by the notion of territorial legislation, the notion of "aesthetic judgment" elaborated in the third *Critique* is remarkably de-territorialized. Kant argues that there is no established framework for pursuing the matter of aesthetic judgment. Accordingly, he claims that aesthetics is not a discipline, claims no realm as properly its own, and has "no field of objects appropriate to it" (*CJ*, Introduction, p. 15).

Reflective judgment is in this respect not a faculty equal to those of cognition and morality, which address properly formed object-spheres. He insists that reflective judgment exercises jurisdiction over "no peculiar realm" (p. 14). Having delimited the object-spheres proper to the first two *Critiques*, Kant explains that judgment occupies an indeterminate "middle ground." As between the two relatively secure and established fields of epistemology and morality, aesthetic or reflective judgment constitutes a middle articulation (*Mittleglied*) that is specific to neither one:

> now comes *judgment*, which in the order of our cognitive faculties forms a middle term between understanding and reason. Has *it* got independent *a priori* principles? If so, are they constitutive, or are they merely regulative, thus indicating no special realm? And do they give a rule of *a priori* to the feeling of pleasure and displeasure, as the middle term between the faculties of cognition and desire, just as understanding prescribes laws *a priori* for the former and reason for the latter? This is the topic to which the present Critique is devoted. (*CJ*, Preface, p. 4)

Insofar as reflective judgment itself can be "located" at all, it is situated in the great "gulf" (*Kluft*) that threatens the unity of experience by separating the work of epistemology and the world of fact from the world of value or the "kingdom of ends" projected by the free, unencumbered will:

> between the realm of the natural concept, as the sensible, and the realm of the concept of freedom, as the supersensible, there is a great gulf [*Kluft*] fixed, so that it is not possible to pass from the former to the latter (by means of the theoretical employment of reason), just as if they were so many separate worlds, the first of which is powerless to exercise influence on the second: still the latter is *meant* to influence the former. (*CJ*, Introduction, p. 14)

Not surprisingly, poststructuralist readers of Kant have focused great powers of concentration on the question of this "gulf" and the aporias it conjures up. In "Parergon," for instance, Derrida describes aesthetic judgment in terms of the impossible mediation of the theoretical and practical realms. "Since the *Mittleglied* also forms the articulation of the theoretical and the practical (in the Kantian sense), we are plunging into a place that is *neither* theoretical *nor* practical or else *both* theoretical *and* practical. Art (in general), or rather the beautiful, if it takes place, is inscribed here. But this *here*, this place is announced as a place deprived of place. It runs the risk, in taking place, of not having its own proper domain . . . The *Mittleglied*, intermediary member, must in effect be treated as a separable part, a particular part (*als ein besonderer Theil*). But also as a nonparticular, nondetachable part, since it forms the articulation between two others; one can even say, anticipating Hegel, an originary part (*Ur-teil*)" ("Parergon," p. 38).

The indeterminacy of aesthetic judgment in Kant can be associated with the larger project of boundary distinction, which is a concern that governs the entire Kantian critical project. Kant's purpose as an enlightened thinker is not just to increase the store of knowledge, but to secure and to legitimize what we claim to know. As is widely recognized, the Kantian project, including Kant's epistemology and his ethics, is driven by the need to mark off the various fields of cognition as a way to establish the legitimacy of each.[37] For Heidegger, this tendency is identified as the foundation of all science in the modern age: "Every science is, as research, grounded in the projection of *a circumscribed object-sphere* and is therefore necessarily a science of individualized character. Every individualized science must, moreover, in the development of its projected plan by means of its methodology, *particularize itself into specific fields of investigation* . . . Specialization is not the consequence but the foundation of the progress of all research."[38] Whereas a thinker like Habermas endorses the fact that each of the separate spheres of knowledge has come to develop a logic of its own in the culture of enlightened modernity, Kant's third *Critique* confronts the failure of the separation of the spheres. As stated in the Preface to the first edition of the first *Critique*, the need to set limits is a result of reason's "natural" tendency to transgress its bounds; it is a means to restrain the errancy that Kant locates in reason's desire to fathom truths that lie beyond its capacity: "Human reason has this peculiar fate that in one species of its knowledge it is burdened by questions which, as prescribed by the very nature of reason itself, it is not able to ignore, but which, as transcending all its powers, it is also not able to answer" (*Critique of Pure Reason*, A vii, p.7). The work of "critique" is in this respect both negative and positive. Kant says

[37] For Hannah Arendt, this suggests the policing function of the Kantian critique. See also Howard Caygill, *Art of Judgment* (Oxford: Blackwell, 1989).
[38] Heidegger, "The Age of the World Picture," p. 123; emphasis added.

that "critique limits speculative reason, it is indeed *negative*"; but he goes on to aver that to deny the positive character of critique "would be like saying the police are of no positive benefit, inasmuch as their main business is merely to prevent the violence of which citizens stand in mutual fear, in order that each may pursue his vocation in peace and security" (*Critique of Pure Reason*, B xxv, pp. 26–27).

Kant's interest in establishing limits stands at the heart of his conception of the critical nature of philosophy and follows directly from what he describes elsewhere as the failure of "metaphysics" before him. By his own account, Kant initiates the project of rational critique at a moment when metaphysics appears to be in a state of serious and irreversible decline: "Time was when metaphysics was entitled the Queen of all the sciences . . . Now, however, the changed fashion of the time brings her only scorn; a matron outcast and forsaken, she mourns like Hecuba" (*Critique of Pure Reason*, A viii, pp. 7–8). Kant's attempt is not to rehabilitate old-fashioned metaphysics, but to replace metaphysics by a project of critique, which is based on *Selbstdenken*, thinking for oneself. The problem of reflective judgment broached in the third *Critique* is a further consequence of the impossibility of "metaphysics" in the Enlightened, modern age, and a further reflection on the need to assess the consequences of this fact for the subject's own powers of self-assertion (i.e. of *Selbstdenken*).[39] Whereas "metaphysics" would require the closure of a system in which the difference between theoretical and practical reason could be reflected upon and the principles underwriting that distinction in turn justified, the notion of a reflective "critique" registers the difficulty of recovering what is lost in the distinction between theoretical and practical reason. As Derrida says, "it is in the critique that, precisely, the critical suspension is produced, the *krinein*, the in-between, the question of knowing whether the theory of judgment is theoretical *or* practical, and whether it is then referred to a regulatory or constitutive instance. But the system of pure philosophy *will have had* to include the critical

---

[39] For Kant, the self-assertion of reason yields freedom from nature: "reason has insight only into that which it produces after a plan of its own, and . . . must not allow itself to be kept, as it were, in nature's leading-strings, but must itself show the way with principles of judgment based upon fixed laws, constraining nature to give answer to questions of reason's own determining." *Critique of Pure Reason*, B xiii.

within itself, and construct a general discourse which will get the
better of the detachable and account for it. This system of pure
philosophy is what Kant calls *metaphysics*. It is not yet possible.
Only the critique can have a program that is currently possible"
("Parergon," p. 39).

There are further ramifications of these facts. Kant's critical
project is elaborated in terms of a legislative fiction in which
reason pretends all at once to be the accused, the judge, and the
witness in a quasi-judicial process. A critique of pure reason, for
instance, involves a "tribunal" (*Critique of Pure Reason*, A xii, p.20)
in which reason acts as a self-appointed "judge" who "compels
the witness to answer questions which he has himself formulated" (B xiii, p.20). The task of this tribunal, as Kant spells out
later in the first *Critique*, is to prevent us from lapsing into the war
of opinions:

The critique of pure reason can be regarded as the true tribunal for all
disputes of pure reason; for it is not involved in these disputes – disputes
which are immediately concerned with objects – but is directed to the
determining and estimating of the rights of reason in general, in accordance with the principles of their first institution.

In the absence of this critique reason is, as it were, in the state of nature,
and can establish and secure its assertions and claims only through *war*
. . . As Hobbes maintains, the state of nature is a state of injustice and
violence, and we have no option save to abandon it and submit ourselves
to the constraint of law, which limits our freedom solely in order that it
may be consistent with the freedom of others and with the common good
of all.

This freedom will carry with it the right to submit openly for discussion
the thoughts and doubts with which we find ourselves unable to deal,
and to do so without being decried as troublesome and dangerous
citizens. This is one of the original rights of human reason, which recognizes no other judge than that universal human reason in which everyone
has his say.     (*Critique of Pure Reason*, A 751–53, B 779–81; pp. 601–02)

In the third *Critique* the notion of legislatively controlled territories is part of the still wider fiction that construes reason as an
arbiter, whose judgment is called for by the antinomic nature of
the circumstances facing it. Moreover, the questions associated
with the legislative authority of reason and with the division of
phenomenal and noumenal worlds are never resolved in Kant's
first *Critique*. On the one hand, the interest at work in critical
philosophy requires a series of boundary distinctions that cannot

be justified by any final judgment; and yet to renounce the interest sustaining those distinctions would be to renounce critical philosophy and the demand for judgment altogether. Thus it is little surprise to find that these questions reappear in the *Critique of Judgment*, where the faculty of reflective judgment is called upon to address the need for a principle or faculty which would arbitrate between the claims of the others (see *CJ*, Preface, p. 3). Indeed, Kant goes so far as to say that such a function is integral to any system of rational knowledge, arguing in a passage already adduced that "in the division of a rational science the difference between objects that require different principles for their cognition is *the difference on which everything turns*" (*CJ*, Introduction, p. 9; emphasis added).

The image that weighs so heavily in the Introduction to the third *Critique*, of a fissure, gap, or gulf (*Kluft*) between the causality of nature and the realm of moral freedom, which reflective judgment is called upon to bridge, thus engages the more general legislative, judicial fiction governing Kant's critical enterprise that roots in the notion that the faculties of cognition define or delimit proper "territories" and "realms" over which they exercise governance.[40] In the *Foundations of the Metaphysics of Morals*, Kant proposes the not unrelated fiction that there exists a "division of labor" among the philosophical faculties, where the notion of such a division serves to underwrite the purity of philosophy and to distinguish its conceptual labor from all other forms of human work. This distinction in turn confirms the Enlightenment's progressive, self-justifying interpretation of itself as having achieved

---

[40] Kant explains this in terms of the juridical fiction of a "territory" or "realm" of experience over which the various faculties have jurisdiction. "Concepts, so far as they are referred to objects apart from the question of whether knowledge of them is possible or not, have their field, which is determined simply by the relation in which their Object stands to our faculty of cognition in general. – The part of a field in which knowledge is possible for us, is a territory (*territorium*) for these concepts and the requisite cognitive faculty. The part of the territory over which they exercise legislative authority is the realm (*ditio*) of these concepts, and their appropriate cognitive faculty" (*CJ*, Introduction, p. 12). Kant goes on to explain that "Understanding and reason, therefore, have two distinct jurisdictions over one and the same territory of experience" (p. 13). The difficulty lies in the fact that "neither can interfere with the other. For the concept of freedom just as little disturbs the legislation of nature, as the concept of nature influences legislation through the concept of freedom . . . Still, how does it happen that these two different realms do not form *one* realm, seeing that, while they do not limit each other in their legislation, they continually do so in their effects in the sensible world?" (*ibid.*).

a definitive distance from the "barbaric" civilizations of the past. It is a central instance of the myth that "progress" in the arts and sciences is achieved when, as Habermas says, each separate sphere of culture is allowed to develop according to its own inner logic:

All crafts, handiworks, and arts have gained by the division of labor, for when one person does not do everything, but each limits himself to a particular job which is distinguished from all the others by the treatment it requires, he can do it with greater perfection and with more facility. Where work is not thus differentiated and divided, where everyone is a jack-of-all-trades, the crafts remain at a barbaric level. It might be worth considering whether pure philosophy in each of its parts does not require a man particularly devoted to it, and whether it would not be better for the learned profession as a whole to warn those who are in the habit of catering to the taste of the public by mixing up the empirical with the rational in all sorts of proportions which they do not themselves know.[41]

In the third *Critique* Kant argues that reflective judgment provides us with the "mediating concept" – with a concept that "makes possible the transition from the pure theoretical [legislation of understanding] to the pure practical [legislation of reason] and from conformity of law in accordance with the former to final ends in accordance with the latter . . . This concept makes possible the transition from the realm of the concept of nature to that of the concept of freedom" (*CJ*, Introduction, p. 38). As a "middle term," reflective judgment is expected to shuttle back and forth between the otherwise distinct domains of pure theoretical reason (cognition) and pure practical reason (morality), for the purpose of proving the relevance of freedom in a world of objects causally ordered and to show that nature stands ready to accommodate the ends proposed by morality. But at the same time, Kant in the third *Critique* refuses to offer any determination of this middle term. Specifically, he refuses to locate or limit the work of judgment with respect to any specific class of objects, whether "fictional," "imaginary," or "aesthetic." As Adorno writes in *Aesthetic Theory*, "despite the programmatic idea of building a bridge between theoretical and practical pure reason, the faculty of judgment turns out to be *sui generis* in relation to both forms of reason"

[41] Kant, *Foundations of the Metaphysics of Morals*, trans. Robert Paul Wolff (Indianapolis, IN: Bobbs-Merrill, 1969), p. 5.

(p. 16). In Kant, the faculty of reflective judgment is defined by its refusal to control a specific object-domain.[42] The theory of reflective judgment thus recognizes the existence of legislative principles that constitute and legitimize fields of knowledge as bounded territories; but at the same time it calls into question the ability of any system to justify or ground the principle of differentiation itself. Because Kant has equal respect for the principle of boundary distinction and for the desire to link knowledge-domains, reflective judgment holds open the possibility of a rational critique while recognizing that the problem of boundary distinction cannot be resolved *überhaupt*.

As Derrida has pointed out, Kant imagines the pure philosopher as the "good architect" who wishes to bridge the gaps created by the critical system but who must prepare the way for this philosophical architecture by locating "first principles," by "clearing the ground": "The architect of reason searches, probes, prepares the ground. In search of the bedrock, the ultimate *Grund* on which to raise the whole of metaphysics" ("Parergon," p. 40). In the third *Critique*, however, Kant is faced with the fact that this architectural philosophy must presuppose the very same aesthetics which it underpins.[43] As a result Kant is faced also with the fact that any proof or derivation of the principle that would allow us to bridge this gap, any demonstration of the interest in recovering the unity of experience, is impossible to justify. Thus it seems that there is no "ground," but only the appearance of an abyss, a place of gathering negative interest, non-interest, or dis-interest, created by the separation or refusal of the determinate interests of fact and value. Although the "interest" at work in the third *Critique* is one of communication, it is not built upon the ground of linguistic universals; it would be more accurate to say that "communica-

---

[42] The theory of reflective judgment developed in the third *Critique* contains a critical force insofar as it enables what Lyotard describes as the "presentation" of that which is proper to one domain to be made outside its boundaries. Jean-François Lyotard, *The Differend: Phrases in Dispute*, trans. Georges van den Abbeele (Minneapolis: University of Minnesota Press, 1988), especially pp. 131–33.

[43] There is at least one step in Derrida's argument on this point that is, at best, implicit, namely, the reading of architecture as aesthetic rather than structural. The issue is of some importance insofar as Derrida suggests that the aesthetic is revealed in the failures, flaws, or gaps of the structure: taken as an aesthetic concept, this notion of "architecture" depends upon a concept of structure as opaque, flawed, or "dislocated."

tion" is a figure for those gaps that cannot be bridged. To think in Kantian terms, it may be the *wish* of critical philosophy to reconcile the separate realms of nature and free will. Similarly, it may be the desire of reflective judgment to advance a "higher" critique of reason by deducing the principle according to which the various faculties are divided from one another and their proper territories secured. Indeed, Kant speaks with conviction about the unity of the world of "experience." But what Kant in fact concludes is that the derivation of the "higher" principle of reflective judgment and the corresponding proof of the unity of experience remain opaque. According to Kant, we know these must exist, we may remember or presuppose them to exist, but we cannot demonstrate to the satisfaction of reason that they do in fact exist. Thus Kant also says that aesthetics offers a sign of the *impossibility* of conjoining the worlds of nature and of freedom. Indeed, Kant explicitly states that "it is not possible to throw a bridge from the one realm to the other" (*CJ*, Introduction, p. 37).

Kant's conception of reflective judgments as representing a form of knowledge that proceeds without concepts is likewise typical of the negative or counterfactual principles that are invoked in order to isolate the problem of aesthetic judgment and to establish the purity of aesthetic pleasure throughout the third *Critique*.[44] Not only is aesthetics without a territory of its own and aesthetic judgments without concept. Aesthetic pleasure is said to be without interest in the existence of the object. Aesthetic judgments give us knowledge of no "thing." (Its proximity to what Nietzsche terms nihilism is most apparent here.) Indeed, one could go so far as to say that Kant would like to avoid understanding aesthetics in relation to any form of productive praxis whatsoever. Derrida thus interprets Kant as saying that "this critique of taste does not concern production; it has in view neither 'education' nor 'culture,' which can do very well without it" ("Parergon," p. 42). In point of fact, Kant does not dissociate fine art from production in general. Rather, he aligns the products of fine art with a special mode of production, namely, one whose aim is to please "in the mere estimate of it" and not in sensation or by means of a concept (*CJ*, sec. 45, p. 167). Kant thinks of art as

[44] On Derrida's account, it is equivalent to the effort to make a "pure" or "bloodless" cut. See "Le sans du coup pure" ("The Sans of the Pure Cut") in "Parergon," pp. 83–118.

pursuing those purposes that remain when the pleasures of sense and concept have been winnowed away. Not surprisingly, Kant's notion of "fine art" seems underdetermined. Artworks demonstrate a purposiveness that is without purpose and excite a pleasure that is not within the bounds of the agreeable, the useful, or the good. Already in the *Observations on the Feeling of the Beautiful and the Sublime* of 1764 Kant had distinguished the "finer feeling" associated with the beautiful and the sublime from the pleasure felt in the gratification of inclinations, but the *Critique of Judgment* goes much farther in the effort to purify aesthetic pleasure. Pure judgments of taste are also independent of charm and emotion. Not surprisingly, Adorno calls Kant's an aesthetics of "castrated hedonism," a theory of "pleasure without pleasure," and challenges that Kant's position "fails to do justice either to artistic experience wherein satisfaction is a subordinate moment in a larger whole, or to the material-corporeal interest, i.e. repressed and unsatisfied needs that resonate in their aesthetic negations – the works of art – turning them into something more than empty patterns . . . In Kant . . . enjoyment comes in the guise of disinterestedness, a guise that makes enjoyment unrecognizable" (*Aesthetic Theory*, pp. 16, 18).

But it would be a mistake to think that the disinterested stance required by pure aesthetic pleasure is not itself impelled by a very powerful and distinct interest.[45] Indeed, it is the particular *interest* of aesthetic disinterest that the third *Critique* struggles to sustain. It is this same interest that Adorno confronts head-on when he suggests that "if Kant's disinterestedness is to be more than a synonym for indifference, it has to have a trace of untamed interest somewhere. Indeed, there is much to be said for the thesis that the dignity of works of art depends upon the magnitude of the interest from which they were wrested."[46] For Kant, there is in fact

---

[45] See Arendt's *Lectures on Kant's Political Philosophy*, p. 73 and *CJ* sec. 41. Derrida: the formula of "disinterested pleasure" is too well known, too received, "*as is the refusal it has never ceased to provoke*. Anger of Nietzsche and Artaud: disinterest or uninterestedness are supererogatory. Meditative murmur from Heidegger, at the end of *The Origin*: pleasure is superfluous or insufficient" ("Parergon," p. 46).

[46] Adorno, *Aesthetic Theory*, p. 16. For Derrida, the (dis)interest at issue in Kant's third *Critique* helps situate the problem of the non-closure of the Enlightenment in the context of an (un)economic interest. See Derrida, "Economimesis," *Diacritics*, 2, 2 (1981). Bill Readings wrote of Lyotard that "the effects art produces do not add up to new truth, the little narratives do not form a metanarrative of

a pervasive interest in establishing the purity and incommensurability of aesthetic pleasure, and the peculiar nature of this (dis)interest can help shed light on the question of the critical role of art with respect to a world governed otherwise by the categorical apportionment of theory and practice, fact and value, "is" and "ought." On the one hand, Kant recognizes the injury done to the concept of experience as a whole by this apportionment. For this reason, he wants to locate in aesthetics a form of judgment that would bridge these gaps; but if the notion of "aesthetic judgment" is not merely to multiply the number of spheres into which experience has been partitioned, then aesthetics must also renounce its identity as a coequal faculty and dissociate itself from any particular object-sphere. Thus while aesthetics has a critical function with respect to the division of experience inherited from the first two critiques, Kant is loathe to ascribe aesthetics a territory or an interest of its own. This can help explain the need to resist the tendency to take aesthetic judgments either as statements of fact or as quasi-moral commands and, moreover, can help locate the particular interest of aesthetic judgments in that very resistance.

The claims "It is beautiful" and "It is sublime" (which are, quite remarkably, the only two examples Kant offers of claims of taste) may, as we have said, take the same form as assertions of epistemological facts. Likewise, they may bear a formal resemblance to claims of moral value. As Hannah Arendt noted, prior to 1770 Kant had planned to write not a critique of aesthetic judgment, but rather a "Critique of Moral Taste."[47] To be sure, there are moral implications that Kant himself wished to draw from the third *Critique*, but in the 1790 *Critique of Judgment* Kant takes pains to distinguish aesthetic judgment from both moral and epistemological claims, but only by resolutely prescribing what aesthetic judgment is *not*. This negativity contributes to the peculiar "interest" of the third *Critique*. While Kant's first instinct may be to deny the disciplinary independence of aesthetics, to

cultural transformation, because they are *aneconomic*. There is no bottom line. Artistic invention does not produce anything that would not itself be subject to further displacement by aesthetic innovation." *Introducing Lyotard* (New York: Routledge, 1991), p. 73.

[47] Hannah Arendt, *Lectures on Kant's Political Philosophy*, p. 10. See also Lewis White Beck, *A Commentary on Kant's Critique of Practical Reason* (Chicago: University of Chicago Press, 1960), p. 6.

ignore the constitution of "art" as an autonomous field, and to insist on the disinterestedness of claims of taste, he is driven to sustain an "interest" in aesthetic disinterestedness throughout the third *Critique*, if only in order to keep claims of taste from being read as unjustified statements of fact or as unprincipled assertions of moral obligation. Moreover, since the unity of experience – like the common ground which we share with others – can only be remembered or presupposed, but cannot be proved, the critical force of judgments of taste derives from the fact that they attempt to carve out a space that lies in between what can be known cognitively and what is commanded morally. The force of the claims these judgments make lies in the fact that they rest neither on assertions of empirical fact nor on moral commands, but only on a "conditionality" that calls upon us to judge "as if" we were in possession of a common world of experience and shared a common sense. Thus Kant goes on in section 19 to remark that "we are *suitors* for the agreement of every one else, because we are fortified with a ground common to all" (p. 82; emphasis added).

The powerful interest that governs the third *Critique* is lodged in the image of the gap, gulf, or separation of realms that divides our interests in the world of appearances (nature) from our interest in achieving existence in a "realm of ends." The difference between these interests creates the worry that human freedom may stand at odds with the causality of the natural world and be unrealizable in it. This problem must be addressed if the notion of agency is to have any sense of belonging to a meaningful world at all;[48] but it cannot be addressed by any of the means available for

---

[48] An important footnote in the first *Critique* confirms Hans Blumenberg's observation in *The Genesis of the Copernican World* that what is asserted in the *Critique of Pure Reason* requires the second *Critique* if it is to have more than theoretical validity. Kant writes that: "To *know* an object I must be able to prove its possibility, either from its actuality as attested by experience, or *a priori* by means of reason. But I can *think* whatever I please, provided only that I do not contradict myself, that is, provided my concept is a possible thought. This suffices for the possibility of the concept, even though I may not be able to answer for there being, in the sum of all possibilities, an object corresponding to it. But something more is required before I can ascribe to such a concept objective validity, that is, real possibility . . . This something more need not, however, be sought in the theoretical sources of knowledge; it may lie in those that are practical." *Critique of Pure Reason*, B xxvi, n. See Blumenberg, *Genesis of the Copernican World*, trans. Robert M. Wallace (Cambridge, MA: MIT Press, 1987).

distinguishing between appearances and things-in-themselves. Moreover, the form of judgment it requires is said to operate according to an *a priori* principle that cannot be proved empirically or demonstrated morally and is assertable only conditionally. The interest sustaining reflective judgment is, as Adorno would say, a *"sui generis"* reflection of the difficulty involved in establishing a principle that would conclusively validate the distinct interests of theory and practice – i.e., validate them as distinct. Similarly, it is a reflection of the problems posed by any attempt to reconstruct the unity of experience by reuniting these interests as one. Just as any potentially unifying or differentiating principle cannot itself be theoretical or practical, neither can it form the basis for a third (aesthetic) realm with an interest entirely and properly its own, for the problems of difference, of boundary distinction, and of figuration would then only be multiplied or deferred, not resolved. We would be faced with an infinite regress of judgment, always needing a further principle in order to perform the task for which reflective judgment was designed. As Kant discovers, our relationship to "experience as a whole," like the relationship between the third *Critique* and the Kantian system itself, cannot be secured in any determinate way. It is conditional. There is no position from within the critical system to view "experience as a whole." One is drawn to say that our vision of "experience as a whole" is ultimately opaque,[49] or perhaps more accurately, that "experience as a whole" is unsurveyable. In refusing to be determined according to the concepts of either cognition or morality, reflective aesthetic judgment is a primary instance of the particular difficulty produced by the necessary but unsustainable division within the world of "experience," which was central to the Enlightenment's own epistemological and moral agendas.

As Kant argues in the *Foundations of the Metaphysics of Morals*, it would be contrary to the goals of enlightened critical thinking to derive the laws that prescribe what *ought* to be done from

[49] I should clarify that "opacity" and "indeterminacy" do not mean incoherence. Indeed, there have been various attempts on the part of analytical philosophers to restructure the argument of the third *Critique* as a coherent whole. Among the best known of these in recent years is Paul Guyer's in *Kant and the Claims of Taste* (Cambridge, MA: Harvard University Press, 1979). But there are others, among which I would include Bernstein's reading in *The Fate of Art*.

instances of what actually *is* the case, for to derive values from the world of fact might leave us with impure and unreliable forms of value; without thinking about value from the standpoint of the pure will, there would be no way to exclude the "interested" values of egoism and no way to protect against the "materialism, fatalism, atheism, free-thinking, fanaticism, and superstition" that Kant names in the Preface to the second edition of the *Critique of Pure Reason* (B xxxiv, p.32).[50] Kant nonetheless recognizes that there is something that is sacrificed in making the distinction between theory (cognition) and practical reason (morality). This is something that only the affects can reveal and that only taste can claim to know. Insofar as sections 20–22 of the *Critique of Judgment* identify "common sense" (the *sensus communis aestheticus*) as the missing foundation or ground of the judgments we make about the beautiful and the sublime, then what is sacrificed by the Enlightenment division of theory and practice is the shareability of experience.

To ground reflective judgments in the transcendental conditions required for communicability, as Habermas seeks to do, or to reconstruct the possibility of community out of the "publicity" of critical judgments, as Hannah Arendt suggested in her reading of Kant's third *Critique*, is to formalize what Kant characterizes as a "judgment of feeling" (*CJ*, sec. 20, p.82). It is, moreover, to ignore the fact that in making claims of taste we are always in the position of *seeking* the assent of others. For Kant, we are "suitors" for the assent of everyone else: "the assertion is not that every one *will* fall in with our judgment, but rather that every one *ought* to agree with it . . . Here common sense is a mere ideal norm" (*CJ*, sec. 22, p. 84).[51] If, according to Kant, the universal ground for claims of taste lies in a shared feeling (*sensus communis aestheticus*),

[50] Kant carries forward Plato's separation of geometry from physics, or more technically, the separation of the noetic from the sensory (Plato's *chorismos*). As Hans-Georg Gadamer observed, "this severance of the noetic from the sensory, of true insight from mere points of view – this chorismos, in other words – is the truth of moral consciousness as such." *The Relevance of the Beautiful*, trans. Nicholas Walker (Cambridge and New York: Cambridge University Press, 1986), p. 18.

[51] In an extension of this argument, Kant proposes that "the universal communicability of a feeling presupposes a common sense . . . we assume a common sense as the necessary condition of the universal communicability of our knowledge, which is presupposed in every logic and every principle of knowledge that is not one of scepticism" (*CJ*, sec. 21, p. 84).

then it is the task of beauty to recall that feeling, just as it is the task of claims of taste to call the community it references into being. This is why claims of taste cannot be proved in any conventional sense, or why their proof seems to be circular. In soliciting the assent of others we are in effect creating the ground on which our community with others rests. But since we do not create this common ground *ex nihilo*, it makes more sense to say that we are remembering or re-creating it – which means that this (common) ground is not only projected but also presupposed. Hence: "The judgment of taste . . . depends on our presupposing the existence of a common sense" (*CJ*, sec. 20, p. 83).

On the account that Arendt proposes in her reading of the third *Critique*, claims of taste are asserted from the perspective of an "enlarged mentality" that comes from thinking from the other's standpoint: "communicability obviously depends on the enlarged mentality; one can communicate only if one is able to think from the other person's standpoint; otherwise one will never meet him, never speak in such a way that he understands" (*Lectures on Kant's Political Philosophy*, p. 74). And yet Arendt vacillates on this point, perhaps reflecting an aporia in Kant's own thinking, when she also says that "one's community sense also makes it possible to enlarge one's mentality" (p. 73). I will discuss Arendt's interpretation of Kant in greater detail in chapter 4. For now it should be enough to say that the *Critique of Judgment* is itself structured around an unresolved and unresolvable aporia that invokes a "common sense" or "common ground" of experience whose existence is thought of as both remembered and as yet to be created. In making aesthetic judgements, we look as if in two directions at once: on the one hand we "remember" the unity of experience and the commonness of our purposes in the world, which present themselves to us through the lens of the pleasurable and painful experiences of the beautiful and the sublime; and on the other hand we judge things "as if" from the perspective of our (lost) common sense, and on this basis solicit or demand the assent of everyone else ("the subject must regard [aesthetic pleasure] as resting on what he may also presuppose in every other person; and therefore he must believe that he has reason for demanding a similar delight from every one" [*CJ*, sec. 6, p. 51]). As Kant says in the passage just cited, and as he repeats in section 20, this "remembered" common sense must be presupposed for the analysis of judgments of taste.[52] In contrast to Habermas, who is sometimes cast as a Kantian with a communicative bent, Kant himself takes the affective substance of a community (the "community sense") not just as the product of communication but also as its enabling possibility.

Our participation in judgments that refer to this "common sense" incites the memory of a knowledge that was itself once conceived as pleasurable. As Kant describes it, this moment was filled with the passions of wonder and awe. These are the wonder and the awe associated first with cognition and then with recognition – in the case at hand, with the recognition of the fact that the particularities of experience can indeed be coordinated. Wonder and awe are a first, affective, response to the recognition of an order in nature. (It bears noting that in Aristotle wonder – *thauma* – is the affect closest to epistemic thought. It constitutes the cognitive *pathos* characteristic of the beginning of philosophical inquiry.) Although the affects associated with this initial cognition have been deadened by the layers of routine, conceptual thinking that have been deposited over it, Kant nonetheless suggests that every act of cognition replicates this first excitement, even if in an extremely diminished mode: every act of knowledge recalls the wonder or awe produced at our original recognition of the orderliness of nature: "just as if it were a lucky chance that favoured us, we are rejoiced (properly speaking relieved of a want) where we meet with such systematic unity under empirical laws" (*CJ*, Introduction, pp. 23–24).[53] We recall this wonder when we recognize a unity in the empirical laws of nature, as happens fleetingly in our ordinary acts of cognition:

We do not, and cannot, find in ourselves the slightest effect on the feeling of pleasure from the coincidence of perceptions with the laws in accordance with the universal concepts of nature (the Categories), since in their case understanding necessarily follows the bent of its own nature without ulterior aim. But, while this is so, the discovery, on the other hand, that two or more empirical heterogeneous laws of nature are allied under one principle that embraces them both, is the ground of a very appreciable

---

[52] As Bernstein says in *The Fate of Art*, "It is present by virtue of its absence. As remembered/presupposed, common sense is constitutive of the judgement of taste; as not existent, it is regulative" (p. 60).

[53] But whether we glimpse this unity or not, Kant goes on immediately to say that "we must necessarily assume the presence of such a unity, apart from any ability on our part to apprehend or prove its existence" (*CJ*, Introduction, p. 24).

pleasure, often even of admiration, and such, too, as does not wear off even though we are already familiar enough with its object. It is true that we no longer notice any decided pleasure in the comprehensibility of nature, or in the unity of its divisions into genera and species, without which the empirical concepts, that afford us our knowledge of nature in its particular laws, would not be possible. Still it is certain that the pleasure appeared in due course, and only by reason of the most ordinary experience being impossible without it, has it become gradually fused with simple cognition, and no longer arrests particular attention. Something, then, that makes us attentive in our estimate of nature to its finality for our understanding . . . is required, in order that, on meeting with success, pleasure may be felt in this their accord with our cognitive faculty. (*CJ*, Introduction, pp. 27–28)

The pleasure we take in the beautiful is rooted in the original pleasure Kant describes in this passage. (In Wittgenstein's 1938 lectures on aesthetics, he reminded his students that terms like "fine," "lovely," etc., were first used as interjections.[54]) As Rodolphe Gasché has noted, the speculative germs of the third *Critique* lie in the hypothesis of the "immemorial identity" of pleasure and cognition referred to above. For Gasché the crucial passage is paragraph 76 of the third *Critique*:

Here Kant, after having recognized that ordinary human knowledge is reduced to subsuming the particular within the universal, and that this kind of knowledge, whereby the particular is condemned to remain contingent, is inadequate to nature as a whole, declares himself compelled to posit hypothetically the possibility of a higher form of cognition for which this opposition of the universal and the particular would no longer exist, a sort of *intellectus archetypus* anterior to the antinomies of understanding . . . The *intellectus archetypus*, in contrast to the derivative mode of human intuition, is original. It is an intellect that itself gives existence to its objects. It is, in other words, a nondiscursive intellect, linking things as heterogeneous as the intellect and the intuition, which for Kant is the privilege of the primordial being alone. This intellect is characterized by intuitive intellection beyond the antinomies of understanding and reflexive thinking.[55]

---

[54] Ludwig Wittgenstein, *Lectures and Conversations on Aesthetics, Psychology and Religious Belief*, ed. Cyril Barrett (Berkeley: University of California Press, n.d.), p. 3.

[55] Rodolphe Gasché, *The Tain of the Mirror* (Cambridge, MA: Harvard University Press, 1986), p. 29. Gasché adduces a relevant passage from *Faith and Knowledge* in which Hegel says that "It is an 'archetypal (*urbildlich*) intellect' for which 'the possibility of the parts, etc., as to their character and integration is dependent on the whole.' Kant also recognizes that we are necessarily driven to this idea. The *Idea* of this archetypal intuitive intellect is at bottom nothing else but the *same Idea* of the transcendental imagination" (cited in Gasché, *The Tain of the Mirror*, p. 29).

In Kant, it is the genius who carries on the work of this "archetypal intellect." But, as the third *Critique* makes abundantly clear, it is the burden of taste to bring discipline and rule to genius; taste, for instance, asks for a justification of what the genius claims to know by "original intuition." The tensions between terms like genius and taste pervade the third *Critique*. We are drawn to the genius as a means to re-create the powers of the *intellectus archetypus*, which itself remains inaccessible; but we are also confronted with the need to bring the original intuition of the genius under the rule of taste. When Kant says that we are "suitors for agreement from every one else" he signals the way in which that process might occur.

If the pleasure Kant describes contains a memory or trace of what it was like to grasp the ordered purposiveness of nature in a single act of cognition, then the difficulty raised by the claim of section 59 of the third *Critique*, and likewise the challenge for any subsequent theory of judgment, lies in the fact that beauty, as we know it now, remains a "symbol" of morality. Beauty provides the indication of an original convergence of facts and values, of the coordination of human purposes with the natural world, a reminder of the possibility of universal agreement; but it remains a figure nonetheless and, as Kant is quick to point out, figures are not susceptible to rational proof. They must be apprehended by intuitive or affective means.[56]

The conditions that have determined beauty as we know it now to be a figure, symbol, or memory of the mutual transparency of facts and values are those that Adorno describes under the heading of "rationalization" and "reification." An understanding of the historical roots of these processes in the mechanisms of modern capitalism and bureaucratic organization goes a long distance toward explaining the motives behind an interest in aesthetic reflection as a critical response to that history; hence the critical potential that members of the Frankfurt School have sometimes associated with art. But Kant's own interest lies in understanding the anomalous place of pleasure and pain with respect to what is called "experience as a whole." And, as we have already begun to

---

[56] As Derrida's reading of Kant's third *Critique* amply demonstrates, the project of reflective judgment is itself sustained by a figural structure that is well at work before the theory that would justify it is in place. See "Parergon," in *The Truth in Painting*, pp. 15–147.

see, Kant recognizes that the best that can be hoped for in respect of a conclusive derivation of the transcendental principle of aesthetic judgment is not a "solution" to the division of cognition and morality or a proof of the unity of experience, but rather a clear articulation of what amounts to an antinomy – that the principle of the universal validity of claims of taste must indeed exist, but that the principle cannot be *shown* to exist. Indeed, Kant concludes the Preface to the third *Critique* with an avowal of "the difficulty of unraveling a problem so involved" as the principle of aesthetic judgment. He only hopes that this difficulty may serve to excuse "a certain amount of hardly avoidable obscurity in its solution, provided that the accuracy of our statement of the principle is proved with all requisite clearness" (pp. 6–7).[57] If the third *Critique* was meant to bring the project of critical philosophy to a close, then, by Kant's own admission, the problem of aesthetic judgment succeeds at best in uncovering an antinomy that cannot be finally resolved.[58]

In Kant, the indeterminacy of aesthetic reflection and the particular dis-interestedness of aesthetic pleasure represent ways in which the Enlightenment subject begins to understand the separation of cognitive fact and moral value as a necessary distortion of the unity of experience. That distortion is necessary if the subject is to resist the temptation merely to disregard the claims of critical reason, which aims at a sharp distinction between the worlds of phenomenal and noumenal experience, between "is" and "ought." But it remains a distortion nonetheless, for Kant insists

[57] Kant returns to the issue in section 57, "Solution of the antinomy of taste," where he nonetheless pursues the issue to the point where he believes it orients us undeniably toward the "supersensible" realm: "If, however, our deduction [of the principle of reflective judgment] is at least credited with having been worked out on correct lines, even though it may not have been sufficiently clear in all its details, three ideas stand out in evidence. *Firstly*, there is the supersensible in general, without further determination, as substrate of nature; *secondly*, this same supersensible as principle of the subjective finality of nature for our cognitive faculties; *thirdly*, the same supersensible again, as principle of the ends of freedom, and principle of the common accord of these ends with freedom in the moral sphere" (*CJ*, sec. 57, p. 215). The principal problem with this statement is that now we do not know whether the "supersensible substrate" is part of the problem or part of the solution to it. On the "difficulty" of judgment and the finally aporetic status of the problem in Kant, see Caygill, *Art of Judgment*.

[58] Caygill explains this *aporia* as Kant's continuation of Aristotle's restatement of what is undecidable in the Platonic dialogues.

that the world of experience is in fact one. In the problem of aesthetic reflective judgment, Kant's Enlightenment subject begins to look back, from the "as if" position of its lost or presupposed common sense, upon what it has cost to establish the legitimacy of knowledge by means of the systematic separation of value from fact. In so doing, Kant finds that the unity of experience can be remembered or projected, not cognitively known or proved, but only felt, and that judgments of taste, which invoke a truly common sense, must operate from a perspective that is itself fictional, figural, or "as if." To say this much is to suggest that the Enlightenment desire to speak rationally and objectively about the world as a whole stands in a strange but necessary kinship with those modes of discourse (e.g. fiction and figure) commonly understood as antithetical to it.[59] It suggests that the "truth" of the Enlightenment as a form of systematic thinking lies in the discovery that the unity of experience cannot be proved within the system of critical thinking but must be represented by a form of fiction that has feeling at its base. The figure of a "division of worlds" thus represents a necessary but nonetheless perspectival or contingent consequence of Kant's own understanding of the relationship between natural causality and human freedom – necessary, Kant says, in order to keep us from taking the objects of sense-knowledge as categorically and not merely empirically true; but contingent and perspectival nonetheless, because the world of experience, which comprises the empirical and the transcendental, is said to be one. The third *Critique* moves between the labor involved in searching in the discourse about our feelings of pleasure and pain for the universal laws that govern claims of taste and the imaginative, "as if," not-quite-moral obligation to re-create the conditions necessary to the commonality such laws presuppose.[60]

---

[59] The Lacanian formulation that this fact would seem to demand is: the Truth has the structure of a fiction. This formulation is cited in Slavoj Žižek, *The Sublime Object of Ideology* (London: Verso, 1989), p. 191. Gloss: "Truth is an empty *place*, and the effect of Truth is produced when, quite by chance, some piece of 'fiction' (symbolically structured knowledge) finds itself occupying this place" (*ibid.*).

[60] This movement between lost universals and imaginative re-creation is in turn embodied in the aesthetic object insofar as it is one whose existence according to Kant does not – cannot – interest us, as if to confirm the suggestion that aesthetic objects are themselves positioned somewhere in between the nullity of non-existence and the inviolability of pure fantasy. On the loss of universal laws in relation to mourning in the third *Critique*, see Derrida's "Parergon."

By virtue of the indeterminate position of aesthetic judgments, which are more forceful than mere predictions about taste but considerably more fragile than factual claims or moral commands, the *Critique of Judgment* brings to light the critical potential that lies in what might be described as the "constitutive opacity" of the Kantian system. As the principal examples of reflective judgment, claims of taste represent salient instances in which Kant reflects critically upon the division of experience necessary to the system of critical philosophy, not so much returning us to "experience as a whole" but rather acknowledging the need for affect where reason cannot prove the unity of experience or the shareability of a common world.

# 3

❖❖❖❖❖❖❖❖❖❖❖❖❖❖❖❖❖❖❖❖❖❖❖❖❖❖❖❖❖❖❖❖❖❖❖❖❖❖❖❖❖❖❖❖❖❖❖

# The difficulty of art

❖❖❖❖❖❖❖❖❖❖❖❖❖❖❖❖❖❖❖❖❖❖❖❖❖❖❖❖❖❖❖❖❖❖❖❖❖❖❖❖❖❖❖❖❖❖❖

Beauty and truth are in one way the same.　　　　　G. W. F. Hegel[1]

Art remains for us a thing of the past.　　　　　　G. W. F. Hegel[2]

Everything about art has become problematic: its inner life, its relation to society, even its right to exist.　　　　　Theodor Adorno[3]

Art – this is merely a word to which nothing real any longer corresponds.
　　　　　　　　　　　　　　　　　　　　Martin Heidegger[4]

Of all the riddles of aesthetic theory, none is as puzzling as the fact that what is arguably the pivotal work in the field – Kant's third *Critique* – contains no sustained or systematic theory of art. As Adorno bluntly remarked, "pre-Hegelian, including Kantian, aesthetics had no emphatic conception of the work of art, relegating it to the status of some kind of sublimated means of enjoyment."[5]

---

[1] Georg Hegel, *Lectures on Aesthetics*, trans. T. M. Knox (Oxford: Clarendon Press, 1975), vol. I, p. 111. (Hereafter cited as *LA*.)

[2] *Ibid.*, p. 11.

[3] Theodor Adorno, *Aesthetic Theory*, ed. Gretel Adorno and Rolf Tiedemann, trans. C. Lenhardt (London: Routledge and Kegan Paul, 1984), p. 1. (Hereafter cited as *AT*.)

[4] Martin Heidegger, "The Origin of the Work of Art," in *Poetry, Language, Thought*, trans. Albert Hofstadter (New York: Harper and Row, 1971), p. 17. (Hereafter cited as OWA.)

[5] Adorno, *AT*, pp. 485–86. But even Adorno recognizes the sacrifice of enjoyment as the fate of art in an Enlightened age: "the enjoyment of art and manual labor break apart as the world of prehistory is left behind." "The Concept of Enlightenment," in Max Horkheimer and Theodor Adorno, *Dialectic of Enlighten-*

Although Kant does offer some remarks on the subjects of "art" and "fine art" in sections 43–47 of the *Critique of Judgment*, he largely eschews a discussion of art as a mode of productive praxis and refuses to treat the aesthetic field as comprised of objects to be understood in terms of the circumstances of their social conditioning or material making. Although the feelings of pleasure and pain that Kant associates with the beautiful and the sublime may be incited by nature or by art,[6] what Kant is willing to count as "art" excludes any form of handicraft or "industrial art" (section 43).[7] Moreover, Kant makes an effort to distinguish the "transcendental" analysis of aesthetic judgment from a study of the history or culture of taste. Aesthetic judgment does not in Kant's sense refer to the specific choices we make about works of art. "The present investigation of taste," he writes, "[is] not being undertaken with a view to the formation or culture of taste, (which will pursue its course in the future, as in the past, independently of such inquiries,) but [is] being merely directed to its transcendental aspects" (*CJ*, Preface, p. 6). In so saying, Kant defines the field of aesthetics as a domain in which our particular feelings of pleasure and pain are endowed with a universality that is independent of the laws of cognition and morality.[8] But the difficulty of aesthetic

*ment*, trans. John Cumming (New York: Continuum, 1995), p. 34. For Horkheimer and Adorno, the theft of enjoyment roots in the sensory deprivation required of alienated labor: "as proprietor [Odysseus] cannot yield to the temptation to self-abandonment, so, as proprietor, he finally renounces even participation in labor, and ultimately even its management, whereas his men . . . cannot enjoy their labor because it is performed under pressure, in desperation, with senses stopped by force" (p. 35).

6 Immanuel Kant, *Critique of Judgment*, trans. James Creed Meredith (Oxford: Clarendon, 1986), Preface, p. 5. (Henceforth abbreviated as *CJ*.)

7 Heidegger essentially repeats Kant when, in the course of writing on Nietzsche, he says that "the beautiful can pertain to either nature or art." Heidegger, *Nietzsche, 1: The Will to Power as Art*, trans. David Farrell Krell (New York and San Francisco: Harper and Row, 1979), p. 78. Heidegger also echoes Kant (though modifying him so as to include handiwork) when, in the course of his discussion of poetry and technology, he asks "how does bringing-forth happen, be it in nature or in handwork and art?" See "The Question Concerning Technology," in *The Question Concerning Technology and Other Essays*, trans. William Lovitt (New York: Harper and Row, 1979), p. 78.

8 Cf. Tony Bennett, who defines "aesthetic discourse" in terms of "the many variants of philosophical aesthetics which exhibit related properties in their attempts to distinguish some unique faculty, lodged within and constitutive of human subjectivity, which would serve as a basis for establishing the potential, if not actual, universality of aesthetic judgment. Aesthetic discourse . . . construes the aesthetic as a distinctive mode of the subject's mental relation to reality." *Outside Literature* (London: Routledge, 1990), p. 150.

judgment lies in the fact that these universals do not pre-exist the particulars in question: the universals must either be found (by soliciting the agreement of others) or made (in the creative work of the genius). Respecting the difficulty of aesthetic judgment in this regard means rejecting the temptation to ground the universality of taste in any of the forms of "false necessity" such as "nature" or "culture" might provide. Taste, while universal, is also more contingent on particulars than either of these notions would allow. It is, in Kant's estimation, a faculty requiring originality rather than imitation. (Kant: "Taste must be an original faculty, whereas one who imitates a model, while showing skill commensurable with his success, only displays taste himself as a critic of this model" [*CJ*, sec. 17, p. 75].)

In view of the difficulties presented by Kant's theory of aesthetic judgment, it is not surprising to find that considerable energy has been expended upon historicist corrections of the third *Critique*. In reaction to the "metaphysical" assumptions behind what Kant has to say about a delight that is pure, free, and independent of all interest, these corrective efforts represent attempts to ground reflective judgment in something considerably more objective and concrete. Moreover, Kant's emphasis on the universality of judgment and on the purity of aesthetic pleasure has sometimes been read as a suppression of the historical specificity of the problems of aesthetic judgment. In Adorno's view, for instance, one cannot hope to understand "art" without comprehending the history of its autonomy in the modern world, and this autonomy is rooted in the facts of capitalist production and bureaucratic praxis. The separation of aesthetic pleasure from cognition (the true) and morality (the good) is for Adorno a socially determined phenomenon. (In his later writings Adorno nonetheless recognizes the critical potential of Kant's stance in the face of such facts: "[Kant's position] not only expresses the idea that current praxis denies happiness, but also carries the connotation that happiness is something beyond praxis. The chasm between praxis and happiness is surveyed and measured by the power of negativity of the work of art" [*AT*, pp. 17–18].)

Kant's emphasis on the disinterestedness of aesthetic pleasure has likewise been taken as an attempt to exclude the political interests that shape the "universal" face of claims of taste.[9] Among thinkers in the tradition of Marx and Althusser, Kantian aesthetic theory has often been cast as part of a concealed effort on the part of idealist philosophy to confer legitimacy upon a political order driven by the interests of the modern state. Terry Eagleton's account of the "ideology of the aesthetic" is a case in point. Eagleton regards the universal validity that Kant attributes to claims of taste as an extension of the powers of the absolutist state over the physical locus of pleasures and pains – the body – which Eagleton claims that Kant systematically neglects. "The body," he says, "cannot be figured or represented within the frame of Kantian aesthetics; and Kant ends up accordingly with a formalist ethics, an abstract theory of political rights, and a 'subjective' but non-sensuous aesthetics."[10] Let us set aside what Eagleton here claims about Kant's neglect of the body – which seems questionable in light of Kant's engagements with thinkers such as Epicurus and Burke on the issues of "health" and "well being."[11] The point of Eagleton's argument is that the rational and universalizing element in aesthetic theory serves as but the thinnest mask for absolutist power. More specifically, Eagleton proposes that aesthetic theory was born in the eighteenth century in response to a "crisis" in the logic of absolutism. This "crisis" was revealed in the absolutist state's need to gain control of all of "subjective" life, including the life of the senses: "[absolutist] power needs for its own purposes to take account of 'sensible' life, for without an understanding of this no dominion can be secure. The world of feelings and sensations can surely not just be sundered to the 'subjective,' to what Kant scornfully termed the 'egoism of taste'; instead, it must be brought within the majestic scope of reason itself . . . Reason must find some way of penetrating the world of perception, but in doing so must not put at risk its own absolute power" (*Ideology of the Aesthetic*, p. 15).

These and similar attempts to historicize aesthetics are designed to save the theory of reflective judgment from "abstraction" and to reduce what is sometimes regarded as the formalism of

[9] Pierre Bourdieu's *La Distinction* (Paris: Minuit, 1979) dissociates aesthetics from both these strategies by conceiving the exercise of "taste" as a matter of social praxis that bears no trace of transcendental principles. Such a critique of the Kantian notion of taste solves the problem of the third *Critique* by eliminating its source.

[10] Terry Eagleton, *The Ideology of the Aesthetic* (Oxford: Blackwell, 1990), p. 21.

[11] On related topics, see Susan Meld Shell, *The Embodiment of Reason: Kant on Spirit, Generation, and Community* (Chicago: University of Chicago Press, 1996).

Kant's third *Critique* by referring us to the historical and political interests it may conceal. In part by appealing to a notion of ideology as a mode of distortion rooted in the negation of the material basis of consciousness, such efforts purport to "correct" Kant's aesthetic theory by specifying both the political circumstances of its genesis and the social objects of its analysis, thus offering a determinate point of reference for what in Kant may seem not just indeterminate, but hopelessly vague and abstract. But post-Kantian attempts to complete the theory of reflective judgment by reference to history hardly succeed in resolving the difficulties that Kant himself encountered in attempting to address the problem of taste. Foremost among these is the difficulty of thinking the particular in advance of the universal. Indeed, by ascribing a set of social and historical motives to Kant's theory of judgment, historicist critics of Kant's third *Critique* tend to equate the problem of aesthetic judgment with the rise of art as an autonomous object-sphere and with the social and political interests that condition it. In the process, however, they may not see that the notion of "interest" itself sets in motion a version of the very problem Kant sought to address in the theory of reflective judgment – that of a systematic gap or distortion, a fundamental irreconcilability – in the relationship between the world of phenomena and the realm of "transcendental" truth.

In short, an analysis of aesthetic judgment in strictly historicist terms tends to suppress the difficulty that Kant found to be inherent in the attempt to think categorically about the validity of claims that originate in subjective particulars. Just as Kant's notion of aesthetic reflection can seem empty and abstract without an awareness of the social conditions underlying the autonomous work of art, an analysis of the social construction of the aesthetic field must face the question of judgment raised by Kant in the third *Critique*: how can the particulars that originate in the "experiences" of pleasure and pain assert a validity that is independent of the categories that seem to stand waiting for them in advance? How can these particulars "create" their own universals?

The limitations of a strictly historicist critique of aesthetics become further apparent when we recognize that a given phenomenon (e.g. art, taste) can never be fully contextualized within history, no matter how concretely "historical" it may appear.

Despite efforts to read judgments of taste in strictly historical terms, something that escapes history, something at the level of the universal, always remains. Indeed, Marx himself recognized the dilemma of aesthetic universality in his discussion of Greek art in the Introduction to the *Grundrisse*. There, Marx noted that although Homer's poetry was thoroughly conditioned by its time, it has nonetheless retained a "universal" appeal. Marx's problem was not to explain how Homer's poems were possible within the context of early Greek society but rather to account for the "universal" admiration they continued to arouse. The universality of Greek art would seem to be an embarrassment for Marx, who otherwise insists on the irreducibility of the concrete, material circumstances of human action. Marx's solution to this dilemma, which nonetheless follows the theory of judgment outlined in Hegel's *Logic*, was to take the historical particular as *itself* the universal.[12] As Adorno pithily remarked, no doubt thinking of Marx, singularity misrepresents itself in pretending that it is *not* in fact a universal (*AT*, p. 195). To wit, Marx suggests that the universality of Homer's poetry derives from its attachment to specific historical conditions. Elaborating on Marx, Slavoj Žižek takes Marx's solution as reason to suspect that the historicist insistence upon particularity must be *inherently* incomplete, i.e., not wholly determined or determinable by its context: what is lacking from the particular, paradoxically, is the universal.[13] But since the universal is likewise thought to be "completed" by the historical particular, it would be more accurate to think that what Kant calls "aesthetic judgment" is in fact the difficulty created by the intersection of two lacks, each one standing in need of, hence appealing to, the other: "The point is thus not that we, the observing subjects embedded in our particular situation, can never comprehend the set of particular circumstances which determine the Other, the object of our scrutiny; the deficiency is 'ontological,' not merely 'epistemological' – this Other is already in itself not wholly

---

[12] Hegel: "In its abstract terms a Judgment is expressible in the proposition 'The individual is the universal.'" *Hegel's Logic*, trans. William Wallace (Oxford: Oxford University Press, 1975), p. 231.

[13] Slavoj Žižek, *The Indivisible Remainder: An Essay on Schelling and Related Matters* (London: Verso, 1996), pp. 214–15. As he goes on to say, each of these positions within the social-symbolic field is bound to misperceive itself as universal, as encompassing not only itself but also all other particular totalities (epochs, societies, etc.).

determined by circumstances. It is this very overlapping of the two deficiencies (or, in Lacanese: the intersection of the two lacks) that opens up the dimension of universality" (*Indivisible Remainder*, p. 214). Expanding upon what is essentially Kant's formulation of the difficulty of aesthetic judgment in the third *Critique*, Žižek writes that "here, it is as if Universal and Particular change places – we have a series of Universals, of universal interpretive matrices, which are all answers to the 'absolute particularity' of the traumatic Real, of the imbalance of an antagonism which throws out of joint, and thereby 'particularizes', the neutral-universal frame" (*Indivisible Remainder*, p. 217). From Žižek's Lacanian perspective, judgment may be called upon to resolve (but in fact only deepens) the "traumatic antagonism" in the structure of what Kant calls "experience." The very existence of such an antagonism forces Žižek to suspend all the usual assumptions about the relationship between universals and particulars.

The Lacanian formulation can nonetheless shed some light on the historical specificity of autonomous art: the category of "art" comes into being within the culture of enlightened modernity not as the effect of any determinate set of causes but only as the consequence of an impossibility – specifically, as a consequence of the impossibility of constituting the "whole" of experience by bridging the "two worlds" that Kant had set apart in the first two critiques. Indeed, even Kant recognizes that art cannot unify but can at best render possible a transition between them (*CJ*, Introduction, p. 14). In historicist accounts of the theory of aesthetic reflection, however, the problem of reflective judgment is subsumed within a determinate logic, where it is explained as the historical consequence of a deep-structure "cause." Similarly, the theory of judgment is reduced to the status of an historical particular to be treated in terms of its place under such universal categories as "class" and "state." While reference to history can indeed help us move from a discussion of the problem of taste in its "transcendental" aspect to an analysis of the configuration of the aesthetic field within the culture of enlightened modernity, such an analysis may end up saying very little about the central difficulty of the aesthetic reflective judgment and its importance for contemporary thought.

What, then, are the alternatives to an historicist critique of art? In pursuing this question I want to examine some central moments in aesthetic theory after Kant's third *Critique*, including Hegel's *Lectures on Aesthetics*, Heidegger's essay "The Origin of the Work of Art," and Paul de Man's analysis of Hegel in "Sign and Symbol in Hegel's *Aesthetics*." These texts all remain indebted to Kant's characterization of aesthetic judgment as having a critical value that outstrips the determinate logic to be found in the domains of cognition and morality; likewise they lead to a rethinking of the logic of production that governs much historicist criticism.

In Heidegger, for instance, the forms of "production" that dominate the culture of the West are themselves taken to be a suppressed or forgotten form of the disclosive "making" (*poiēsis*) associated originally with the generative processes of the natural world (*physis*). Heidegger reverses the historicist attempt to grant priority to "production" over "art" when he writes that "the road toward the determination of the thingly reality of the work [of art] leads not from thing to work but from work to thing."[14] Whereas the Kantian critique of judgment is concerned with the problem of the proof of a universal concept (taste) that originates in particulars and suggests that the universality of taste is guaranteed both practically and theoretically by the particularities of feeling (pleasure, pain), Heidegger asks how the notion of "art" as such (i.e., as a designation for the category of things beautiful as opposed to things true or good) could have come about. Why was art drawn into the ambit of the aesthetic (rather than the practical, the useful, the moral, etc.)? The Heideggerean answer to these questions, given most succinctly in the essay "The Age of the World View," is clear enough. Since the origin of "art" as we know it coincides with the culture of enlightened modernity, an understanding of the separation of beauty from truth must involve nothing less than a critical comprehension of modernity, where modernity is understood as the culture for which "truth" means the knowledge of objects by means of representations. Heidegger's aesthetic critique of modernity amounts to an effort to "think back" from the (historical) fact of art's constitution as an autonomous object-sphere to the (original) moment of a truth that was itself a form of revealing. Thus despite what may seem to be a naive historicism on Heidegger's part (derived in part at least from Hegel's admiration of the Greeks), Heidegger's archaeology

---

[14] Heidegger, "The Origin of the Work of Art," p. 39.

of the aesthetic can in turn help frame a central paradox of Hegel's assertions about art. According to the first of Hegel's claims, art is the "sensuous appearance of the idea,"[15] a form of showing forth (*scheinen*) that constitutes spirit's equivalent to nature; according to the second claim, however, art is "a thing of the past." The latter view articulates the problem of aesthetics by locating the "death of art" in what would seem to be historical terms; the former recalls the immanence of beauty and truth from what would seem to be a transcendental point of view. What we think of as the culture of enlightened modernity, in which the difficulty of art is made emphatically clear, can be understood in terms of the constitutive antagonism between these two.[16]

## Art and the circle of feeling and truth

I want to proceed with a discussion of the "difficulty" of art by recalling certain crucial points about Kant's encounter with the theoretical limitations of reflective judgment. Kant's specific interest in the problem of aesthetic judgment lies in testing the validity of the claims that we make in response to the subjective feelings that are incited by occasions of the beautiful and the sublime. What is paramount and paradoxical about these feelings for Kant lies in the fact that they command universal assent even though they cannot be grasped by conceptual thought. The ambition of the third *Critique* is to locate in aesthetic judgment a form of knowledge that does not subordinate the affects (pleasure, pain) to the governance of universal laws but that begins from particulars and proceeds to find the concepts according to which they can be phrased with categorical validity. Insofar as Kant's aesthetic particulars incite claims that seek the agreement of all, they solicit an interest that is neither empirical nor transcendental. Rather, the validity of judgments that are grounded in our particular responses to moments of beauty and sublimity supports Kant's

---

[15] Hegel, *Lectures on Aesthetics*, vol. I, p. 39.
[16] Regarding Hegel's assertion that "art is for us a thing of the past," Paul de Man argues that this cannot be falsified or confirmed by historical investigation. With Heidegger, he takes Hegel's insight into the eclipse of "great art" as a sign of the inability of "aesthetics" adequately to determine a sphere of objects. See "Sign and Symbol in Hegel's Aesthetics," *Critical Inquiry*, 8 (1982). For related reflections on art see Arthur Danto, *After the End of Art* (Princeton, NJ: Princeton University Press, 1997).

conviction that the concept-driven fields of cognition and morality cannot possibly account for all there is of knowledge. Aesthetic judgment represents a form of knowledge that gives us the cognition of no thing (there is no class of "things beautiful" that it is the task of aesthetic reflection to delimit); aesthetic reflection is in fact defined by the *limits* of those modes of knowledge (e.g. cognition) that consist in the logical determination of a "thing."[17]

The particular difficulty that arises in the course of Kant's attempt to provide a derivation for the theory of aesthetic reflective judgment lies in the fact that although claims of taste are recognized as satisfying the demand for categorical validity, their validity cannot be proved. Or rather, their proof requires reference to a notion of "community sense" (*sensus communis*) which must itself be established by such claims. For this reason, Kant's theory of aesthetic judgment appears to be profoundly circular. Kant's circularity here anticipates the efforts of post-Enlightenment thinkers such as Wittgenstein to explain rationality in terms of the notion of "language games," in which utterances are validated by the communities and contexts they themselves create. Kant's argument about the problem of establishing a first unit of measurement in section 26, for instance, anticipates Wittgenstein's analysis in the *Philosophical Investigations* of how we follow signs. Kant notes that every unit of measurement must make reference to some other unit if it is to have any meaning at all; but if this is so, then what is the source of the first unit of measurement? "As the magnitude of the measure has to be assumed as a known quantity if, to form an estimate of this, we must again have recourse to numbers involving another standard for their unit, and consequently must again proceed mathematically, we can never arrive at a first or fundamental measure, and so cannot get any definite concept of a given magnitude" (*CJ*, sec. 26, p. 98). Whereas analytical philosophers like Paul Guyer have tended to approach Kant with the expectation that the circularity in the reasoning of the third *Critique* can in fact be resolved,[18] it may be the case that this circularity is basic to any form of judgment that

---

17 Though she makes no mention of aesthetics *per se*, Drucilla Cornell's book *The Philosophy of the Limit* (New York: Routledge, 1992), provides an insightful study of deconstruction as a philosophy of the limit.

18 The most prominent example of this is *Kant and the Claims of Taste* (Cambridge, MA: Harvard University Press, 1979).

say that the notion of aesthetic reflective judgment is not a "theory" at all, but an expression of the impossible desire for an independent grounding of the circle (read: the whole).[25] It is the site, not only of reflection, but of infinite reflection. Insofar as we are able to grasp the whole in conceptual or theoretical terms, art reveals something to be missing from it – the quality or mode of our relationship to the whole, all of which Kant figures as the "feeling" associated with a pleasure that figures recognition and a pain that figures loss. Insofar as aesthetic judgment takes its bearings by particular pleasures and pains, it must proceed without the benefit of criteria, without universal "grounds" (Kant: "it is throwing away labor to look for a principle of taste that affords a universal criterion of the beautiful by definite concepts," *CJ*, sec. 17, p. 75). Aesthetic reflection involves a form of judgment that is necessarily incomplete insofar as it requires not just the application of criteria or rules, but their discovery; its work is infinite because one can never know which objects will fit these rules: "one cannot determine a priori what object will be in accordance with taste or not – one must find out the object that is so" (*CJ*, Introduction, p. 32).

So understood, the circularity of aesthetic judgment may seem to resemble the circularity of hermeneutics. Indeed, none other than the "father" of modern hermeneutics, August Boekh, defined hermeneutic understanding as "the knowing of the known."[26] Derrida nonetheless suggests that there is a difference between a "vicious hermeneutic circle" and the circle that is established by a work of art: "this hermeneutical circle has only the (logical, formal, derived) appearance of a vicious circle," Derrida writes; "it is not a question of escaping it but on the contrary of engaging it and going all round" ("Parergon," p. 32). To state the case somewhat more explicitly than Derrida, hermeneutics argues that judgments of particulars require the preexistence of the "whole" they go to comprise; artworks instantiate the fact that what the theoretically conceived "whole" is forever missing is the force of our feeling or reflection upon it. In Kant's

25 For a powerful argument in support of this view, see Stanley Rosen, *The Limits of Analysis* (New York: Basic Books, 1980).
26 August Boeckh, *On Interpretation and Criticism*, trans. John Paul Pritchard (Norman: University of Oklahoma Press, 1968), pp. 51–52, 53. See also Hans-Georg Gadamer, *Philosophical Hermeneutics*, trans. David E. Linge (Berkeley: University of California Press, 1976), p. 45.

language, cognition and morality fail to incorporate the "affective element" (pleasure, pain) that accompanies any conceptual representation. The "difficulty" or "impossibility" of art as what Hegel will later call the "sensuous appearance of the idea" is a consequence of this fact.

The difference between the hermeneutic circle and the circularity of aesthetic judgment is likewise central to Heidegger's essays "The Origin of the Work of Art" and "The Question Concerning Technology." The hermeneutic circle is fashioned from a chain of signs, each of which incorporates a judgment that is contingent upon a prior construction of the whole which cannot logically be completed until after the fact. In hermeneutics, one asks for the truth and is given a sign; and when one asks again for the truth in place of this second sign, one is given still another sign; indeed, it seems that a sign is "always already" standing in place of the truth. Hermeneutics thus leads dialectically to the notion that the truth is itself a sign, or what Nietzsche described as "an army of metaphors."[27] In Heidegger's notion of "art," by contrast, we meet the desire for a self-revealing or self-grounding truth, one that would speak without the mediation of signs – a solution to the problem of infinite reflection made available by appeal to an archaic conception of art not as situated in a world, but as disclosive of it, in the way that calls to mind the self-disclosive quality of an organic whole, of *physis*: "to be a work [of art] means to set up a world."[28] What remains to be seen is the degree to which Heidegger's understanding of art as world-disclosive conceals the problem of world-loss.

To be sure, Heidegger's "world" has very little to do with what we ordinarily think of as a realm of objects, and even less with the world of "experience" in the Kantian sense. Indeed, Heidegger is particularly sensitive to the ways in which the notion of "experience" stands at the center of an equally problematic circle in Kant. Specifically, Heidegger notes that Kant's proof of the unity of intuition and thought consists in "showing that the principles of pure understanding are made possible by that which they ought

[27] Friedrich Nietzsche, "On Truth and Lies in a Nonmoral Sense," in *Philosophy and Truth*, trans. and ed. Daniel Brezeale (Atlantic Highlands, NJ: Humanities Press, 1979), p. 84. What hermeneutics cannot capture is the self-reflective awareness that accompanies the "dawning" of this truth.

[28] As Bernstein has discussed in *The Fate of Art*, it is the work of genius.

to make possible – experience." As he goes on to say, "this is an obvious circle. Certainly, and for the understanding of the process of the proof and of the character of what we are discussing it is indispensable not only to suspect this circle and so to create doubts about the clearness of the proof, but to recognize the circle clearly and to carry it out as such."[29] Heidegger's "world" is by contrast characterized as "the ever-*nonobjective* to which we are subject as long as the paths of birth and death, blessing and curse keep us transported into Being" (OWA, p. 44; emphasis added). Indeed, this is an apt description of what Kant had to say not about "experience" but about the appropriate subjects of poetry: "the poet essays the task of interpreting to sense the rational ideas of invisible beings, the kingdom of the blessed, hell, eternity, creation, etc." (*CJ*, sec. 49, p. 176). For Heidegger, we respond to the world-disclosive power of art when we refuse to ask art to be "about" anything in the world at all. We respond to art's apophantic power, similarly, when we respect the disinterestedness of the pleasures and pains that the beautiful and the sublime call forth, i.e., when we resist the temptation to attach interest to a determinate *telos* or goal. As Horkheimer and Adorno argue in a passage of "The Concept of Enlightenment" that is highly suggestive of Heidegger, "the work of art . . . posits its own, self-enclosed area, which is withdrawn from the context of profane existence, and in which special laws apply . . . every work of art describes its own circumference which closes it off from actuality" (p. 19).

If the theory of aesthetic reflection can help us understand the claims of judgments that are set within a field that is "objectless," then is there anything at all to be said about "art" as a mode of productive praxis? Surprisingly, the matters of production and praxis are never far afield in the discussion of "pure" aesthetic pleasure and reflective judgment, even in Kant. But Kant famously defines the purposiveness of art as being "without purpose." "Art" represents a form of work that is directed toward no determinate goal and that produces no objects – not just because the model of production does not apply to art but because the work of art is no mere "thing." Kant's position on these matters has been taken by historicist critics like Eagleton as part of an attempt to save art from

[29] Heidegger, *What Is a Thing?*, trans. Eugene T. Gendlin (South Bend, IN: Regnery/Gateway, 1967), p. 224.

vulgar appreciation and to defend it against efforts at ideological appropriation.[30] Likewise, in discussing the "philosophical disenfranchisement" of art, Arthur Danto has suggested that Kant's aesthetics serve to license art to represent potentially threatening kinds of experience – including the "wonder" and "fear" that are the strongest forms of the pleasure and pain that concern Kant – by insulating these experiences from the realm of lived experience.[31] To be sure, Kant treats the fear associated with the sublime as a *faux* fear, but Danto seems to regard Kant as concerned with the "culture of taste" rather than with aesthetic judgments. Indeed, it would be better to say that Kant thinks of aesthetic pleasure and pain as reflective modes of the end-directed forms of agency and attention that we ordinarily bring to bear upon nature or the world of objects. By focusing on the purposelessness of aesthetic agency and the disinterestedness of aesthetic pleasure, Kant attempts to view purposiveness and agency as modes of being or qualities in their "passive" or "receptive" mode; hence their affinities with what Aristotle described as the *pathē*. We respect the subjective mode of the agency that is at play in works of art when we refuse to ask art to move us to act upon the world, and we respond to the universality of that form of agency when we purge it from all interest associated with the agreeable and the good.

While Kant freely admits that "art has always got a definite intention of producing something" (*CJ*, sec. 45, p. 167), he goes on to say that this is not the production of a definite object and certainly not production according to a concept or plan. Moreover, Kant argues that the "work" of fine art must be clothed "with the aspect of nature" (p. 167), which is to say that it must occur "without a trace appearing of the artist having always had the rule present to him and of its having fettered his mental powers" (p. 167); it must be production as if by genius, which sets its own rules. "The way in which a product of art seems like nature," Kant says, "is by the presence of perfect exactness in the agreement with rules prescribing how alone the product can be what it is intended to be, but *with absence of laboured effect*" (p. 167; emphasis added). Kant's insistence on the purposelessness of

[30] See Mark Edmundson, *Literature Against Philosophy, Plato to Derrida* (Cambridge: Cambridge University Press, 1995), p. 7.
[31] Arthur Danto, "The Philosophical Disenfranchisement of Art," in *The Philosophical Disenfranchisement of Art* (New York: Columbia University Press, 1986).

aesthetic production and on the disinterestedness of aesthetic pleasure is not meant to efface the effects of labor or to diminish the role of agents in the process of production but rather to isolate what pertains irreducibly to the subject in the peculiar mode of production that is characteristic of art.

Hegel's *Lectures on Aesthetics* attempts to press on with the tasks begun in Kant's theory of reflective judgment; but Hegel does so by associating "art" with a specific domain of objects having an historical organization. What may be the most striking feature of the *Lectures* is that Hegel, unlike Kant, begins from the premise that aesthetics deal with the beauty that is specific to fine art. Whereas Kant does not distinguish between nature and art, Hegel's lectures presuppose the existence of art. By beginning in this way, the analysis of subjective feeling that defined the domain of "aesthetics" in the work of figures like Baumgarten, Wolff, and Kant himself, and which concentrated on the passions of admiration (wonder) and fear, is placed in relation to a specific class of objects that are regarded as culturally fashioned products. As Paul de Man observed in his essay on Hegel's *Lectures on Aesthetics*, we tend to act as "orthodox" (i.e., historicist) Hegelians in approaching aesthetics in terms of the formal or stylistic differences between the Hellenic and the Christian era or between the Hebraic and the Hellenic world.[32] We are Hegelian in a similarly historicist fashion when we try to systematize the relationships between the various forms or genres of art, or when we attempt to comprehend a particular style as a mode of expression that corresponds to some moment in the progress, development, or regression of a collective or individual consciousness.[33]

---

[32] De Man is not the only one to make this observation. See also Michael Fried, *Three American Painters* (Cambridge, MA: The Fogg Museum of Harvard University, 1965), p. 7.

[33] "Sign and Symbol in Hegel's Aesthetics," p. 763. Consider Lukács's thesis of the epic genealogy of the novel in *The Theory of the Novel*, as well as his development of a typology of novelistic form, as examples of the way in which Hegel's *Lectures on Aesthetics* has given rise to historicist interpretations of art. This is not to say that *The Theory of the Novel* is a strictly historicist text. As I have argued elsewhere, it is Lukács's ambition to sustain a perspective that is at once historical and philosophical. See *The Subject of Modernity* (Cambridge: Cambridge University Press, 1992). On the interpretation of other critics, however, *The Theory of the Novel* makes sense only as an historicist text. See Jay M. Bernstein, *The Philosophy of the Novel: Lukács, Marxism, and the Dialectics of Form* (Minneapolis: University of Minnesota Press, 1984).

But the task of Hegel's *Lectures on Aesthetics* is not simply to show that art is historical, and even less to subordinate art to the worldly discourses of production and praxis, but to relate the particular form of making that is visible in art to the larger story of consciousness as it is set to work in the world, impelled by desire and seeking satisfaction (closure). Thus the *Lectures* aim to show the ways in which art is not just an object sought by desire-driven consciousness, but is itself a consequence or effect of desire in action. Moreover, the task of aesthetic theory as Hegel conceives it is to reestablish the place of the passions (or "passive powers") of pleasure and pain among such predominantly "active" categories as "production" and "praxis." In the process, Hegel aims to disclose how the object-world is in fact permeated by human consciousness. The recovery of the truth of art is, for Hegel, the recovery of consciousness from the object-world.

The tension in Hegel's *Lectures on Aesthetics* between the memorial role of art and philosophy's supersession of art by the powers of dialectical thought has likewise been overlooked by critics who focus on the claims that Hegel makes about the various stages of art – the symbolic, the classical, and the romantic. To be sure, de Man's own work represents a signal instance of the deconstructive effort to question the historicist use of Hegel. De Man is particularly intent on resisting the suggestion of passages like the one below, in which Hegel proposes that art can build a bridge between the realms of "meaning" and "form":

If consciousness does advance out of the immediately intuited identity between the Absolute and its externally posited existence, then what confronts us as the essential point is the cleavage between the hitherto united aspects, i.e. the battle between meaning and shape, which immediately provokes the attempt to heal the breach again by building the separated parts together in a fanciful way. It is with this attempt alone that there arises the proper need for art. For if the content of ideas is established independently, in present reality, then thereby the task is set before spirit of giving for contemplation and perception – in a renewed mode produced by spirit – a richly fanciful shape to universal ideas and in this activity creating artistic productions. (*LA*, vol. I, p. 333)

Hegel holds the view that art has its origins as an irreducible form of particularization that nonetheless retains the power to act upon the universal, if not in fact to guarantee its existence; specifically, Hegel regards art as the manifestation or showing (*scheinen*) of the universal in sensuous form. This is possible in Hegel's sense if, and only if, the particularization that occurs in art is understood as *poiēsis* in the strong form, namely, as a form of making that rivals that of nature. As Heidegger suggests in "The Question Concerning Technology," *poiēsis* was originally bound to the *physis* or "showing forth" of the natural world; both represent forms of what has since come to be called "production."[34] But since, unlike Heidegger's Greeks, Hegel regards "nature" as the locus of a lack that only spirit can fill (e.g., as incapable in itself of granting recognition to or of satisfying the human subject), it is hardly a surprise to find that the purposiveness of "nature" must for Hegel be described in terms of art.[35] Not only in Hegel, but throughout Romantic aesthetics, nature is *already* art insofar as it mimes the labor of the genius, whose work involves the production of particulars which in turn create universal rules.

In "The Origin of the Work of Art" Heidegger calls Hegel's *Lectures* "the most comprehensive reflection on the nature of art that the West possesses – comprehensive because it stems from metaphysics."[36] But the meaning of Heidegger's claim is not immediately apparent. First, Hegel's *Lectures* are heavily indebted to Kant on certain key points. Moreover, Hegel's *Lectures* appear to be historically rather than metaphysically grounded. The sense of Heidegger's remark lies in the claim that the effort of the *Lectures on Aesthetics* is to reestablish a fundamental connection between art and truth. Hegel expresses the truth of art as the correspondence between beauty ("sensuality") and truth (the "Idea"). Over the course of the *Lectures*, Hegel's definition of "art" as "the sensory appearance of the idea" ("das Sinnliche Scheinen der Idee") is qualified and refined to reflect Hegel's belief that art calls for cognition and judgment to supplement

---

34 Heidegger, "The Question Concerning Technology," p. 10.
35 When Fredric Jameson defines "postmodernism" as the moment "when the modernization process is complete and nature is gone for good," he is in fact articulating a position that begins in Hegel, if not before. See Jameson, *Postmodernism or, The Cultural Logic of Late Capitalism* (Durham, NC: Duke University Press, 1991), p. ix. The difference between Hegel and postmodernism on this point has to do with whether Hegel remains nostalgic for the "nature" that is supplanted by art. On the basis of the *Phenomenology*, it seems clear that spirit has needs (such as those of recognition) that cannot possibly be met by nature: in order to satisfy its needs, spirit is obliged to leave nature behind.
36 Heidegger, Epilogue to OWA, p. 79.

sense experience (e. g., "what is now aroused in us by works of art is not just immediate enjoyment but our judgment also" [*LA*, vol. I, p. 11]).[37] Indeed, the Hegelian claim that art is the "sensuous appearance of the Idea" contains the traces of a falsehood that Hegel himself would have been among the first to recognize. As Hegel says in the *Lectures on the Philosophy of Religion*, nothing in the world is unmediated; and as Hegel amply demonstrates in the *Phenomenology* – which begins with a critique of the immediacy of sense-certainty – immediacy itself is mediated.[38] Nonetheless, Hegel regards sensuous particularity as somehow central to the work of art: the sensuous particularity of art serves to displace the conditions of its formation by the force of its appearance, such that its appearance in effect becomes a "creation" of its universal character.

How can the sensuous immediacy of art be related to Hegel's project in the *Phenomenology* to understand the unfolding of truth through the workings of self-conscious spirit, which involves a process of constant, internal mediation? And how may it be reconciled with the *Phenomenology*'s effort to articulate the logic of appearances in their totality? The meaning of Hegel's claims about the sensuous immediacy of art can best be understood against the background of the distinction that Hegel attempts to draw between "art" and "nature." The "subject" of the *Phenomenology* is defined in terms of the distance between the givenness of nature and the lack that consciousness, as a "higher" form of nature, transforms into desire. In the *Lectures on Aesthetics*, art plays a crucial role in revealing the further complexities of this relationship. In the *Lectures*, Hegel delimits the field of art by reference to the lack ("deficiencies") of nature, which art, as a product of spirit, is said to supersede (*LA*, vol. I, p. 152). In point of fact, art is only one stage in what Hegel thinks of as the "surpassing" of nature, and not necessarily the highest one; philosophy is a more advanced moment in this same process, since it aims to

---

[37] Hegel argues that art solicits an *intellectual* interest both in its content and in its means of presentation: "Art invites us to intellectual consideration, and that not for the purpose of creating art again, but for knowing philosophically what art is" (*LA*, vol. I, p. 11). In the philosophy of aesthetics, this intellectual interest assumes a discursive form. It is a consequence of the claim that our interest in art must be intellectual, and represents nothing more than what art itself demands.

[38] See Hegel, *Lectures on the Philosophy of Religion*, trans. E. B. Speirs and J. B. Sanderson (New York: Humanities Press, 1962), vol. I, p. 162.

present a comprehensive perspective on the truth in discursive form.

As far as the "deficiencies" of nature are concerned, the *Lectures on Aesthetics* show two to be prominent in Hegel's mind. First, Hegel says that the component parts of nature ("the reality of the independent differences and their equally independent objectified unity as such") require unification under some concept, which transforms these differences into something that is in fact more than a concept – nature's "animating soul" ( *LA*, vol. 1, p. 118). In this, he echoes section 49 of Kant's third *Critique*, which defines "soul" (*Geist*) in an "aesthetical" sense as signifying "the animating principle in the mind" (*CJ*, sec. 49, p. 175). According to Kant, the aesthetic faculty has the power to put this "animating" principle into play, directing it toward ends that are final, organizing in a form of activity that is "self-maintaining" and which strengthens and reinforces itself for this same purpose (*CJ*, sec. 49, p. 175).[39] Second, Hegel argues that the things of the natural world are "dependent" or "restricted" in ways that art as a product of the spirit is not. Art is said to be "higher" than nature because it is a fruit of the productivity of the spirit working in "freedom." In characterizing art at the very beginning of the *Lectures*, Hegel writes that "the beauty of art is *higher* than nature. The beauty of art is beauty *born of the spirit and born again*, and the higher the spirit and its productions stand above nature and its phenomena the higher too is the beauty of art above nature and its phenomena" (*LA*, vol. 1, p. 2).

The *Lectures on Aesthetics* nonetheless begins with a full-blown discussion of the beauty of nature, ostensibly devoted to establishing the superiority of art by reference to its various "deficiencies,"[40] but in reality incorporating nature within the realm of "spirit" that Hegel claims is characteristic of art. For instance, Hegel wishes to establish the unity of nature as conceptually and not sensuously determined. To this end, he observes that when nature is regarded in its "organic" quality, its components ap-

[39] Likewise, in the *Anthropology* Kant remarks that "spirit sets the imagination into motion," i.e., animates it. See *Anthropology from a Pragmatic Point of View*, trans. Victor Lyle Dowdell (Carbondale: Southern Illinois University Press, 1978), p. 124.

[40] According to Gadamer, it may be that Heinrich Gustav Hotho's versions of the *Lectures* ascribes too much autonomy to natural beauty. See Hans-Georg Gadamer, *Truth and Method* (New York: Continuum, 1975), pp. 504–05.

pear as "members" of a whole: "they are no longer sundered, existing independently, but they have genuine existence only in their ideal unity" (*LA*, vol. i, p. 118). But he then goes on to say that "only in such an organic articulation does there dwell in the members the ideal unity of the Concept which is their support and their immanent soul" (*ibid.*), so that the function of the "concept" is not just to unify nature but in fact to structure, support, and finally to animate it. (Cf. Kant: "'Soul' [*Geist*] in an aesthetical sense, signifies the animating principle in the mind."[41]) Indeed, the conceptual "unity" of nature is established by the figure of animate "organicity" – which is also to say that Hegel's "nature" is spiritualized by virtue of an analogy in which the organic is associated with the self-determining purposiveness of life and the inorganic with purposelessness and with death. For instance, the "life" that Hegel associates with nature shows itself in the capacity for free spontaneous movement (*LA*, vol. i, p. 122), which inorganic matter does not have. This purposiveness of the natural world serves to distinguish it categorically from the realm of dead matter: "natural appearance alone is an existence of the Idea, the Idea in natural form as Life. Dead, inorganic nature is not adequate to the Idea, and only the living organism is an actuality of the Idea. For in life, in the first place, the reality of the Concept's distinctions is present as real; secondly, however, there is the negation of these as merely real distinctions, in that the ideal subjectivity of the Concept subdues this reality to itself; thirdly, there is the soulful qua the affirmative form which has the power to maintain itself, as form, in its content" (*LA*, vol. i, p. 118). Indeed, Hegel cannot resist attributing a purposiveness to nature and goes so far as to find a "soulfulness," an "inner animation," and a "free force" at work in it; moreover, he attempts to transform nature's materiality into meaning by aligning it with the free productivity that is characteristic of art: "So, for example, the natural crystal amazes us by its regular shape,

[41] Kant, *CJ*, sec. 49, p. 175. See John H. Zammito's discussion of *Geist* in Kant in *The Genesis of Kant's Critique of Judgment* (Chicago: University of Chicago Press, 1992), pp. 301–05. Zammito devotes special attention to Kant's elaboration of a theory of *Geist* in advance of the third *Critique*, specifically in the *Reflections on Anthropology* of the late 1770s (Kant had lectured regularly on anthropology at Königsberg beginning in the fall semester of 1772). Kant develops the matter in the *Anthropology from a Pragmatic Point of View*. See also chapter 7 below on the relationship between *Geist* as an "animating principle," the *Lebensgefühl* of sec. 1 of the third *Critique*, and Nietzsche's "Wille zur Macht."

produced not by any external, mechanical, influence, but by an inner vocation and free force of its own, free on the part of the object itself" (p. 130).

Hegel's effort to "animate" nature thus represents an attempt to overcome its pure materiality and thereby to create the impression that nature in fact has meaning for, speaks to, the subject. (Cf. Kant, who speaks of the "charms of natural beauty" as embodying "a language in which nature speaks to us and which has the semblance of a higher meaning" [*CJ*, sec. 42, p. 161].[42]) In thus "animating" nature according to what Kant describes as the "aesthetic" principle of *Geist*, Hegel aims to defeat the prospect of a materiality that would leave no room for the generation of a symbolic order of meaning. He attempts to situate the subject in a realm capable of reflecting desire rather than just drive. (As Lacan liked to point out, the generation of meaning requires negation – the symbolic "death" of the thing at the hands of the symbol.) In the example at hand, however, the crystal remains dependent upon and limited by its materiality in ways that, on Hegel's account, the work of art is not. Nonetheless, the "ideal" of nature is that of an "aesthetic" whole – which is to say that it involves precisely the kind of spontaneity that is said to characterize art. (For Kant, the materiality associated with the aesthetic is determined by the semblance of purposiveness: "that whereby this principle [*Geist*] animates the psychic substance [*Seele*] – the material which it employs for that purpose – is that which sets the mental powers into a swing that is final, i.e., into a play which is self-maintaining and which strengthens those powers for such activity" [*CJ*, sec. 49, p. 175].)

In addressing the artwork as a sensuous object that is also a product of human desire, Hegel substantially revises Kant's distinction between "making" (*facere*) and "acting" (*agere*). For Kant, "making" implies action in accordance with a plan, and involves deliberation, whereas "acting" does not. In Kant's example, a beehive gives no evidence of deliberation and so remains unidentifiable as a product of making: "although we are pleased to call what bees produce (their regularly constructed cells) a work of art, we only do so on the strength of an analogy with art; that is to

---

[42] Kant's own reflections on organic form are most fully developed in the *Critique of Teleological Judgment*, which contains the synthesis of Kant's biological reflections.

say, as soon as we call to mind that no rational deliberation forms the basis of their labor, we say that it is a product of their nature (of instinct), and it is only to their Creator that we ascribe it as an art" (*CJ*, sec. 43, p. 163). In Aristotelian terms, the "making" of the beehive would not constitute a *technē*. "Art" is said to be the instance of a special kind of making: it involves a plan or design as well as some formal arrangement of the physical properties of matter so as to impart the semblance of a purposiveness that could not be achieved through natural means alone. Yet this purposiveness is deflected from any determinate goal; hence it appears as "without purpose."

Likewise, Hegel's description of the "suspension of desire" in the apprehension of art represents an extension of Kant's thesis of the disinterestedness that characterizes aesthetic pleasure. Just as art does not involve the making of objects that are what Heidegger would call "mere things," the mode of apprehension appropriate to art requires a deflection of the "natural" course of desire. For instance, the appetitive interest that we ordinarily bring to the sensuous world – which on Hegel's account drives us ultimately to negate or destroy and consume it – must be arrested when dealing with the work of art. (Adorno traces the arresting of "natural" desire along lines that lead from Kant to Freud, likening the taboo that prohibits us from taking an "animal-like" attitude toward art to the repression of a primal urge.[43]) Although a sensuous and material element may be present in and even necessary for art, the deflection of appetite confirms the power of art to "negate" the sensuous world; it transforms the object in question into what Hegel calls "pure appearance" (*LA*, vol. 1, p. 38). As a "pure appearance" art cannot be reduced to a cause, and least of all to a material or efficient cause. Indeed, art is the closest thing in Hegel's thought to something that would seem categorically impossible, given the dialectical determinations that can be brought to bear upon almost any other "thing": a pure effect or appearance that reveals consciousness in action, that shows reflection as a form of deflection, that constitutes a seemingly "objective" representation of the force of the understanding itself. In other words, art exemplifies a mode of agency whose "end" lies in the very affects that arise in re-

---

[43] Adorno, *AT*, p. 16.

sponse to it, not in the production of a "thing."[44] It is "purpose-less" in this sense.

Not surprisingly, then, Hegel calculates that the work of art is not sensuous in the same way that the material world is, and argues that we do not relate to it with the same set of interests that we bring to the material world: "The practical desire rates organic and inorganic individual things in nature, which can serve its purpose, higher than works of art which show themselves useless to serve it and are enjoyable only by other forms of the spirit" (*LA*, vol. I, p. 37.). But neither is art merely a matter of ideas, to be apprehended cognitively. Taking his lead from Kant, who speaks of judgment as a "middle term" between under-standing and reason (*CJ*, Preface, p. 4), Hegel strives to express the indeterminacy of art by saying that it occupies a "middle ground." For Hegel this means that art cannot be reduced to the "immediacy" of the sensuous world or to pure ideality. Art has a sensuous existence but does not have a purely natural life – in part because it has *more* than a merely "natural" life; it is also feeling and thought: "the work of art, though it has a sensuous existence, does not require in this respect a sensuously concrete being and a natural life; indeed it ought not to remain on this level, seeing that it is meant to satisfy purely spiritual interests and exclude all desire from itself" (*LA*, vol. I, p. 37). In Adorno's terminology in the *Aesthetic Theory*, art contains a "plus" (sur-plus) of meaning over nature, which is, however, meaningful only on the basis of an analogy with art: "nature's beauty con-sists in appearing to say more than she is . . . the idea behind art is to wrest this 'plus' from its contingent setting in nature, appro-priating nature's appearance and making it determinate, which means among other things negating its unreality."[45]

---

[44] Cf. Stanley Cavell, who glosses Kant's "speaking of beauty as if it were a property of things" as follows: "Only 'as if' because it cannot be an ordinary property of things; its presence or absence cannot be established in the way ordinary properties are; that is, they cannot be established publicly, and we don't know (there aren't any) causal conditions, or usable rules, for producing, or altering, or erasing, or increasing this 'property.' Then why not just say it *isn't* a property of an object? I suppose there would be no reason not to say this, if we could find another way of recording our conviction that it is one, anyway that what we are pointing to is *there*, in the object; and our knowledge that men make objects that create this response in us, and make them exactly with the idea that they will create it." "Aesthetic Problems of Modern Philosophy," in *Must We Mean What We Say?* (Cambridge: Cambridge University Press, 1969), p. 89, n.

[45] Adorno, *AT*, p. 116.

Yet it proves quite difficult for art to maintain its position in this "middle ground," in part because the notion of a "middle ground" conjures up a spatial location for something that, as "pure appearance," occupies no determinate place. In an attempt to resolve this issue, Hegel resorts to the language of development, suggesting that art is always in process, that it is involved in becoming and overcoming, that it partakes of the "not yet" and the "no longer," ceaselessly aspiring to become pure thought by overcoming its material nature, but remaining nonetheless tethered to the conditions of its sensuous existence: "the sensuous aspect of a work of art, in comparison with the immediate existence of things in nature, is elevated to a pure appearance, and the work of art stands in the *middle* between immediate sensuousness and ideal thought. It is *not yet* pure thought, but, despite its sensuousness, is *no longer* a purely material existent either, like stones, plants, and organic life" (*LA*, vol. 1, p. 38). Unable to say exactly how art is the "sensuous manifestation of the idea," Hegel suggests that art is the sensuous world in the process of becoming Idea.

The second of Hegel's most notorious claims seems to fly even more directly in the face of the avowed purpose of the *Aesthetics* to treat the beauty specific to works of fine art. It nonetheless provides a key to understanding how the difficulty of aesthetic reflective judgment visible in Kant can be linked to a series of post-Enlightenment reflections on art, not least among which is Adorno's analysis of the "problematic" status of art in the *Aesthetic Theory*. In what may well be the most enigmatic claim of the *Lectures*, Hegel says that art is no longer possible in the present age, that when regarded in its "highest vocation" art is "a thing of the past" (*LA*, vol. 1, p. 11).[46] What can be the meaning of such an assertion in relation to Hegel's claim that art is the "sensuous appearance of the idea"? And what might this assertion mean for a philosophy (namely, aesthetics) that seeks to assess the beauty specific to art? Is Hegel's analysis of art as "the

[46] Adorno takes up Hegel's claim explicitly in Appendix I to the *Aesthetic Theory*: "Beginning with Hegel, doomsday prophecies tended to be part of an elitist and authoritarian philosophy of culture, rather than of artistic experience itself. This pattern of dealing with innovation by means of repressive decree, as it were, foreshadowed subsequent totalitarian practices" (*AT*, p. 441).

one reality adequate to beauty" contradicted by this claim about the impossibility of art in the present age?

In "The Origin of the Work of Art" and also in the volumes on Nietzsche Heidegger points out that Hegel's claim cannot possibly mean that art as such no longer exists. As Adorno notes at the beginning of *Aesthetic Theory*, modern (and especially modernist) culture has in fact witnessed a great expansion of art. For Heidegger, the question raised by Hegel's *Lectures* is rather more pointed: "is art still an essential and necessary way in which that truth happens that is decisive for our historical existence, or is art no longer of this character? If, however, it is such no longer, then there remains the question why this is so" (OWA, p. 80). When Tolstoy asked "What is art?" and then proceeded to reject most of the art of the past, he was in fact echoing Hegel's claim. When Stanley Cavell adds that Tolstoy's question is grammatically related to the question "What is the *importance* of art?," he was implicitly following Hegel and Heidegger both.[47]

Hegel's understanding of the eclipse of art (or, following Heidegger, the eclipse of the "importance" of art) may be read within the context of an historical analysis in which Hegel identifies the culture of ancient Greece as the moment when the truth (Hegel's "Idea") was revealed sensuously and immediately, and not in the abstract or through the powers of conceptual representation. For reasons not unrelated to these, Hegel stresses the kinship between religion and art. On this account, the history of art in the enlightened, modern age is the record of a fall away from the immediate satisfaction of spiritual needs that Hegel believes was possible in the ancient world (and, Hegel adds, in theocentric cultures): "art no longer affords that satisfaction of spiritual needs which earlier ages and nations sought in it, and found in it alone, a satisfaction that, at least on the part of religion, was most intimately linked with art. The beautiful days of Greek art, like the golden age of the later Middle Ages, are gone" (*LA*, vol. 1, p. 10). Hegel's account of the eclipse of art is thus part of his critique of modernity: art in its original sense, as an immediate bearer of truth, is impossible in the modern age; moreover, the consequences of this impossibility determine our relationship to the past as one of a

47 Leo Tolstoy, *What Is Art?*, trans. Almyer Maude (Indianapolis, IN: Bobbs-Merrill, 1960). Cavell, *The World Viewed: Reflections on the Ontology of Film*, enlarged edition (Cambridge, MA: Harvard University Press, 1979), pp. 3–4.

loss that is coupled with an impossible desire to grasp the transcendental signified in a sensuously immediate form.

Heidegger's reflections in "The Origin of the Work of Art" and in "The Age of the World Picture" invite a related interpretation. In "The Age of the World Picture" Heidegger argues that an "essential phenomenon" of the modern period lies in art's moving into the purview of aesthetics.[48] In Heidegger's view, as in Hegel's, the distance between the era of "great art," when art was "the truth of beings setting itself to work" (OWA, p. 36), and the condition of "art" in the present (modern) age, is determined by a history in which ancient Greece stands as the fundamental point of reference for a mode of truth that was self-disclosive and where modernity names the moment when truth was drawn within the field of representational thinking (Heidegger's *Gestell*). Heidegger thus remains a Hegelian when he writes that "in Greece, at the outset of the destining of the West, the arts soared to the supreme height of the revealing granted them. They brought the presence [*Gegenwart*] of the gods, brought the dialogue of divine and human destinings, to radiance."[49] On this account, the history of art ever since has been one of loss and decay; it has determined a fate from which, in Heidegger's words, only a god could save us: "World-withdrawal and world-decay can never be undone. The works are no longer the same as they once were. It is they themselves, to be sure, that we encounter there, but they themselves are gone by. As bygone works they stand over against us as in the realm of tradition and conservation. Henceforth they remain merely objects. Their standing before us is still indeed a consequence of, but no longer the same as, their former self-subsistence. This self-subsistence has fled from them. The whole art industry, even if carried to the extreme and exercised in every way for the sake of works themselves, extends only to the object-being of the works. But this does not constitute their work-being" (OWA, p. 41).

To be sure, Hegel's and Heidegger's images of antiquity could easily be falsified by an historical analysis of the culture of the ancient world. While we may be able to recognize a genre like the ancient epic as having a value that was at once cognitive and

---

[48] Heidegger, "The Age of the World Picture," in *The Question Concerning Technology and Other Essays*, p. 116.
[49] "The Question Concerning Technology," p. 34.

truth. (Here, Hegel reveals himself as far closer an antecedent of Nietzsche than is commonly assumed.)

Following this train of thought, Hegel suggests that Enlightenment culture has become so pervaded by the conditions of "reflection" (read: conceptual thought, science) that it would be impossible to imagine the circumstances in which art could be regarded as the "sensuous manifestation of the idea." In Hegel's view, the idea of an aesthetic revolution against the conditions of reflection grossly underestimates the difficulty of the problems involved and misconstrues the power of art: "it is not, as might be supposed, merely that the practising artist himself is infected by the loud voice of reflection all around him and by the opinions and judgments on art that have become customary everywhere . . . the point is that our whole spiritual culture is of such a kind that [the artist] himself stands within the world of reflection and its relations, and could not by any act of will and decision abstract himself from it; nor could he by special education or removal from the relations of life contrive and organize a special solitude to replace what he has lost." For this reason Hegel concludes that art is impossible in the present age, that "the conditions of our present time are not favorable to art" (*LA*, vol. I, pp. 10, 11). (Hegel's argument is essentially repeated in Heidegger's essay "The Question Concerning Technology," where Heidegger claims that technology – "enframing," *Gestell* – drives out every other possibility of revealing, including that of *poiēsis*.)

As Hegel sees it, the strictly conceptual determination of our relationship to the sensuous world has implications for all aspects of social life. In a culture where "reflection" prevails, the free, concrete particularities of experience are subsumed under general laws and rules that are given in advance. Insofar as it is through these general laws that sensuous particulars become available to us, "reflection" negates everything that is concrete about the particularities in question. Following Kant's analysis of the logic of subsumptive (determinant) judgments,[53] and anticipating the post-positivist critique of empiricism, Hegel argues that while

---

[53] This is not to suggest that Hegel does nothing more than reject the logic of subsumptive judgments. Adorno argues the point forcefully in "The Experiential Content of Hegel's Philosophy," in *Hegel: Three Studies*, trans. Shierry Weber Nicholson (Cambridge, MA: MIT Press, 1993). He also makes the point that in Hegel the inadequacy of all isolated particular definitions is also the inadequacy of the reality grasped in those definitions.

scientific knowledge may indeed begin from an engagement with sensuous particulars – i.e., from an engagement with *this* color, size, temperature, smell, or shape – the knowledge appropriate to science is bound to end up privileging the universal over and against the particular. In the process of achieving what science calls "knowledge" the particularity of the particular is effaced. Heidegger advances a related argument when he contrasts *empeiria* (*experientia*) with the modern, Kantian notion of "experience," which founds and is in turn founded upon the notion of scientific experiment. For Aristotle, *empeiria* meant "the observation of things themselves, their qualities and modifications under changing conditions," whereas experiment "begins with the laying down of a law as a basis."[54] For what Hegel calls "science," as for what Kant calls "cognition," "this isolated sensuous thing has as such no further bearing on the spirit, inasmuch as intelligence goes straight for the universal, the law, the thought and concept of the object; on this account not only does it turn its back on the object in its immediate individuality, but transforms it within; out of something sensuously concrete it makes an abstraction, something thought, and so something essentially other than what that same object was in its sensuous appearance" (*LA*, vol. I, p. 37). If any trace of particularity remains within "science," it must be that of an instance that relates to the general rule in the mode of mere illustration or example. Moreover, the particular must be removed from its context in order to serve as a truthful trace of it.[55] The particular is liable to become a mere part, standing in a metonymic relationship to the whole, which all these particulars together cannot comprise: as a part, the particular stands for the dismemberment of the totality that is "organically" whole, while the whole must in turn be thought of as the impossible object comprised of the summation of such mere parts.[56]

Hegel's critique of scientific cognition follows Kant's contras-

[54] Heidegger, "The Age of the World Picture," p. 121.

[55] On the root meaning of the "example" as something excerpted or cut out, see John Lyons, *Exemplum* (Princeton, NJ: Princeton University Press, 1989).

[56] Cf. Susan Stewart: "Here we find the structure of Freud's description of the genesis of the fetish: a part of the body is substituted for the whole, or an object is substituted for the part, until finally, and inversely, the whole body can become object, substituting for the whole. Thus we have the systematic transformation of the object into its own impossibility." *On Longing: Narratives of the Miniature, the Gigantic, the Souvenir, the Collection* (1984; rpt. Durham, NC: Duke University Press, 1993), p. 135.

tive presentation of art and science in relation to the category of genius.[57] Kant says that the talent of genius is that of an "exemplary validity"; genius sets its own rules, whereas in science "clearly known rules must take the lead and determine the procedure" (*CJ*, sec. 49, p. 180). Hegel's critique of empiricism moreover makes it abundantly clear that the task he sees for aesthetics is not simply to recover the particular in naked isolation from the (conceptual or natural) whole. Like those brands of historicism that insist upon the primacy of the concrete and the particular over and against the abstractions of "theory," empiricism is guided by the misleading belief that we can grasp the particular in itself. In Hegel's critique, empiricism falsely denies the role of universal concepts and laws in mediating the particularity of experience: "empiricism is not merely an observing, hearing, feeling, etc., a perception of the individual; for it really sets to work to find the species, the universal, to discover laws. Now because it does this, it comes within the territory of the concept."[58] Indeed, Hegel is willing to favor the notion of "reflection" if by so doing the naive conception of experience associated with empiricism can be overturned.

Hegel's critique of empiricism is closely related to what Adorno criticizes as the response of "bourgeois culture" to the dominance of concepts. Like Rorty's later neo-pragmatism, "bourgeois nominalism" aims to liberate consciousness from the concept's claim of universality.[59] Adorno suggests that it does so by demystifying the concept, deflating its pretensions, making it appear as a mere

---

[57] So too for a thinker like Coleridge the poetic genius demonstrates an essentially organic creativity. Christopher Norris provides a good account of the deconstructive critique of organicity in chapter 2 of *Paul de Man: Deconstruction and the Critique of Aesthetic Ideology* (New York: Routledge, 1988), pp. 28–64.

[58] Hegel, *Lectures on the History of Philosophy*, trans. E. S. Haldane and Frances Simson (New York: Humanities Press, 1955), vol. III, p. 176. Adorno comments: "Hegel's antipositivist insight has been redeemed by modern science only to the extent that Gestalt theory has shown that there is no such thing as an isolated, unqualified sensory 'this thing here'; it is always already structured." Adorno, "The Experiential Content of Hegel's Philosophy," in *Hegel: Three Studies*, p. 58.

[59] What is false in Rorty's pragmatism lies in the belief that our particular interests and aims can be isolated from all overarching or underlying (i.e. "metaphysical") structures of consciousness. Indeed, Rorty's attempt to deflate the metaphysical notion of truth by invoking the pragmatist motto that truth is simply "what works" in the way of ideas still makes reference to the notions of purposiveness and efficacy that would be meaningless and incommunicable were it not for the mediation of the conceptual husks that Rorty wishes to discard.

abbreviation for the particularities which it embraces. But nominalism falls into the all too familiar trap of "solving" the problem posed by the third *Critique* – that of relating particulars to universals – by accepting a monistic concept of experience; to wit, nominalism restricts our interest to the world of particulars, to phenomena. As Adorno perspicuously warned, nominalism is thus inclined to make a fetish of particulars; he sees this as a special danger in bourgeois culture, where the power of concepts is so easily degraded: "nominalism encourages the bourgeoisie to be suspicious of everything that would restrain isolated individuals in their pursuit of happiness, the unreflective pursuit of their own advantage, as being mere illusion. Nothing should remove the blinders of the particular, the belief that its contingency is its law. 'What's a concept anyway?' – this gesture always expresses something else as well: that the individual has money to earn and that is more important than anything else. If the concept were to be autonomous in such a way that it did not exhaust itself in the particulars of which it is composed, the bourgeois principle of individuation would be shaken to its core" (*AT*, pp. 112–13).

In the *Lectures on Aesthetics*, Hegel nonetheless remains attached to the idea that the very existence of art, however difficult or fraught, is bound up with its sensuous particularity. What kind of particularity then is this and how, in acknowledging it, can we avoid the reductive nominalism associated with an interest in particulars, historical or otherwise? Though reflection may preclude any encounter with the "sensuous appearance of the idea," Hegel continues to believe that art can and does play a role in the culture of enlightened modernity. What can this be?

One answer to these questions is that art serves a "memorial" role, that in a culture of "reflection" art allows us to see what it might have been like to make universal claims on the basis of sensuous particulars, without the prior mediation of concepts. This "memory" is, of course, but a version of the Kantian "as if." Just as Kant imagines an archaic moment when knowledge was itself a pleasurable experience, Hegel imagines that art has the power to remind us of what it would be like for the truth to reveal itself in a sensuously apprehensible form. In Hegel, art "remembers" the conditions under which feelings of pleasure and pain can assert their priority over the universal laws to which they are otherwise subsumed. He suggests that art has the power to show what it might be like to credit the passions and the affects with the world-disclosive power that Heidegger later ascribed to *poiēsis*. The particularity of art is for Hegel one in which the universal is revealed in the senses' analogues, the feelings; it is that of a universal that stands at one remove from the concrete: "for artistic interest and production we demand in general . . . a quality of life in which the universal is not present in the form of law and maxim, but which *gives the impression* of being one with the senses and the feelings, just as the universal and the rational is contained in the imagination by being brought into unity with a concrete sensuous appearance" (*LA*, vol. I, p. 10; emphasis added). While art may indeed be a "thing of the past," and while art may no longer count as "the highest mode in which truth fashions an existence for itself" (*LA*, vol. I, p. 103), art recalls its connection, if only by similitude, to the truth as the "sensuous manifestation of the idea." The "utopian" function of art, the promise of its power to project a world in which the differentiation of universal and particular would truly wither away, can be understood as a function of its "memorial" role. Adorno advances a closely related claim when he proposes that art is "an unconscious form of historiography, the memory of what has been vanquished or repressed, perhaps an anticipation of what is possible" (*AT*, p. 366), or again when he writes that "art wills what has never existed so far, but at the same time all art is one big *déjà vu*" (*AT*, p. 195).

Phrased in slightly different terms, one could say that art is licensed to disclose the truth, but only – necessarily – in a fictional or hypothetical mode. Adorno's "memory" and "anticipation" are themselves figures or signs of an immediate relationship to the world of appearances that is impossible to achieve.[60] Indeed, I would go so far as to suggest that even the feelings of pleasure and pain summoned up by the beautiful and the sublime are unintelligible apart from the "as if" – not because such feelings are simulacra of their "real" counterparts but because they allow us to comprehend imaginatively conditions that we could not otherwise apprehend. By virtue of its apparent impossibility in the present age, the "as if" structure of art allows us to grasp the

---

[60] Precisely because art is consigned to the realm of the "as if," however, the disclosive power of figures and signs must be indirect; it occurs through what Heidegger would call "concealment."

fundamental insight of Kant's theory of aesthetic judgment: the paradox of a truth that is at once subjectively grounded in our apprehension of sensuous particulars, but also universally true.

## Postscript

Hegel's analysis of art in the *Lectures on Aesthetics* is complicated by what Hegel regards as the philosophical "overcoming" of the fate by which art is consigned to the realm of the "as if." By overcoming this fate, philosophy aims to defeat the "as if," to supersede discourse in the "hypothetical" mode, to deny its provisionality, and thereby to present itself as an articulation of absolute knowing. As Arthur Danto has pointed out, art serves in Hegel's system to pave the way for philosophical discourse; once philosophy comes into being, art can be surpassed by articulations of knowledge that conform to the inherent clarity of the concept rather than to sense-experience. Art thus appears as a "thing of the past" not only because of the "alienation" associated with the culture of reflection but also in view of the promise of a full philosophical articulation of the Idea. As Danto is quick to indicate, Hegel's position on this issue is by no means unique: "this is a cosmic way of achieving the second stage of the platonic program, which has always been to substitute philosophy for art. And to dignify art, patronizingly, as philosophy in one of its self-alienated forms, thirsting for clarity as to its own nature as all of us thirst for clarity as to our own."[61] Indeed, Hegel's concept of philosophy seems designed to accomplish through the power of concepts what he says is impossible for art to achieve – the "sensuous appearance of the idea."[62] In a passage that harkens

[61] Danto, "Philosophical Disenfranchisement," p. 16. Mark Edmundson notes that art is obliged to submit to a kind of "philosophical therapy" in which it "overcomes its fixation on the merely particular and rises into the world of the evolving idea, the world of spirit. Where artistic id was there philosophical ego shall be." Edmundson, *Literature Against Philosophy*, p. 8.

[62] In *Truth and Method* Gadamer observes that Hegel's concept of philosophy vies with and attempts to supersede art as the "bridge" between the worlds of sensuous matter and pure ideas. For his own part, Hegel claims that it is religion that transcends art. He regards religion as an advance over art because religion adds worship to what art offers. (See *LA*, vol. 1, pp. 103–04.) For this same reason, Hegel argues that the manifestation of truth in a sensuous form is unable to satisfy what spirit desires (p. 105). But religion still thinks in terms of images; so philosophy, which aspires to be a kind of imageless thinking, must in turn transcend religion.

back to Kant's analysis of the problem of the division of worlds created by the separation of "things" from "things-in-themselves," but that goes further than Kant in outlining a reconciliation of these two worlds, Hegel writes that

Spiritual culture, the modern intellect, produces this opposition in man which makes him an amphibious animal, because he now has to live in two worlds which contradict one another. The result is now that consciousness wanders about in this contradiction, and, driven from one side to the other, cannot find satisfaction for itself in either the one or the other. For on the one side we see man imprisoned in the common world of reality, hard pressed by nature, enmeshed in matter, sensuous ends and their passions. On the other side, he lifts himself to eternal ideas, to a realm of thought and freedom, gives to himself, as *will*, universal laws and prescriptions, strips the world of its enlivened and flowering reality and dissolves it into abstractions . . . If general culture has run into such a contradiction, it becomes the task of philosophy to supersede the oppositions, i.e. to show that neither the one alternative in its abstraction, nor the other in the like one-sidedness, possesses truth, but that they are both self-dissolving . . . *Philosophy affords a reflective insight into the essence of the opposition only in so far as it shows how truth is just the dissolving of opposition and, at that, not in the sense, as may be supposed, that the opposition and its two sides do not exist at all, but that they exist reconciled.*

(*LA*, vol. I, pp. 54–55; emphasis added)

Writing in response to this ambition, it has been the task of deconstructive thinkers like de Man and Derrida to show that the project of philosophy is ideological insofar as it fails to recognize its inseparability from art. Indeed, Michael Sprinker has argued that ideology was a constant preoccupation of de Man's aesthetic critique,[63] the point of which is to say that philosophy itself is bound to exist in the mode of the "as if" – i.e., in the mode of the alienated (read: mediated and mediating) sign. (Cf. Horkheimer and Adorno, who write that "dialectic . . . interprets every image as writing."[64]) In de Man's case, philosophy remains fundamentally aesthetic insofar as reflection (including reflection in the strictly Hegelian sense) never yields a properly constructed object-domain.

De Man frames the aesthetic critique of philosophy in terms of the difference between the "sign" and the "symbol," a difference that goes back at least to Horkheimer and Adorno's *Dialectic of*

---

[63] Michael Sprinker, *Imaginary Relations* (London: Verso, 1987).
[64] Horkheimer and Adorno, "The Concept of Enlightenment," p. 24.

*Enlightenment*, where the mediating function of the sign is aligned with the renunciation of a mimetic participation in the animate world: "As a system of signs, language is required to resign itself to calculation in order to know nature, and must discard the claim to be like her" (p. 18). As early as the essay on "The Dead-End of Formalist Criticism" in *Blindness and Insight*, for instance, de Man takes I. A. Richards to task for naively believing that there could be "a perfect continuity between the sign and the thing signified."[65] The fate of art, de Man says, is one with the sign, as opposed to the symbol. Unlike the symbol, which bears an "essential" correspondence with the content it expresses, the sign is characterized by the conventional and contingent nature of its existence; its coherence is assured only by means of the "as if."

Echoing notions that reach back at least to Saussure, de Man writes that "in the case of the sign, the proper content of the perception and the content of which it is a sign have nothing to do with each other" ("Sign and Symbol," p. 766). This contingency cuts two ways. On the one hand, the "arbitrariness" of the sign allows the subject the freedom to display its agency within the world. The aesthetic "sign" thus becomes a vehicle for the projection of human power: "the thinking subject is kept distinct from the perceiving subject, in a manner that is reminiscent of (or that anticipates) the distinction . . . between sign and symbol. Just as the sign refuses to be in the service of sensory perceptions but uses them instead for its own purposes, thought, unlike perception, appropriates the world and literally 'subjects' it to its own powers . . . thought subsumes the infinite singularity and individuation of the perceived world under ordering principles that lay claim to generality. The agent of this appropriation is language" ("Sign and Symbol," pp. 767–68). But because of the sign's alienated quality, the freedom that attaches to these powers is also an

[65] Behind the work of Richards stands the same Enlightenment tradition that associates beauty and aesthetic truth with human subjectivity and not with anything that is categorically and universally true. Unaware of his own links to this same tradition, no doubt, de Man objected that "Richards insists continually on the fact that criticism does not deal with any given material object but with a consciousness (or an experience) of this object, and he quotes Hume to this effect: 'Beauty is no quality in things themselves; it exists merely in the mind which contemplates them.'" De Man, *Blindness and Insight: Essays in the Rhetoric of Contemporary Criticism*, 2nd edn. (Minneapolis: University of Minnesota Press, 1983), p. 233. For de Man, Richards's thinking represents something like a category mistake that stems from the confusion of "symbol" and "sign."

ideological site, the source of a possible "coercion": "to the extent that the sign is entirely independent with regard to the objective, natural properties of the entity toward which it points and instead posits properties by means of its own powers, the sign illustrates the capacity of the intellect to 'use' the perceived world for its own purposes, to efface its properties and to put others in their stead. This activity of the intellect is both a freedom, and a coercion, since it does violence, as it were, to the world" ("Sign and Symbol," p. 767).[66] The power of the sign is "coercive" rather than merely appropriative insofar as it makes reference to and mimes the operations of the symbol. While critics of modernity conventionally point out that the "alienation" of consciousness from nature is strategic insofar as it allows the human being to become "master and possessor" of the natural world, de Man's interpretation of the coercive force of the sign is best understood in relation to the romantic desire for a world that would answer to our powers of cognition and desire. Like Aristotle's *technē*, which approximates the causality and conformity to law exhibited by nature in the growth of organisms, the sign has as its founding fiction the notion that the subject can indeed find the form of its own purposiveness reflected in the external world.

Thus de Man reads the notion of a speaking sign as a form of what Horkheimer and Adorno called "myth." On both accounts, the danger of myth lies in its anthropomorphism, in the temptation to forget that the sign operates within the realm of the "as if," that it is strictly representational or, in Derrida's sense, citational; de Man: "the sign does not *actually* say what it means to say or, to drop the misleading anthropomorphic metaphor of a *speaking* sign endowed with a voice, the predication involved in a sign is always citational" (*ibid.*). As Adorno said in *Aesthetic Theory*, "while nature's language is mute, art tries to make this muteness speak."[67] Mediated by Hegel's *Lectures on Aesthetics*, de Man's theory of the sign is representative of deconstruction's critical

---

[66] So, too, the Aristotelian notion of *technē* is potentially coercive and appropriative: insofar as it is not natural, a *technē* finds in particulars the properties through which matter can become *its* material, the material cause of its *poiēsis* or production.

[67] Adorno continues: "In so doing art is constantly exposed to the danger of failure because of the insurmountable contradiction between the notion of teaching nature to speak – a Herculean effort – and the fact that such a result cannot be willed or intended" (*AT*, p. 115).

response to this attempted seduction. Deconstruction maintains a critical stance insofar as it remains faithful to the Enlightenment effort to establish the subject's ability to reflect upon the seductions of "mythical" speech. De Man's aesthetics may thus be skeptical but, as Habermas said of Horkheimer and Adorno, it seeks to enlighten nonetheless. Specifically, the deconstructive "enlightenment" represents a continuation of the project to disenchant the world through an eradication of all anthropomorphism from the "as if" nature of the sign. Philosophy may thus be entwined with art, but it remains critical insofar as it hopes to identify and distance itself from the fiction of the "living sign."[68]

[68] Thus when J. Hillis Miller traces the ethics of narrative from the myth of Pygmalion in Ovid's *Metamorphoses* through modernist texts, he follows de Man in identifying the guilt associated with narrative as deriving from the anthropomorphizing fiction of a "living sign." See Hillis Miller, *Versions of Pygmalion* (Cambridge, MA: Harvard University Press, 1990).

# 4

❖❖❖❖❖❖❖❖❖❖❖❖❖❖❖❖❖❖❖❖❖❖❖❖❖❖❖❖❖❖❖❖❖❖❖❖❖❖❖❖❖❖❖❖❖❖

# Communication and transformation: aesthetics and politics in Habermas and Arendt

❖❖❖❖❖❖❖❖❖❖❖❖❖❖❖❖❖❖❖❖❖❖❖❖❖❖❖❖❖❖❖❖❖❖❖❖❖❖❖❖❖❖❖❖❖❖

The whole factual world of human affairs depends for its reality and its continued existence, first, upon the presence of others who have seen and heard and will remember, and, second, on the transformation of the intangible into the tangibility of things.                    Hannah Arendt[1]

In an essay first published along with *The Contest of the Faculties* in 1798, Kant took up the "old question" that has widely been recognized as central to the historical self-understanding of the Enlightenment: "Is the Human Race Constantly Progressing?"[2] Kant's response to this question, and the subsequent engagement of that response (whether explicitly or implicitly) by a range of thinkers including Habermas and Arendt, is particularly important for understanding the relationship between the political ambitions of contemporary critical theory and the theory of aesthetic reflection. Kant's essay is crucial, first, because it offers a complex and decisive stance on questions that are central to the Enlightenment's vision of morality as the existence of humanity in a true "kingdom of ends," and second, because it trades the stringent requirement of obedience to the moral law as the price of entry

---

[1] Hannah Arendt, *The Human Condition* (Chicago: University of Chicago Press, 1958), p. 95. (Hereafter cited as *HC*.)

[2] Immanuel Kant, "An Old Question Raised Again: Is the Human Race Constantly Progressing?," in Lewis White Beck, ed., *Kant on History* (Indianapolis, IN: Bobbs-Merrill, 1963), pp. 137–54. (Hereafter referred to as *P* and *OH*, respectively.)

into that kingdom for what would seem to be the more malleable demands of reflective judgment, by asking not how we must *act* in order to behave in accordance with the moral law but where (and with whom) we should *stand* in order to move from our engagement in particular actions and events to a comprehension of the shape of history as a whole. When faced with the events of history, which do not in and of themselves demonstrate any apparent order,[3] Kant was led to ground the progressive moral vision of the Enlightenment on principles that could most accurately be called "aesthetic." Specifically, Kant was impelled to stake his belief in progress on our ability to recognize and judge the meaning of a process whose completed or "perfected" form cannot be held in view.[4] "Progress" is thus an idea that admits no *direct* representation. It can be approximated only by means of signs. As the discussion of "hypotyposis" in section 59 of the third *Critique* confirms, the process of figuration is central to the work of aesthetic judgment; figuration provides terms for judgment where no pre-existing criteria can be invoked.

Not surprisingly, however, what for Kant turns out to be a matter of aesthetic judgment, involving fundamental questions about figuration and the imagination, is initially formulated as a question about cognition.[5] Specifically, that question is what kind of knowledge about the shape of history in its totality might be consistent with the principles of Enlightenment and, specifically, with the Enlightenment's suspicion of false signs, mystifications, and superstitious beliefs. Kant is not just interested in asserting dogmatically that the human race is progressing toward the better or in sustaining the hope that humanity is bound toward moral

---

[3] Kant outlines three models of history, determined according to the play of good and evil in each. The first is "terroristic" and indicates decline and disintegration. The second is "eudemonistic" and proceeds according to the free will of the subject-agent. The third is "abderitic" and is exemplified by those who "reverse the plan of progress, build in order to demolish, and impose upon themselves the hopeless effort of rolling the stone of Sisyphus uphill in order to let it roll back down again" (*P*, p. 140).

[4] As Kant explains in section 15 of the *Critique of Judgment*, judgments of taste are likewise independent of the concept of perfection. Hence one immediate link between historical knowledge and judgments of taste. *Critique of Judgment*, trans. James Creed Meredith (Oxford: Clarendon Press, 1986). (Hereafter cited as *CJ*.)

[5] Jean-François Lyotard takes up this subject in his discussion of the *differend* in Kant in *The Differend: Phrases in Dispute*, trans. Georges van den Abbeele (Minneapolis: University of Minnesota Press, 1988), pp. 161–71.

perfection, but in validating that claim and in establishing the stance from which it could be known as true.[6] The demand to know history as a whole poses special problems precisely because we must learn to read signs as indications of a totality we cannot possibly comprehend and can only represent as lawful and coherent in retrospect. Indeed, Kant freely admits that the problem posed by the question of progress in history is that the much vaunted Copernican turn in knowledge does not seem to apply to it. If we are unable to see what Kant in another essay calls the "end of all things," and if we must therefore judge the shape of history by fragments, then it would seem that we would require a fragment of human history "drawn not from past but from future time, therefore a predictive history" (*P*, p. 137). As Kant goes on to say, "these actions, of course man can *see*, but not *foresee* with certitude (for the divine eye there is no distinction in this matter); because, in the final analysis, man requires coherency according to natural laws, but with respect to his future free actions he must dispense with this guidance or direction" (*P*, p. 142). Knowledge of the shape of history as a whole would seem to require not just the memory of a totality that has been lost, but an insight into a totality that is yet to be established. Moreover, the activity of seeing is not easily reconciled with the power of foreseeing, just as the coherence of natural laws (the world accessible by "seeing") is not in any obvious way amenable to the realization of pure freedom (which leads us to the kingdom of ends by means of a kind of "foreseeing"). We are not capable of executing a "Copernican turn" with respect to our knowledge of history as a whole, for that would require "the standpoint of Providence which is situated beyond all human wisdom, and which likewise extends to the free actions of man" (*P*, p. 142). Indeed, the question of progress represents a signal point at which the process of transcendental

---

[6] In the first *Critique*, Kant writes that "the touchstone whereby we decide whether our holding a thing to be true is conviction or mere persuasion is . . . the possibility of communicating it and of finding it to be valid for all human reason. For there is then at least a presumption that the ground of the agreement of all judgments with each other, notwithstanding the differing characters of individuals, rests upon the common ground, namely, upon the object." *Critique of Pure Reason*, trans. Norman Kemp Smith (New York: St. Martin's Press, 1965), A 820, B 848 (p. 645). This means that establishing the validity of these signs is dependent upon creating a space for communication about them. The only "present" space in which the validity of these signs can be established is that of a communicative community, or what Arendt calls the "public sphere."

reflection discovers the condition of its own impossibility in Kant. In order to know the shape of history as a whole we would thus seem forced to claim "divinatory" or "premonitory" powers. Kant calls the power of prediction in history "divinatory" if it is not based on any known laws; if it can only be acquired by supernatural means it is called "premonitory."

On one level, Kant's analysis of the role of "divination" and "premonition" in historical knowledge reflects the logic of an Enlightenment that sought to root out superstition as well as all other forms of false belief. Kant offers the following definition: "emancipation from superstition is called *enlightenment*; for although this term applies also to emancipation from prejudices generally, still superstition deserves pre-eminently [*in sensu eminenti*] to be called a prejudice" (*CJ*, sec. 40, p. 152.) But against that skepticism is staked the Enlightenment faith in moral progress, which Kant says requires a knowledge of future time. When faced with this question Kant reasons that the question of *a priori* knowledge in history is satisfiable only "if the diviner himself creates and contrives the events which he announced in advance" (*P*, p. 137). Freedom is clearly a precondition of progress, which suggests on one level that history can be assessed as a function of morality. But in this instance what seems to require a privileged, premonitory form of knowledge is demoted to the status of an event that is *merely* caused – i.e., caused by a self-interested will. Progress and freedom thus remain at odds.

Kant provides two examples of such self-fulfilling prophecies, both of which raise fundamental questions about the role of progress in his conception of history. In each of these instances, Kant suggests that the modern state is not so much the coming into being of the moral "kingdom of ends" as the secularization of a prior "organic" unity that was founded upon beliefs that stand beyond cognition. The question that remains is how to reconceptualize this secularized realm in accordance with the need to validate progress in human history. The first example concerns the role of the Old Testament prophets in predicting the decline of the state founded on the basis of their own directives. If any political state, religious or otherwise, is the objectification of beliefs held in common, then the decline of this particular state is, oddly enough, a confirmation of the prophets' own predictive powers:

It was all very well for the Jewish prophets to prophesy that sooner or later not simply decadence but complete dissolution awaited their state, for they themselves were the authors of this fate. As national leaders they had loaded their constitution with so much ecclesiastical freight, and civil freight tied to it, that their state became utterly unfit to subsist of itself, and especially unfit to subsist together with neighboring nations. Hence the jeremiads of their priests were naturally bound to be lost upon the winds, because the priests obstinately persisted in their design for an untenable constitution created by themselves; and thus they could infallibly foresee the issue. (*P*, pp. 137–38)

In Kant's estimation, those in charge of governing the modern constitutional state (the "politicians") are all too much like these false prophets, secretly creating the false needs whose solutions they alone seem able to satisfy:

our politicians do precisely the same thing and are just as lucky in their prophecies. We must, they say, take men as they are, not as pedants ignorant of the world or good-natured visionaries fancy they ought to be. But in place of that "as they are" it would be better to say what they "have made" them – stubborn and inclined to revolt – through unjust constraint, through perfidious plots placed in the hands of the government; obviously then, if the government allows the reins to relax a little, sad consequences ensue which verify the prophecy of those supposedly sagacious statesmen. (*P*, p. 138)[7]

Kant's second example concerns priests who foretell the decline and destruction of religion, leading ultimately to the coming of the Antichrist. In this case, it is their very own predictions that are the cause of the "mechanical unanimity" that results from the historical transition from the spiritual unity of a religious body to the merely civil state that we know now. Kant's opinion is that the "mechanical unanimity" that can be achieved through a civil constitution can never ensure the "moral disposition" available in a community of sense toward which mankind must be destined if the case in favor of progress is to be made:

Ecclesiastics, too, occasionally prophesy the complete destruction of religion and the immanent appearance of Antichrist; and in doing so they are performing precisely what is requisite to call him up. This happens because they have not seen to impressing on their parishes moral prin-

---

[7] Little wonder, then, that recent political theorists like Roberto Unger have argued that no true revolution will be possible if we do not first identify and overcome false necessity. See especially Part I of Unger's *Politics*, entitled *False Necessity* (Cambridge: Cambridge University Press, 1987).

ciples which lead directly to the better, but rather fabricate into essential duty observances and historical beliefs which are supposed to effect it indirectly; from this, of course, can grow the mechanical unanimity as in a civil constitution, but none in moral disposition. But then they complain about irreligion, which they themselves have caused and thus could predict even without any special talent. (*ibid.*)

In both these instances, the much sought after reconciliation of freedom and necessity occurs by means of an ideological illusion so deep that it cannot be eradicated by means of mere conciliation on the part of the critical judge. As Lyotard explains, it is not sufficient for a judge to dismiss the advocate of determinism and the advocate of freedom by offering an arrangement that would satisfy them both; "rather he constrains them together and positively to exercise joint sovereignty over the sought-for event" (*The Differend*, pp. 164–65). As for the status of this "event," it ought not to be itself the cause of progress but only its index or sign. In Lyotard's terms, "the *Begebenheit* [event] ought to be the probative index of the Idea of free causality" (p. 165). The status of the sign as both indexical and probative solves this dilemma.[8]

The notion of a sign with both indexical and probative value represents one indication of the contradictions involved in the notion of "universal history." Another is to be found in the implicit tension between the inorganic but objective and organic but "spiritual" conceptions of the civil state. Kant's description in this passage of the "mechanical unanimity" of a civil state is resonant with the process that Max Weber described in terms of the "rationalization" of culture and the "disenchantment" of the world.[9] As Habermas sees it, the process of rationalization wrests

---

[8] To illustrate a related point, Žižek recounts a joke about a conscript who tries to evade military service by pretending to be mad: he checks all the pieces of paper he can lay his hands on, constantly repeating "That's not it!" The psychiatrist, finally convinced of his insanity, gives him a written certificate releasing him from military service, whereupon the conscript says cheerfully "That is it!" As Žižek reads the joke, it is a classic case of the symbolic process which appears to create its own cause, the object that sets it in motion. Slavoj Žižek, *The Indivisible Remainder: An Essay on Schelling and Related Matters* (London: Verso, 1996), p. 228.

[9] On "disenchantment," see Weber's essay "Wirtschaftsethik der Weltreligion," translated as chapter IX ("The Social Psychology of the World Religions" – pp. 267–301) in the volume *From Max Weber: Essays in Sociology*, ed. H. H. Gerth and C. Wright Mills (New York: Oxford University Press, 1946), pp. 267–301. In another essay in the Gerth and Mills volume, "Science as a Vocation" ("Wirtschaft als Beruf"), Weber speaks explicitly of the "disenchantment of the world" (p. 155). He makes several other references to the process of world-disenchantment in that essay (e.g., p. 139).

an objective world from mythical thinking and this in turn allows us to make validity claims that would otherwise be groundless. "Only against the background of an objective world, and measured against criticizable claims to truth and efficacy, can beliefs appear as systematically false, action intentions as systematically hopeless, and thoughts as fantasies, as mere imaginings. Only against the background of *a normative reality that has become autonomous*, and measured against the criticizable claim to normative rightness, can intentions, wishes, attitudes, feelings appear as illegitimate or merely idiosyncratic, as nongeneralizable and merely subjective"[10] (emphasis added). But as Habermas is nonetheless aware, and as Weber before him pointed out, the very same process that makes such validity claims possible lays bare the risk that the social order based upon them may be merely "mechanical" in nature. In Hannah Arendt's analysis, the process of rationalization may bring with it the "substitution of behavior for action and its eventual substitution of bureaucracy, the rule of nobody, for personal rulership."[11] Following the thinkers of the Frankfurt School, she characterizes these conditions as typical of politics and society in the modern age.

The modern democratic state is the point at which these seemingly irreducible tensions converge. On the one hand, democratic politics provides a structure through which beliefs can be made representable, negotiable (some would say "communicable"), and open to competing claims. But the genealogy of the democratic state also lies in the materialization of what were once wholly immaterial beliefs and may yield the "mechanization" of a "living community." A "mechanical" unity is opposed to a free state just as the "mechanical" arts described in the third *Critique* are unfree ("in all the free arts something of a compulsory character is still required, or, as it is called, a *mechanism*, without which the *soul*, which in art must be *free*, and which alone gives life to the work, would be bodyless and evanescent" [*CJ*, sec. 43, p. 164]). Both Habermas and Arendt suggest that the dangers of a "mechanical" (i.e. rationalized) unanimity can be avoided as long as enlightened politics works to secure a space in which the com-

---

[10] Jürgen Habermas, *The Theory of Communicative Action vol. 1: Reason and the Rationalization of Society*, trans. Thomas McCarthy (Boston: Beacon Press, 1984), p. 51.
[11] Arendt, *The Human Condition*, p. 45.

munication necessary for the testing of competing beliefs can occur.[12] How can this be accomplished? Both Habermas's and Arendt's accounts of the public sphere draw heavily on the Kantian notion of "publicity" as the bridge between politics and morality. In the essay "What Is Enlightenment?" Kant says that freedom of public expression is a necessary precondition of the exercise of reason: "The public use of one's reason must always be free, and it alone can bring about enlightenment among men . . . By the public use of one's reason I understand the use which a scholar makes of it before the reading public."[13] As far as politics is concerned, the fact that it is public, i.e., conducted in the public sphere, also enables it to be moral.[14] In Kant's terms, "Enlightenment of the masses is the public instruction of the people in its duties and rights vis-à-vis the state to which they belong . . . the prohibition of publicity impedes the progress of a people toward improvement, even in that which applies to the least of its claims, namely its simple, natural right" (*P*, pp. 148–49). For both Habermas and Arendt, the public political sphere is the space in which judgments can be fashioned around the regulative ideal of a common (community) sense, and this in turn allows the participants in the political conversation access to the possibility of mutual recognition.[15] As a communicative space, the polis is for both Habermas and Arendt the place in which recognition can be derived from rationality itself. This is no small accomplishment,

---

[12] Habermas writes that the "world" of the public sphere "was not world in the transcendental sense, as the quintessential concept of all phenomena, as the totality of their synthesis and to that extent identical with 'nature.' Rather, 'world' here pointed to humanity as a species, but in that guise in which its unity presented itself in appearance: the world of a critically debating reading public that at the time was just evolving within the broader bourgeois strata." *The Structural Transformation of the Public Sphere: An Inquiry into a Category of Bourgeois Society*, trans. Thomas Burger with Frederick Lawrence (Cambridge, MA: MIT Press, 1993), p. 106. (Henceforth cited as *STPS*.) In so saying, Habermas in essence repeats the views expressed by Kant in "What is Enlightenment?"

[13] "Answer to the Question: What Is Enlightenment?" in *OH*, p. 5.

[14] For a contrastive reading of Habermas and Arendt on this subject, see Seyla Benhabib, *Situating the Self: Gender, Community, and Postmodernism in Contemporary Ethics* (New York: Routledge, 1992), pp. 89–120 ("Models of Public Space: Hannah Arendt, the Liberal Tradition and Jürgen Habermas").

[15] This is emphasized in Arendt's *Lectures on Kant's Political Philosophy*. In historical terms, Arendt says elsewhere that the private sphere of society becomes public as a function of the rise of the social: "Society is the form in which the fact of mutual dependence for the sake of life and nothing else assumes public significance, and where the activities connected with sheer survival are permitted to appear in public." Arendt, *HC*, p. 48.

but the question that remains is whether the polis, so conceived, is also a space in which transformation can be achieved. Can the goals of recognition – which leads Habermas to think of the polis as a sphere in which normative validity claims are tested – be reconciled with those of transformation (including the radical transformation that would be necessary for passage into the "kingdom of ends"), which would require us to break the very constraints within which the process of recognition takes place?

In Habermas, the need to provide a normative alliance between politics and morality is secured through an historical account of the emergence of the public sphere in early modern Europe. This is an account that is designed to prove the "progressive" version of history. In *The Structural Transformation of the Public Sphere* Habermas identifies the "public" that will constitute the "public sphere" with the addressees, consumers, and critics of art and literature, particularly in France – i.e., with the newly emerging *lecteurs, spectateurs*, and *auditeurs* of literature and art who prized their ability to think for themselves. In Germany and England, the consolidation of the new "public" was facilitated by the emergence of coffee-house culture, built around conversation concerned with questions of taste, and which eventually extended its relevance to "serious" (i.e., political and economic) affairs. As Habermas puts it, "the critical debate ignited by works of literature and art was soon extended to include economic and political disputes, without any guarantee (such as was given in the *salons*) that such debate would be inconsequential" (*STPS*, p. 33).[16] Just as the newspaper facilitated the circulation of information, the coffee houses fomented public discussion among the members of many different social classes.[17] Indeed, Kant himself observed that Enlightened society was made possible by freedom of discourse: "if we attend to the course of conversation in mixed companies consisting not merely of scholars and subtle reasoners but also of business people or women, we notice that besides storytelling and jesting they have another entertainment, namely, arguing."[18]

---

[16] Habermas freely admits that the fact that only men were admitted to coffee-house society may have had something to do with this fact; the style of the *salon*, he argues, was by contrast shaped by women.

[17] The newly emergent "public" comprised members of the court, certain portions of the urban nobility, and a thin layer of the bourgeoisie. See *STPS*, p. 31.

[18] *Critique of Practical Reason*, trans. Lewis White Beck, cited in Habermas, *STPS*, p. 106.

But, as Habermas also recognizes, these historical formations came to have normative consequences: they generated a series of ideals that became attached to our expectations about what human discourse should be. These were formulated as principles by Kant, for whom public conversation was a precondition for the moral and epistemological goals of the Enlightenment insofar as it secures peaceful conversation among men. In Kant's analysis, it is only by virtue of their "publicity" that words and actions can form the basis for critical argument. Kant stakes the moral claims of modern, Enlightened culture on the will of the citizens to converse and argue in a free and open way.

Given Kant's political interests in the construction of a free and open communicative space, in which disagreements could be negotiated, it is nonetheless worth remembering that Kant himself invested substantial faith in the possibility of a radical refashioning of society in the image of the "kingdom of ends." It is not surprising to find that he wished to assess our ability to know the signs of true progress and to recognize in them evidence of advancement toward this goal. Yet it remains clear that such a tack does not avoid the problem of figuration mentioned above, but only heightens it. Indeed, it would be difficult to underestimate the importance of figuration in Kant's thought. In the third *Critique*, for instance, the difference between a "mechanical unanimity" and an "organic totality" comes down to the difference between the figure of a "hand-mill" and that of the "living body": "a monarchical state is represented as a living body when it is governed by constitutional laws, but as a mere machine (like a hand-mill) when it is governed by an individual absolute will" (*CJ*, sec. 59, pp. 222–23). As Kant himself admits, there is no inherent likeness between a despotic state and a hand-mill; and yet such symbols are not altogether arbitrary, just as words are not, in his estimation, "mere marks." In the third *Critique*, Kant ventures that such symbols (which he explains as hypotyposes[19]) work by a process of analogy: they "express concepts without employing a direct intuition for the purpose, but only drawing upon an *analogy* with one, i.e. transferring the reflection upon an object of intuition to quite a new concept, and one with which

---

[19] Kant describes the figure of hypotyposis as "presentation, *subjectio sub adspectum*," *CJ*, sec. 59, p. 221.

perhaps no intuition could ever directly correspond" (*CJ*, sec. 59, p. 223; emphasis added).[20]

How then might one adequately represent the ultimate convergence of the opinions of all, which presumably can occur only in the fullness of time? Lacking the ability to know (i.e., to see or to foresee) the future of the human race, Kant looks to history for a fragment that would in turn point to

the disposition and capacity of the human race to be the cause of its own advance toward the better (since this should be the act of a being endowed with freedom), toward the human race as being the author of this advance. An event must be sought which points to the existence of such a cause and to its effectiveness in the human race, undetermined with regard to time, and which would allow progress toward the better to be concluded as an inevitable consequence. This conclusion then could also be extended to the history of the past (that it has always been in progress) in such a way that that event would have to be considered not itself as the cause of history, but only as an intimation, an historical sign (*signum rememorativum, demonstrativum, prognostikon*) demonstrating the tendency of the human race viewed in its entirety. (*P*, p. 143)

As is well known, Kant located what he thought was a true sign of the progress of the human race in the French Revolution.[21] In a passage that Arendt was fond of citing, and that has subsequently been invoked by Lyotard, Kant argued that what was important about the Revolution was not the overthrow of political institutions and individuals once powerful and great, but rather "the

---

[20] The importance of analogy in the third *Critique* has been signaled by Paul Zammito in *The Genesis of Kant's Critique of Judgment* (Chicago: University of Chicago Press, 1992): "In the absence of any objective reference, reason tries to find the next closest approximation. If it cannot form a determinate insight into its supersensible object, it tries to reason about the relation of this object to the objects of experience, and to bring this relation under logical rules. Hence analogy is the rational form of orientation in the realm of the supersensible" (p. 239).

[21] Lyotard emphasizes the role of hypotyposis (and, in the case of the Revolution as a sign of progress, of "extreme hypotyposis") in Kant's thinking: "the historical-political makes itself present to the assertion ['there is progress'] only through cases, which operate not as exempla and still less as schemata, but as complex hypotyposes, the more complex ones being the surer. The popular enthusiasm for the Revolution is a very validating case for the historical-political phrase, and thus allows for a very sure hypotyposis. This is for the simple reason that it is itself a very improbable hypotyposis (the recognition of the Idea of the republic in a 'formless,' empirical given)." Lyotard calculates the larger implications of this for Kant as follows: "As for the philosophy of history, about which there can be no question in a critical thought, it is an illusion born from the appearance that signs are exempla or schemata" (*The Differend*, p. 171).

mode of thinking [*Denkungsart*] of the spectators which ... manifests such a universal yet disinterested sympathy [*Teilnehmung*]
for the players on one side against those on the other, even at the
risk that this partiality could become very disadvantageous for
them if discovered" (*P*, p. 143). In "The End of All Things" Kant
says that only those actions arising from disinterested motives can
inspire human respect and that without respect there is no true
love (*OH*, p. 84).

In recognizing the actions and events of history as signs and in
judging their meaning, Kant proposes that we occupy the position of the spectators at events played on the world-historical
stage. In so doing, he shifts the emphasis of his thinking on the
question of the symbol to the problem of subject-position. Here
the issues of proximity and distance are brought to the forefront.
It is "in the spectators (who are not engaged in this game themselves)" that Kant finds "a wishful participation that borders
closely on enthusiasm, the very expression of which is fraught
with danger; the sympathy, therefore, can have no other cause
than a moral disposition in the human race" (*P*, p. 144). The one
who occupies the position of the subject-spectator demonstrates
an affective response to and maintains a sympathy for the
players on the stage, but also sustains a detached and disinterested stance, participating in the action only from a distance or,
as Kant says in the passage cited above, "wishfully."[22] In Kant's
estimation, the spectator's sympathy for the players on the stage
demonstrates an ability to take the position of others, and this in
turn confirms the moral predisposition of the human race. The

---

[22] Lyotard reads the enthusiasm of the spectators as an aesthetic analogue of the
republican fervor of the actors in the Revolution, thus raising the question of
whether we are to regard aesthetic judgment as itself analogous to action or as
the site in and through which analogies can be established. The latter is
Lyotard's general position, but in this instance he does not clearly explain how it
can be derived from Kant, whom he suggests sustains the former: "on stage,
among the actors themselves, interests, ordinary passions, and the whole pathos
of empirical (psychical, sociological) causality are forever inextricably bound up
with the interests of pure moral reason and with the call of the Idea of republican law. The spectators, placed on other national stages, which make up the
theatre hall for the spectacle and where absolutism generally reigns, cannot on
the contrary be suspected of having empirical interests in making their sympathies public (*öffentlich*), they even run the risk of suffering repression at the
hands of their governments. That itself guarantees the – at least aesthetic – value
[*sic*] of their feelings. *It must be said of their enthusiasm that it is an aesthetic analogue
of pure, republican fervor*' (*ibid.*, p. 167; emphasis added).

disinterestedness of the spectator guarantees the validity of judgments that could not possibly be confirmed by any individual in
time. (Kant writes that "owing to its universality, this mode of
thinking demonstrates a character of the human race at large and
all at once; owing to its disinterestedness, a moral character of
humanity, at least in its predisposition, a character which not
only permits people to hope for progress toward the better, but *is
already itself progress* insofar as its capacity is sufficient for the
present" [*P*, pp. 143–44; emphasis added].) By occupying the
position of the spectator, Kant proposes that we are able to move
from the specific and immediate events of history (the glories
and atrocities of the French Revolution) to a conclusion regarding
the shape of history as a whole for the human species.[23] As we
shall see in connection with Arendt's reading of Kant, this teleological leap is not cognitive. But neither is it psychological.[24] This
process requires the operation of what Arendt calls the "moral
imagination."

---

[23] Lyotard emphasizes the potential universality of the spectacle when he writes
that "the *Teilnehmung* through desire is not a participation in the act. But it is
worth more, because the feeling of the sublime, for its sake, is in fact spread out
onto all the national stages. Potentially, at least, it is universal. It is not universal in the way a well-formed and validated cognitive phrase may be . . . Like
the feeling of the beautiful, though, it does have an *a priori* which is not a rule
that is universally recognized but a rule awaiting its universality. It is this
universality in abeyance or in suspense that is invoked in the aesthetic judgment" (*ibid.*, pp. 167–68). Jay M. Bernstein believes that Kant's shift from the
stance of the philosophical historian to that of the spectator parallels an aestheticization of the "monstrous" events of human history that protects us from
them by holding us at a safe distance from them: "the philosophical historian
takes up the stance of the aesthetic observer in order to transform what is
empirically ugly and monstrous into beautiful 'historical sign(s)' that reveal
the unfolding teleological progress of the race. It is that stance that blocks the
expression of the enthusiasm that is fraught with danger – the danger of real
participation." *The Fate of Art* (University Park: Pennsylvania State University
Press, 1992), p. 181.

[24] As in Žižek's analysis of Lacan, it turns out that even the most personal beliefs
and the most intimate emotions, such as crying, sorrow, laughter, etc., can be
transferred to others without losing their sincerity. Žižek, *The Sublime Object of
Ideology* (London: Verso, 1989), p. 34. Žižek goes on to say of Greek tragedy that
"we, the spectators, came to the theatre worried, full of everyday problems,
unable to adjust without reserve to the problems of the play, that is to feel the
required fears and compassions – but no problem, there is the Chorus, who feels
the sorrow and the compassion instead of us – or, more precisely, we feel the
required emotions through the medium of the Chorus: 'You are then relieved of
all worries, even if you do not feel anything, the Chorus will do so in your place.'
Even if we, the spectators, are just drowsily watching the show, objectively . . .
we are doing our duty of compassion for the heroes" (pp. 34–35).

Kant's conception of the spectator's position, roundly embraced by Arendt, demonstrates the clear influence of Hume on the subject of "disinterested sympathy" and of Rousseau on the subject of the aesthetic "alienation" of actors on the stage. In the *Treatise on Human Nature*, Hume wrote that "no quality of human nature is more remarkable, both in itself and in its consequences, than that propensity to sympathize with others, and to receive by communication their inclinations and sentiments, however different and contrary to our own."[25] In the "Letter to M. D'Alembert on the Theatre," Rousseau recognized that theatrical actors could be seen as "alienated" from themselves insofar as they give their authentic being to that of the characters they represent: "An actor on the stage, displaying other sentiments than his own, saying only what he is made to say, often representing a chimerical being, annihilates himself, as it were, and is lost in his hero. And, in this forgetting of the man, if something remains of him, it is used as the plaything of the spectators."[26] But Rousseau went on to resolve this issue by transforming the spectators themselves into actors, thereby joining all concerned in a new community in which mutual recognition can be achieved through participation in a common project: "Let the spectators become an entertainment to themselves; make them actors themselves; do it so that each sees and loves himself in the others so that all will be better united" ("Letter to M. D'Alembert on the Theatre," p. 126). Kant's ambition nonetheless differs from Hume's or Rousseau's insofar as the spectator position is for Kant the means by which the events of history can be taken as the signs of a moral truth about the human species.

The notion of great events seen as exemplary signs and witnessed from the spectator's point of view allows Kant to reduce the disparity between the unanimity that resists all efforts at representation on the one hand and the merely historical and therefore partial evidence of that unanimity on the other. For Kant, we are *of* history, actors on the world stage, or at least able to place ourselves in our imagination in the position of those who

[25] David Hume, *A Treatise on Human Nature* (London: Longmans, Green, 1883), Book II, sec. 11.
[26] Rousseau, "Letter to M. D'Alembert on the Theatre," in *Jean-Jacques Rousseau: Politics and the Arts*, trans. Allan Bloom (Ithaca, NY: Cornell University Press, 1968), p. 81.

act (which is to say that we inhabit, in reality or in the imagination, a causal world); but we are also *beyond* the historical world, acting as noumenal subjects toward the moral perfection embodied in reason, or toward what Kant elsewhere calls the true universality of the "final judgment,"[27] the gateway through which we pass into the kingdom of ends. In this way, the purposiveness that Kant attributes to nature and the self-conscious subject in the third *Critique* – which results in the feeling that the purposiveness demonstrated in nature's beauty is somehow meant for us (that its charms are, for example, "chosen . . . with an eye to our taste" [*CJ*, sec. 58, p. 217]) – can be predicated of history, whose subject is itself the human "species." The theory of signs as witnessed by spectators allows Kant to imagine a movement from the specific events of history (which by definition are part of a network of relations that on one level can be seen as the "causes" of progress and as providing a mirror for the subject/actor) to the "beyond" that by definition resists all representation. In Kantian (or, indeed, Arendtian) terms, the French Revolution is not – or not only – the "cause" of progress; as a sign, it transcends what can be said about it as a mere phenomenon.[28] But neither is it in and of itself a moment of pure, noumenal freedom or the passageway through which we pass directly into the kingdom of ends.[29] Rather, as a fragment in which we perceive the whole, it is Kant's way of solving the problem of the unpresentability of the end-state of

---

27 In the essay "The End of All Things," in *OH*, pp. 69–84.
28 Lyotard's concern in addressing this issue is to guard against the "transcendental illusion" of revolutionary politics invited by the French Revolution, which would "confuse what is presentable as an object for a cognitive phrase with what is presentable as an object for a speculative and/or ethical phrase, that is, schemas and examples with *analoga*." See *The Differend*, p. 162. David Carroll says in his commentary on Lyotard that "in the ethical-political realm, no example can be given of the law, no direct presentation can be made of what constitutes justice. But this does not mean that one is totally 'abandoned' by the law and placed in an ethical abyss, left with only subjective whim or the uncontrollable flux of libidinal drives that act in the absence of knowable laws (as, for example, Lyotard had argued in *Economie libidinale*). One is, rather, left with feelings, signs, and *analoga*, and in Levinas's terms, 'hostage' to an obligation that cannot be defined in terms of a knowable law or moral code. What cannot be presented directly is evoked indirectly, presented in terms of its unpresentability, as unpresentable except by means of analogies." *Paraesthetics: Foucault, Lyotard, Derrida* (New York: Methuen, 1987), p. 174.
29 Ronald Beiner discusses the relevance of Nietzsche's notion of the "gateway" in *Thus Spoke Zarathustra* to Arendt in his edition of Arendt's *Lectures on Kant's Political Philosophy* (Chicago: University of Chicago Press, 1982), pp. 144–56. (Henceforth cited as *L*.)

progress.[30] For Arendt, the "completion" of the work of the actor by the spectator is also a solution to the problematic separation of theory and practice that haunts Enlightenment thought:

> in Kant the common distinction or antagonism between theory and practice in political matters is the distinction between the spectator and the actor, and to our surprise we saw that the spectator had precedence; what counted in the French Revolution, what made it a world-historical event, a phenomenon not to be forgotten, were not the deeds and misdeeds of the actors but the opinions, the enthusiastic approbation, of spectators, of persons who themselves were not involved. We also saw that these uninvolved and nonparticipating spectators . . . *were* involved with one another. (*L*, p. 65)

In his third review of Johann Gottfried Herder's *Ideas for a Philosophy of the History of Mankind*, Kant emphasizes that it is the species, not the individual (not even the sum of all individuals), that constitutes the subject of universal history. (Kant avers that in animals "species" means "the characteristic in virtue of which all individuals must *directly* agree with one another."[31]) The "species" is conceptually equivalent to a symbol that stands for an infinity that in its interminability resists representation. Specifically, Kant says that "species" means "the totality of a series of generations proceeding to infinity (the indeterminable) . . . [This] line of descent ceaselessly approaches its concurrent destination . . . [It] is asymptotic in all its parts to this line of destiny, and on the whole coincides with it. In other words, no single member in all of these generations of the human race, but only the species, fully achieves its destination . . . The philosopher would say that the destination of the human race in general is perpetual progress."[32] The notion of the "species" as the subject of history thus serves as a figure whose purpose is to reduce, if not to resolve, the

---

[30] True "progress" for Kant stands for a radical form of agreement, a convergence upon true unanimity, wherein the labor of recognition would be complete and no further transformation possible. Cf. Lyotard's emphasis on the role of the sublimity of the Revolution, as evidenced by the enthusiasm of the spectators, in his discussion of Kant. "Enthusiasm as an 'event of our time' . . . obeys the rule of the aesthetic antinomy. And it is the most contradictory of aesthetics, that of the most extreme sublime. First of all, because the sublime is not only a disinterested pleasure and a universal without a concept, such as taste, but also because it entails a finality of antifinality and a pleasure of pain, as opposed to the feeling of the beautiful whose finality is merely without an end and whose pleasure is due to the free agreement of the faculties with each other" (*The Differend*, p. 169).

[31] Kant, third review of Herder, in *OH*, p. 51; emphasis added.

[32] *Ibid.*, p. 51. Arendt cites this passage in *L*, p. 58.

difficulty of representing the universal agreement implicit in the Kantian notion of progress.

The problems posed by the need to render representable and legible, and hence available for the work of recognition, that which stands beyond all representation – in this instance, the radical agreement of all in the "kingdom of ends" – echo with Kant's efforts in the third *Critique* to negotiate a passageway between the subjective affects and universal claims, and so anticipate the questions that Arendt addresses in terms of judgment and that Habermas phrases in terms of the theory of communicative action. The project of the third *Critique* roots in the fact that, on the one hand, the split between the phenomenal and the noumenal worlds seems categorical and complete, while on the other hand Kant wishes to recognize the possibility of passing from one realm to the other as a way of affording human purposiveness a role in the transformation of the world. In Kant's terms, the purpose of the third *Critique* was to show both that freedom is empowered to achieve its aims in the sensible world *and* that the concept of nature, which is rooted in the notion of necessity or conformity to law, is able to accommodate action in accordance with freedom (see *CJ*, Preface, p. 14).

Kant's desire to find a way of "actualizing" noumenal freedom in the fact-world of cognition and causality involves a building process that cannot be brought to completion within the framework of critical philosophy because the unity of experience can only be reconstructed, remembered, or projected in hope, in feeling, but never attested evidentially as true. The special "difficulty" of aesthetic judgment that follows from this fact is sharpened in Kant's analysis of communication in the third *Critique*. As suggested by the epigraph above, Kant recognizes that enlightened subjects have an interest in communication that shows up in their tendency to exchange ideas about art ("Fine art . . . has the effect of advancing the culture of the mental powers in the interests of social communication" [*CJ*, sec. 44, p. 166]). Since Kant's understanding of communication is closely bound up with the notion of community, this statement implies that art plays a role in advancing the "progress" that is at issue in the essays on history – where "progress" is understood in more or less moral terms, as securing the relationship among members of a community as one of mutual respect. The "purposeless purposiveness" of art models the moral relationship among human beings, where all are regarded as ends in themselves.[33] Thus it is not altogether surprising to find that Kant states that communication has priority over pleasure in aesthetic judgments: "it is the universal capacity for being communicated incident to the mental state in the given representation which, as the subjective condition of the judgment of taste, must be fundamental, with the pleasure in the object as its consequent" (*CJ*, sec. 9, p. 57).

This last remark has nonetheless given philosophers pause, for it seems to contradict what Kant says elsewhere about the contingent and particular (i.e. subjective) character of pleasure and pain, as well as what he says about the subjective element in representations that is "incapable of becoming an element of cognition" (*CJ*, Introduction, p. 29). The solution to this apparent difficulty seems to lie in the fact that the community Kant wishes to invoke is one of "sense" and not of "concept." The communication that is at issue in aesthetic reflective judgments must occur, according to Kant, "without the mediation of concepts" (*CJ*, sec. 39. p. 150). Kant's appeal to the notion of common (community) sense as the point of orientation for such judgments follows from this: "taste can with more justice be called a *sensus communis* than can sound understanding; and that the aesthetic, rather than the intellectual, judgment can bear the name of a public sense, i.e. taking it that we are prepared to use the word 'sense' of an affect that mere reflection has upon the mind; for then by sense we mean the feeling of pleasure. We might even define taste as the faculty of estimating what makes our feeling in a given representation *universally communicable* without the mediation of a concept" (*CJ*, sec. 40, p. 153). In a footnote to section 40 (p. 153), Kant clarifies that he is in fact referring to the *sensus communis aestheticus* ("common feeling") rather than to the *sensus communis logicus*, which designates common human understanding. Pleasure stems from the recognition of the universal

---

[33] The particular element of respect is mirrored even more directly in the sublime: "the intellectual and intrinsically final (moral) good, estimated aesthetically, instead of being represented as beautiful, must rather be represented as sublime, with the result that it arouses . . . a feeling of respect" (*CJ*, "General Remark," p. 123).

communicability of judgments of taste, which seems to indicate the quality of a community that is not determined by any concepts.

The Habermassian theory of communicative action, like the theory of politics that Arendt bases on Kant's third *Critique*, nonetheless elides Kant's reference to the *sensus communis aestheticus* with the *sensus communis logicus*. As a consequence, both Habermas and Arendt understand community as mediated conceptually rather than, as Kant says, aesthetically. Indeed, it is through mediation by concepts that Habermas's theory of communicative action claims to clarify the fundamental ground of human action – to allow for "criticizable claims to truth and efficacy" to be assessed against the background of an objective world, and to measure claims to rightness in terms of a "normative reality" that has become autonomous.[34] Habermas thus does not disagree with Kant that the matter of aesthetics in the culture of Enlightened modernity is centrally one of communication. But the Habermassian notion of communication implies a community of concept rather than of sense. In this respect, Habermas relies upon Hegel's reading of Schiller's "Letters on the Aesthetic Education of Man" in the *Lectures on Aesthetics*, according to which the form of communication implicit in aesthetics has a privileged place in the Enlightenment critique of modernity insofar as it can help repair the divisions characteristic of the rationalized world and encourage the process of collective identity formation. Glossing Schiller's notion of the beautiful, Habermas writes that "all other forms of communication divide society, because they relate exclusively either to the private sensibility or to the private skillfulness of its individual members, that is, to what distinguishes between one man and another; only the communication of the Beautiful unites society, because it relates to what is common to

[34] An alternative way of understanding how a community may be unmediated by a concept is to be found in Aristotle's *Nicomachean Ethics*, where the individual must first be ethical in order to be educated ethically. Hegel draws special attention to the affinity between Aristotle's conception of ethics and Kant's notion of the beautiful as that which is mediated without a concept; in the *Lectures on Aesthetics* he writes that "the beautiful . . . should be that which is put before us without a concept, i.e. without a category of the Understanding, as an object of *universal* pleasure. To estimate the beautiful requires a cultured spirit; the uneducated man has no judgment of the beautiful, since this judgment claims universal validity." *Lectures on Aesthetics*, trans. T. M. Knox (Oxford: Clarendon Press, 1975), vol. I, p. 56.

them all."[35] More specifically, Habermas finds in Schiller the basis for a project of identity formation that takes as its task the reconciliation of the individual and the social whole, though precisely how "communication" performs this work goes unspecified: "The aesthetically reconciled society would have to form a structure of communication 'where [each] dwells quietly in his own hut, communicating with himself and, as soon as he issues from it, with the whole race.'"[36] Habermas praises Schiller because his "aesthetic utopia" is aimed expressly at "revolutionizing the conditions of mutual understanding."

At the same time, Habermas's reading of the aesthetic raises the question of the transformative potential of art. For Schiller, Habermas says, the "aestheticization of the lifeworld is legitimate only in the sense that art operates as a catalyst, as a form of communication, as a medium within which separated moments are rejoined into an uncoerced totality. The social character of the beautiful and of taste are to be confirmed by the fact that art 'leads' everything dissociated in modernity . . . 'out under the open sky of common sense.'"[37] But the thorniest problem posed by Schiller's text, which Habermas seems to ignore, lies in the notion of a radical transformation or "total revolution" of society by means of a transformation of the "whole mode of perception," which would seem to weigh against Habermas's own investment in the theory of communicative action as a conceptual mediation of relations within the polis. And whereas Kant insists that claims of taste maintain a *subjective* universal validity, Habermas concentrates on the way in which the "background of normative validity" itself becomes autonomous and objectified in the modern world. While Kant's interest in the third *Critique* centers on the pleasure associated with communication, rather than on establishing the preconditions for aesthetic validity claims, Habermas takes the notion of "universal communicability" as an explanation of the type of validity claims possible in the modern, Enlightened world. In the process, Habermas casts aesthetic pleasure and the sensuous apprehension of the world aside.

Habermas identifies two possible outcomes that might follow from the project of an aesthetic critique. The first, which he rejects

---

[35] Habermas, *The Philosophical Discourse of Modernity*, trans. Frederick Lawrence (Cambridge, MA: MIT Press, 1987), pp. 48–49.
[36] *Ibid.*, p. 49.    [37] *Ibid.*, p. 50.

out of hand, aligns Kant's notion of a community of sense un-mediated by any concept with the beginnings of a troubling "aestheticization" of the lifeworld characteristic of Surrealism, Dadaism, and postmodernism. As I have already suggested, Habermas's fear that an aesthetic critique of reason may give rise to a series of undisciplined aesthetic practices is unfounded insofar as it obscures the role of "principle" and "rule" in (modern) art. As far as Kant is concerned, however, the project of an aesthetic critique does not depend upon an "aestheticization" of the life-world nor does it envisage the "completion" of the project of Enlightenment in the way indicated by the Habermassian notion of communicative action. (It is Habermas, not Kant, who presses for an articulation of the norms and principles that make com-munication possible.) The second outcome of an aesthetic critique, which Habermas attributes to the older members of the Frankfurt School, such as Herbert Marcuse, has its point of origin in Marx's notion that the senses themselves have a history and are involved in the reproduction and transformation of the social world. This alignment of the sensuous basis of the aesthetic with a critical understanding of transformation effectively grounds the produc-tion and reproduction of the social world in something that the concept cannot entirely subsume. Since society is (re)produced not only in the consciousness of its members but also sensuously, by means of work, the emancipation of consciousness from nature or from social domination must begin with the emancipation of the senses: the "repressive familiarity with the world of given objects" must accordingly be dissolved if society is to be transformed according to such a critique.[38] For a similar reason Habermas appeals to Horkheimer's 1933 call for a materialist theory of society at the conclusion of his essay on "Moral Consciousness and Communicative Action." There he argues that what is needed to move beyond the utopian character of Kant's idea of a perfect constitution of humankind is a materialist theory of society.[39]

[38] It is nonetheless worth noting that for Marcuse, as for Adorno, it is through appearance that art may establish the total revolution envisioned by Schiller. This is because "aesthetic appearance develops reconciling force only as ap-pearance – 'only so long as [Schiller] conscientiously abstains, in theory, from affirming the existence of it, and renounces all attempts, in practice, to bestow existence by means of it'" (*ibid.*, p. 50, citing Marcuse).

[39] Habermas, *Moral Consciousness and Communicative Action*, trans. Christian Len-hardt and Shierry Weber Nicholson (Cambridge, MA: MIT Press, 1990), p. 211.

The plea to understand the notion of "aesthetic critique" in terms of a materialist-oriented theory of communicative action nonetheless raises questions that Habermas himself admits cannot be answered. It seems that Habermas ignores the fact that a materialist theory of society is meant not merely to be a description of facts but an interpretation of those facts in light of a teleological understanding of history, an understanding of where history *ought* to lead, not just a statement about or a prediction of where it will indeed lead. Curiously enough for a project designed to "complete" the work of the Enlightenment, however, Habermas has relatively little to say about the shape of history as a whole, which the notion of completion would seem to imply. Indeed, in "Morality and Ethical Life" Habermas admits that "discourse ethics does not see fit to resort to an objective teleology, least of all to a countervailing force that tries to negate dialectically the irreversible succession of historical events – as was the case, for instance, with the redeeming judgment of the Christian God on the last day" (*Moral Consciousness and Communicative Action*, p. 210). What is the status of a *subjective* teleology, and how can the purposiveness attributed to the subject in this respect help negotiate between the realms of theory and practice?

In Habermas's account, discourse ethics aims to "give up" the problem of closing the gap between the phenomenal (cognitive/theoretical) and noumenal (moral/practical) realms, more or less by declaring this gap to be a metaphysical illusion. In a move that is reminiscent of Wittgenstein, Habermas wishes us to see the problem of theory in relation to practice as no more difficult or strange than that of a language that admits statements of fact as well as statements that are contrary to fact ("the unbridgeable gap Kant saw between the intelligible and the empirical becomes, in discourse ethics, a mere tension manifesting itself in *everyday communication* as the factual force of counterfactual presuppositions"[40]). But it would seem more accurate to say that this appeal to ordinary language and to counterfactual statements as a way to overcome the gap between Kant's two worlds only succeeds in underscoring the difficulty identified by Kant in the third *Critique*, not resolving it. The force of counterfactual propositions made against factual claims, which Habermas identifies as a feature of

---

[40] *Ibid.*, p. 203.

everyday speech, is haunted by the very same problems that Kant found intractable in the third *Critique*. Merely locating this tension within everyday language does little to help with the implications of Kant's claim that the "agreement" being sought in reflective judgments is the (unrepresentable) agreement of *all*. But Habermas himself acknowledges that the kinds of questions raised by Kant in the essays on history and in the third *Critique* remain unanswerable by discourse ethics: "how can we live up to the principle of discourse ethics, which postulates the consent of *all*, if we cannot make restitution for the injustice and pain suffered by previous generations or if we cannot at least promise an equivalent to the day of judgment and its power of redemption?" (*Moral Consciousness and Communicative Action*, p. 210).

Habermas's project to "complete" the Enlightenment through the theory of communicative action is anticipated by Arendt's interpretation of Kant's third *Critique*. In his essay "On the German-Jewish Heritage" Habermas acknowledges his direct debts to Arendt's analysis of Kant's theory of judgment. He describes her rediscovery of Kant's analysis of *Urteilskraft* (judgment power) for a theory of rationality as an achievement of "fundamental importance" and characterizes it as "a first approach to a concept of communicative rationality which is built into speech and action itself" and points toward "an ethics of communicative action which connects practical reason to the idea of a universal discourse."[41] I would argue that Arendt, like Habermas, is tempted to bring closure to the project of critical philosophy found unfinishable by Kant. Unlike Habermas, however, Arendt's interest in Kant in the 1970 *Lectures on Kant's Political Philosophy* represents an attempt to model a political theory directly on the notion of reflective judgment outlined in Kant's third *Critique*. Specifically, Arendt asks us to imagine that what Kant means by "reflective

[41] Habermas, "On the German-Jewish Heritage," *Telos*, 44 (1980), 127–31; the passages cited are from pp. 128 and 130–31. I owe this reference to Ronald Beiner's edition of Arendt's *Lectures on Kant's Political Philosophy*. Additionally, Arendt recognizes the role of communication in ethics. Drawing directly on Kant's aesthetics, she writes that "communicability obviously depends on the enlarged mentality; one can communicate only if one is able to think from the other person's standpoint; otherwise one will never meet him, never speak in such a way that he understands. By communicating one's feelings, one's pleasures and disinterested delights, one tells one's choices and one chooses one's company' (*L*, p. 74).

judgment" in the third *Critique* must take a political form and that Kant's unwritten "Critique of Political Judgment" is implicit in this work. Arendt follows Kant in identifying the capacity for judgment with the position of the spectator and in treating the position of the spectator as both sympathetic and disinterested in the ways described by Kant in the essay on the "old question" of progress. In spite of Arendt's many criticisms of the modern world elaborated in *The Human Condition*, she remained determined to show that a stance that prizes thinking, willing, and above all judging, and that aims at a politics of community, is what underwrites the notion of moral progress dear to Enlightenment thinkers like Kant. Arendt's notion of democratic community as a domain in which recognition can be pursued represents an attempt to salvage politically the commitment to progress that Kant sustains on moral, historical, and above all aesthetic grounds. In Arendt, a democratic politics is dependent upon an account of reflective judgment as the process through which a "community sense" can be built. By politicizing aesthetic reflective judgment, she aims to rescue the possibility of moral progress from the radical discontinuity that is imposed upon it by the apocalyptic image of a "final judgment." Implicitly, she takes it as the task of politics to reduce the radical discontinuity between the events of history and the "final judgment" or "end of all things" in which history as such reaches closure. For her it is the task of politics to make legible what is unpresentable and thereby to transform the "radical agreement" of the kingdom of ends into the process and the space in which we solicit the agreement of others. In so doing, however, Arendt reduces the tension in Kant's late writings between the need to represent that which stands beyond all knowledge and the resistance to representation offered by the totality of a true kingdom of ends. Claude Lefort expresses a related view in the context of his theorization of modern democracy. Arendt, he says, rejects both historicism and the appeal to a human nature, but does so in such a way as to "escape the tension which mobilizes thought . . . all her investigations are therefore subordinated to a clear and distinct idea of what is political and what is not political. Hence the familiar, clear-cut distinctions she makes between the political and the social realms, between the realm of nature, life, necessity, and labour, and the realm of culture, freedom, and action; between the public and the private realm; between the existence of the individual and that of the citizen."[42]

In ascribing a specific political content to what in Kant is radically indeterminate with respect to any particular sphere of social life, Arendt hopes for a closure to the Enlightenment project that Kant himself could not secure, finding what some have described as a "fourth critique" buried in the third, and turning from the indeterminacy of the aesthetic in Kant to a politics that designates democratic community as its field or object-domain.[43] For Kant, by contrast, the confirmation of progress can only be promised "indeterminately and as a contingent event [*Begebenheit*]" (*P*, p. 147). Specifically, the politics that Arendt would claim to derive from Kant's aesthetics is a democratic politics of the beautiful, of common sense, of the *sensus communis logicus*, of (good) taste. If, as Arendt quotes Kant, in making claims of taste we are indeed "suitors for the agreement of everyone else," and if it is this process of "wooing consent" that is a necessary condition for the moral progress of mankind, then the task of politics for Arendt is to provide for the creation of a space in which that discursive process can occur. But in so saying, Arendt is at a loss to give an account of the "passionate participation in the good" or the "genuine enthusiasm" that Kant described as necessary for a moral politics: "genuine enthusiasm always moves only toward what is ideal and, indeed, to what is purely moral, such as the concept of right, and it cannot be grafted onto self-interest" (*P*, p. 145).

The Arendtian interpretation of the problem of reflective judgment represents one of the most important attempts to transpose the Kantian conception of aesthetic judgment into a democratic politics, by focusing on the polis as the space in which the common sense that is revealed in judgments of (good) taste can appear. And yet, for reasons I will outline below, Arendt's account of aesthetic

---

[42] Claude Lefort, *Democracy and Political Theory*, trans. David Mace (Minneapolis: University of Minnesota Press, 1988), p. 6.

[43] Arendt clarifies that "I do not mean to say that Kant, because of the shortness of his life, failed to write the 'fourth *Critique*' but rather that the third *Critique*, the *Critique of Judgment* – which in distinction from the *Critique of Practical Reason* was written spontaneously and not, like the *Critique of Practical Reason*, in answer to critical observations, questions, and provocations – actually should become the book that otherwise is missing in Kant's great work" (*L*, p. 9). The notion that Kant's historical writings comprise a "fourth critique" was first put forward by Renato Composto in *La quarta critica kantiana* (Palermo: Palumbo, 1954).

reflective judgment as political raises a number of questions that her interpretation of Kant seems unable to resolve, and these in turn are important for assessing the efforts of more recent thinkers (among whom I would include Lefort, Ernesto Laclau, and Roberto Unger) to base a democratic politics on transformative ideals (principles) that might also be described as "aesthetic." If the Kantian notion of aesthetic judgment does indeed constitute the basis for understanding democratic politics, then how can the antinomy of taste be preserved in and made fruitful for democratic political life? How can the rationality associated with claims of taste and with the domain of the beautiful be reconciled with the creativity of the genius, whose creativity seems to be "without law"? What is the relationship between the transformative powers of the genius and the state which the genius would found?

Arendt's account of judgment represents one among several recent attempts to make rational and regular the passage between the noumenal and phenomenal worlds, hence to render legible what in Kant is strictly unpresentable, or presentable only by figure, analogy, or metaphor, namely, the encompassing totality or convergence of opinions implicit in the notion of a kingdom of ends. In Arendt, the attempt to regularize this passage becomes evident in, among other places, her interpretation of the Kantian notion of the beautiful, which she pursues in favor of much of what Kant has to say about genius and the sublime. Yet it is the Kantian account of the sublime that best registers the pressure of truly unpresentable ideas – including the idea of the opinion of "everyone else" and the notion of an "enlarged mentality" – upon our existing routines and states of affairs. What Kant imagines as the "final judgment" is potentially sublime insofar as any spatially imagined or materially constituted "thing" that contains an infinity will defeat the powers of reason devoted to representing it. The transposition of infinite, future time into the discursive or "communicative" space of the polis by contrast reduces the disparity between the ongoing process of challenging opinions and testing claims on the one hand and the categorical inclusiveness of a "final judgment" on the other.

To be sure, sublime "enthusiasm" is a troublesome concept that can easily suggest the very opposite of "good taste." As Lyotard points out, sublimity is an *Affekt*, a strong affection (Kant: *animus strenuus*) of extremely painful joy that is, as such, blind and

undeserving of the approval of reason: "Historical-political enthusiasm is thus on the edge of dementia, it is a pathological
outburst, and as such it has in itself no ethical validity, since ethics
requires one's freedom from any motivating pathos; ethics allows
only that apathetic pathos accompanying obligation that is respect" (Lyotard, *The Differend*, pp. 166–67). This enthusiasm
nonetheless conserves an aesthetic validity as what Lyotard calls
an "energetic sign," in which feeling and meaning are combined.
Though the resolution of the aesthetic antinomy of the sublime is
considerably more difficult than that of the beautiful, it is indispensable for Kant's "proof" of the claim that humanity is progressing toward the better, which in turn underlies his conception
of a democratic-republican state. As Lyotard goes on to explain,
"it is not just any aesthetic phrase, but that of the extreme sublime
which is able to supply the proof that humanity is constantly
progressing toward the better. The beautiful is not sufficient, it is
merely a symbol of the good. But, because the feeling of the
sublime is an affective paradox, the paradox of feeling publicly
and as a group that something which is 'formless' alludes to a
beyond of experience, that feeling constitutes an 'as-if presentation' of the Idea of civil society and even of cosmopolitical society,
and thus an 'as-if presentation' of the Idea of morality, right where
that Idea cannot be presented, within experience" (Lyotard, *The
Differend*, p. 170).

In imagining the polis as a discursive space, and in associating
politics with the "public sphere," Arendt's tendency is to refuse
the power of the sublime to hold in check the impulse to ascribe a
fixed object to an unpresentable idea. As Kant insists, "true sublimity must be sought only in the mind of the judging Subject, and
not in the Object of nature that occasions this attitude by the
estimate formed of it."[44] The Arendtian understanding of reflective judgment recoils from the sublime (subjective) moment and
gives us instead an interpretation of the beautiful in which the
object of beauty is itself the moral quality of the "enlarged mentality": seeing from the perspective of everyone else.[45] In so doing,

[44] Kant, *CJ*, sec. 26 (especially p. 104).
[45] It is interesting to note that Richard Rorty loads a similar ethics onto his notion
of the aesthetic (literature): "In my utopia," he writes, "human solidarity would
be seen not as a fact to be recognized by clearing away 'prejudice' or burrowing
down to previously hidden depths but, rather, as a goal to be achieved. It is *to be
achieved not by inquiry but by imagination, the imaginative ability to see strange people*

the difficulties posed by the need to represent the perspectives of "everyone else" are elided,[46] and Arendt diminishes what I take to be the animating tension of the third *Critique*: that while we must be able to reconcile cognition and morality, it remains impossible to construct a permanent bridge between the two. As I hope to suggest, we need to preserve something of this tension if we are not to rob democratic politics, on the one side, of its transformative possibilities and, on the other, of the possibility of its becoming regular and legitimate.

In writing a theory of judgment that is essentially a politicized version of the aesthetic of the beautiful, Arendt's reinterpretation of Kant represents a consequence and continuation of the Enlightenment project to diminish fear and perpetuate the everlasting peace brought by the arbitration of reason. But I would submit that Arendt's resolution of the aporia of reflective judgment is premature, if not false. It avoids the thorniest problems of representation apparent in Kant's essays on history and progress from which Arendt derives her notion of the "spectator's judgment" and draws her to see the polis as an objectification of the *sensus communis logicus* as the best way in which to assure its rationality.[47] Objectification is by her own account the price that must be paid to ensure that subjective elements of consciousness

---

*as fellow sufferers*. Solidarity is not discovered by reflection but created." *Contingency, Irony, and Solidarity* (Cambridge: Cambridge University Press, 1989), p. xvi; emphasis added.

[46] For Kant, judgments of taste take account *a priori* of the mode of representation of everyone else "in order, as it were, to weigh its judgment with the collective reason of mankind, and thereby avoid the illusion arising from subjective and personal conditions which could readily be taken for objective, an illusion that would exert a prejudicial influence upon its judgment" (*CJ*, sec. 40, p. 151). The *a priori* is here balanced by the conditional or hypothetical ("as it were") nature of judgment.

[47] Cf. Lyotard: "The *sensus communis* is thus in aesthetics what the role of practical, reasonable beings is in ethics. It is an appeal to community carried out *a priori* and judged without a rule of direct presentation. However, in the case of moral obligation, the community is required by the mediation of a concept of reason, the Idea of Freedom, while in the phrase of the beautiful, the community of addressors and addressees is called forth immediately, without the mediation of any concept, by feeling alone, inasmuch as this feeling can be shared *a priori*. The community is already there as taste, but it is not yet there as rational consensus" (*The Differend*, p. 169). For Arendt, the task of politics is to provide a "rule of direct presentation" in order to move from the community as taste to the community as rational consensus. In the process, she relies on a series of analogies that are never quite recognized as such: taste is read as moral (through the principle of the "enlarged mentality"), and this morality is in turn read into the politics.

(among which would be included not just reflective judgments, but our memory of the past as well) will in fact endure beyond their own moment: "Without the reification which remembrance needs for its own fulfillment . . . the living activities of action, speech, and thought would lose their reality at the end of each process and disappear as though they had never been. The materialization they have to undergo in order to remain in the world at all is paid for in that always the 'dead letter' replaces something which grew out of and for a fleeting moment indeed existed as the 'living spirit'" (*HC*, p. 95). (In response, one is immediately reminded of Kant's remark in the "Analytic of the Sublime" that "the fear that if we divest this [sublime] representation of everything that can commend it to the senses, it will thereupon be attended only with a cold and lifeless approbation and not with any moving force or emotion, is wholly unwarranted. For when nothing any longer meets the eye of sense, and the unmistakable and ineffaceable idea of morality is left in possession of the field, there would be need rather of tempering the ardour of an unbounded imagination to prevent it from rising to enthusiasm, than of seeking to lend these ideas the aid of images and childish devices for fear of their being wanting in potency" [*CJ*, "General Remark," pp. 127–28].) Arendt's political theory, which by contrast with Kant's aesthetics is deeply rooted in the processes of world-building, is thus by her own account a necessary moment in the "reification of the soul": "Human life, in so far as it is world-building, is engaged in a constant process of reification, and the degree of worldliness of produced things, which all together form the human artifice, depends upon their greater or lesser permanence in the world itself" (*HC*, p. 96). In contrast to Kant's formulation of the sublime as that which is "altogether negative as to what is sensuous" (*CJ*, "General Remark," p. 127), and likewise in contrast to Kant's fascination with the Old Testament's "sublime" ban against the making of graven images ("there is no more sublime passage in the Jewish law than the commandment: Thou shalt not make unto thee any graven image, or any likeness of any thing that is in heaven or earth, or under the earth, &c"; the same holds true, Kant argues, of our representation of the moral law and, indeed, of our "native capacity for morality" [*ibid.*]), Arendt echoes Hegel's claim in the *Lectures on Aesthetics* that art satisfies the need for recognition because it is a form of expression that takes shape as an object that can be made available for all to view:

The universal need for art . . . is man's rational need to lift the inner and outer world into his spiritual consciousness as an object in which he recognizes again his own self. The need for this spiritual freedom he satisfies, on the one hand, by making what is within him explicit to himself, but correspondingly by giving outward reality to this explicit self, and thus in this duplication of himself by bringing what is in him into sight and knowledge for himself and others. This is the free rationality of man in which all acting and knowing, as well as art too, have their basis and necessary origin.[48]

In her lectures on Kant, Arendt speaks of the principle of common sense or "community sense" (*sensus communis*) as that to which we make implicit reference in aesthetic or reflective judgments. Arendt establishes a distinction not between two types of common sense (*sensus communis*) but between common sense and private sense (*sensus privatus*). The "private" senses, like taste and smell, are radically subjective and inward, Arendt says, because "the very objectivity of the seen or heard or touched thing is annihilated in them or at least is not present; they are *inner* senses because the food we taste is inside ourselves, and so, in a way, is the smell of the rose" (*L*, p. 66).[49] On her account these sensations are "not object-bound and cannot be recollected" (*L*, p. 66). Second, she argues that "common sense" refers in Kant both to a norm of reasonableness and to a form of cognition that are open and accessible to all. More precisely, it is the openness and "publicity" of the *sensus communis* that she sees as the guarantee of its reasonableness; likewise, the reasonableness of common sense can claim normative validity because its items can be scrutinized publicly. In contrast to "private sense," the validity of the *sensus communis* depends upon the fact that it represents and makes reference to objects that are open for all to view. As she says in *The Human Condition*, there are some things that need to be displayed publicly if they are to exist at all.[50] For the sake of rationality, Arendt limits

[48] Hegel, *Lectures on Aesthetics*, vol. 1, pp. 32–33.
[49] Arendt's formulation raises interesting questions not addressed by her. Is the taste of the food in the food or in us? Likewise with the smell of the rose: is the smell in the rose or in us? Nonetheless, the thrust of Arendt's argument is clear enough. In arguing that private sense is "rooted" in public sense, we are forced to do precisely what Kant said we must not in matters of claims of taste, namely, ascribe an object to them.     [50] See *HC*, p. 73.

the interest of politics to what can be represented to and by "public reason"; in the process she makes representability a precondition for rationality. The consequences for her own political vision are clear enough. Like Habermas, Arendt favors a politics of rational communication over a politics of radical transformation, even if her own interest in the phenomenon of revolution would seem to require her to reckon with the force of ideas (i.e., of feelings) that lie beyond all representation. Reading her work in light of Kant's late writings nonetheless forces us to grapple with the tension between rationality as communication grounded in common sense and a transformative vision that relies on the feelings generated by those things that stand beyond all possible representation, including the notion of the "agreement of all."

In Kant, claims of taste begin from purely subjective experiences and yet claim universal validity. This suggests that there must be a linkage between the "private" and "public" (common) senses. For Kant, the problem of this linkage defines the antinomy of taste. It is expressed in the tension between the following commonplace propositions: on the one hand that "everyone has his own taste" (or, in another formulation, that "there is no disputing about taste"), while on the other hand that there could be no such thing as contention about taste were there not also a hope of coming to agreement (*CJ*, sec. 56, p. 205). The tension between these propositions means that "one must be able to reckon on grounds of judgment that possess *more than private validity* and are thus not merely subjective" (*ibid.*). It does not, however, mean reflective judgments negate everything that is truly private and subjective about claims of taste, namely, the experiences of pleasure and pain in which they originate. For Arendt, by contrast, the antinomy of taste is resolved by *rooting* private sense in community sense, which in turn requires her to presuppose the existence of community sense. In the process, what begins as something so "private" that it annihilates its objects is transformed into something publicly communicable. Arendt calls the process of this transformation "reflection":

common sense is community sense, *sensus communis*, as distinguished from *sensus privatus*. This *sensus communis* is what judgment appeals to in everyone, and it is this possible appeal that gives judgments their special validity. The it-pleases-or-displeases-me, which as a feeling seems so

utterly private and noncommunicative, is actually rooted in this community sense and is therefore open to communication once it has been
*transformed by reflection, which takes all others and their feelings into account*
. . . When one judges, one judges as a member of a community.

(*L*, p. 72; emphasis added)

And yet Arendt's reliance on the notion of "reflection" in this
passage and others like it raises at least as many problems as it
solves, for the mechanism of reflection she describes, like her
notion of the *sensus communis*, in fact *presupposes* the totality of
sense that it is the task of judgment to create. How can one put
oneself in the place of *everyone else*, if that all-inclusive community
has yet to be formed? The notion of "everyone else" is an indeterminate norm. Conversely, in taking the feelings of all others into
account, what becomes of the "private sense" that served as the
provocation for reflective aesthetic judgment in the first place?

These questions cannot easily be escaped because Arendt relies
on the idea that reflection on "all others and their feelings" is the
way in which taste can make its claims moral. (Arendt quotes
Kant as saying that taste represents "egoism overcome" [*L*, p. 67].)
In this context Arendt embraces the Kantian principle of the
"enlarged mentality" developed in section 41 of the *Critique of
Judgment*, which Kant posits as one of the three "maxims" of the
Enlightenment ("put oneself in thought in the place of everyone
else" [*L*, p. 71]). Communicability is for Arendt the test of one's
ability to adopt an "enlarged mentality" and thereby to stand in
the position of all others. But what does it mean for Arendt to
presuppose the existence of a "community sense" and to treat it as
a faculty that *enables* one to adopt the stance of everyone else
(Arendt: "one's community sense makes it possible to enlarge
one's mentality" [*L*, p. 73])? The answer can only be that Arendt
takes the notion of common sense as an intuitive given.

On the one hand, Arendt wishes to historicize Kant's notion of
communication, just as much as Habermas does. The context for
her discussion of judgment is not nature but the polis, which is
itself historical. Her demonstration of the role of judgments of
taste in the making of a rational (i.e. peacefully communicative)
community represents a way of remembering and thereby carrying forward the discursive ideals embodied in the ancient Greek
polis. The prevailing model of judgment in modernity (which she
links to the writings of Gracián in the Baroque and Cicero in

Antiquity), is one that privileges the testing and negotiating of claims as a way to form the "community sense" that might otherwise be lost to history, or available only in memory. Because it is in principle open to all the "community sense" ensures the rationality and objectivity of the discourse of the polis. For Arendt, claims of taste depend upon the publicity and objectivity of the "community sense," both of which require representability.

Arendt's commitment to the representability of the *sensus communis* in the polis and in the objectivity of reflective judgment should nonetheless be set in contrast with Kant's account of the indeterminacy of reflective judgments and the fragility of claims of taste. Recall that, in making claims of taste, Kant says we invoke concepts from which nothing can be known or proved about the object, and also that such objects are themselves indeterminable and useless for knowledge (*CJ*, sec. 57, p. 208). Although the principle of reflective judgment rests on an underlying *a priori* concept, this is a concept from which we cognize no "thing" (*CJ*, Preface, p. 5).[51] And yet Kant goes on to suggest that there may indeed be something valid in the way of knowledge that we communicate in making aesthetic judgments, thus holding out the possibility that the power of beauty is to show that not all knowledge must be the knowledge of "things."

Arendt's account of this aspect of Kant's aesthetics depends heavily on a theory of the imagination. If the imagination has a privileged role in Arendt's account of judgments of taste, this is because it allows us to judge objects that are not quite "objects," or at any rate that are not directly present to the senses. The power of the imagination is to render representable and thereby knowable that which is not present before us. In the imagination, Arendt says, "one judges objects that are no longer present, that are removed from immediate sense perception and therefore no longer affect one directly, and yet, though the object is removed from one's outward senses, it now becomes an object for one's inward senses. When one represents something to oneself that is absent, one closes, as it were, those senses by which objects in their objectivity are given to one" (*L*, p. 68). The

---

[51] In section 9 Kant argues that when we call something beautiful, beauty is to be regarded as "a quality of the object forming part of its inherent determination according to concepts; although beauty is for itself, apart from any reference to the feeling of the Subject, nothing" (*CJ*, sec. 9, p. 59).

imagination is in turn the key to the mechanism of "reflection" that transforms private sense into the Arendtian *sensus communis*. As with Kant's notion of the historical sign, the imagination allows us to represent the point at which all possible lines of argument, all perspectives, will converge and yield the final and complete agreement of all. Arendt nonetheless insists that in no case is the imagination radically creative. In her view, not even the genius can create that which does not exist; in her example, the genius can only rearrange what already exists. The genius produces the centaur out of the given, the horse and the man (*L*, p. 79).

On the basis of a narrow and literal reading of Kant it would be tempting to say that beauty itself constitutes a form of freedom that does not presently exist, and to think that beauty, like the religious states Kant describes in the essay on progress, or the "community" that Arendt grounds in the *sensus communis*, is the materialization of things that are essentially immaterial and unrepresentable. In the case of beauty, these would be the ideas and concepts of morality; in the case of politics, this would be the "agreement of all" that is presupposed in free and open conversation. Kant says that "the poet essays the task of interpreting to sense the rational ideas of invisible beings, the kingdom of the blessed, hell, eternity, creation, etc. Or again, as to things of which examples occur in experience, e.g., death, envy, and all vices, as also love, fame, and the like, transgressing the limits of experience he attempts with the aid of imagination . . . to body them forth to sense with a completeness of which nature affords no parallel" (*CJ*, sec. 49, pp. 176–77). Here Kant himself may lead us to think of the beautiful as something objective and material, whereas we know that he believes it must be subjective. We must therefore be cautious not to take beauty as itself the representation of what is unpresentable – whether this begins in the purely private experiences of pleasure and pain, or, in judgments (claims) of taste, attempts to reflect upon the opinions and feelings of "everyone else." To do so would be to elide the appearance of beauty as the "symbol of morality" with the exercise of reflective judgment in claims of taste and to overlook the fact that were we indeed faced with the appearance of the kingdom of ends in the form of the beautiful, reflective judgments would be unnecessary. Similarly, one could reason that if the experiences of "private sense" are indeed rooted in the community sense, claims of taste would be superfluous.[52]

In Kant, the origins of Enlightenment in peaceful conversation among members of the polis stand in clear and yet unresolved tension with the radical transformation required to bring us into the kingdom of ends. Even within the sphere of what Kant means by communication there is a tension between the *sensus communis* and the force of the (unpresentable) agreement of all, and this tension is preserved in the third *Critique*. An account of reflective judgment that would reflect the transformative power of the aesthetic would be one in which beauty would be seen either as a memory of our first excitement upon finding the unity of nature as a whole compressed into a single act of cognition, or as the projection of a truly universal accord that in its totality defies representation. It would likewise be an account in which both the pleasures remembered in the beautiful and the common sense presupposed by judgments of taste are paired with the pain felt at the inability to represent our convergence upon a true unanimity or to represent what is beyond all knowledge (in Arendt's terms, the opinions and feelings of "everyone else"). In short, such an account would be one in which the pleasure associated with the beautiful would be coupled with the pain characteristic of the sublime, where the pain of the sublime derives specifically from our feeling overwhelmed by the presentation of the unpresentable (in Kant's words, the "absolutely great" [*CJ*, p. 94]). (Recall that in characterizing the spectators of world history Kant echoes the language of the sublime in saying that their experience "borders closely on enthusiasm, the very expression of which is *fraught with danger*" [*P*, p. 144].) Unlike more recent critical theory, which has focused on the sublime almost to the exclusion of the beautiful in discussing the *Critique of Judgment*, Arendt was drawn to those moments where Kant himself seemed to recoil from its pain and power, as in all those instances in which he emphasizes that the fear raised in us is a *faux* fear ("the *astonishment* amounting almost to terror, the awe and thrill of devout feeling, that takes hold of one when gazing upon the prospect of mountains ascending to

---

[52] As Bernstein has argued, in a completely rational universe judgments of taste would be unnecessary, just as in a strictly causal universe of "facts," judgments of taste would be impossible. Bernstein, *The Fate of Art*, pp. 37–38.

heaven, deep ravines and torrents raging there, deep-shadowed solitudes that invite to brooding melancholy, and the like – all this, when we are assured of our own safety, is *not actual fear"* [*CJ*, "General Remark,"* pp. 120–21; emphasis added]), or where he turns from representations of the violence of war to the far more comforting (and comfortable) image of bourgeois peace and commerce, as in the remarks on war in *Perpetual Peace* and in section 28 of the *Critique of Judgment* (e.g.: "War itself, provided it is conducted with order and a sacred respect for the rights of citizens, has something sublime about it . . . On the other hand, a long peace favors the predominance of a mere commercial spirit, and with it a debasing self-interest, cowardice, and effeminacy, and tends to degrade the character of the nation" [*CJ*, sec. 28, pp. 112–13]).

Arendt's tendency to privilege the beautiful over the sublime must be seen as part of her larger effort to construct a rational politics. For this effort, she takes her bearings by Kant's claim that taste represents a way of bringing the potentially fearsome power of the legislator-genius under the control of something like the "rule of law." Taste is according to Kant "the discipline (or corrective [training]) of genius":

it severely clips its wings, and makes it orderly . . . it gives it guidance, directing and controlling its flight . . . It introduces a clearness and order into the plenitude of thought, and in so doing gives stability to the ideas, and qualifies them at once for permanent and universal approval, for being followed by others . . . Where the interests of both these clash in a product, and there has to be a sacrifice of something, then it should rather be on the side of genius.     (*CJ*, sec. 50, p. 183; see *L*, p. 62)

Though Arendt might wish it otherwise, Kant insists that there can be "no *objective* rule of taste . . . it is only throwing away labor to look for a principle of taste that affords a universal criterion" (*CJ*, sec. 17, p. 75; emphasis added). But as Kant's own remarks on the relationship between genius and taste make plain, this does not go to say that taste has no rule or produces no objects at all. On the contrary, genius is defined as the capacity for the production of beautiful objects (*CJ*, sec. 48, p. 172). Moreover, Arendt emphasizes those elements in Kant's theory of taste that locate the very possibility of aesthetic reflective judgment in mankind's "sociability," which for Kant is both a point of departure (as in the "original compact" referred to in section 41 of the *Critique of*

*Judgment*) and the "highest end" intended for man (as in the "Conjectural Beginning of Human History"[53]). Referencing section 41 of the third *Critique*, Arendt draws on Kant in order to explain how the possibility for aesthetic reflective judgments must be grounded in "sociability," which is in turn constitutive of human nature:

> If we admit that the impulse to society is natural to mankind, and that the suitability for and the propensity towards it, i.e. *sociability*, is a property essential to the requirements of man as a creature intended for society, and one, therefore, that belongs to *humanity*, it is inevitable that we should also look upon taste in the light of a faculty for estimating whatever enables us to communicate even our feeling to every one else, and hence as a means of promoting that upon which the natural inclination of every one is set. (*CJ*, sec. 41, p. 155)

That this sociability is "constitutive" on Kant's account is apparent from the fact that from the communicability of judgments of taste one can infer an "original compact" among members of the human species: "a regard to universal communicability is a thing which every one expects and requires from every one else, just as if it were part of an original compact dictated by humanity itself" (*CJ*, sec. 41, p. 155). In a memorable passage that is important insofar as it confirms Arendt's own understanding of the social basis of taste, Kant speculated that a person abandoned on a desert island would neither seek adornments nor be inclined to look for flowers for decoration. "Only in society does it occur to him to be not merely a man, but a man refined under the manner of his kind (the beginning of civilization) – for that is the estimate formed of one who has the bent and turn for communicating his pleasure to others, and who is not quite satisfied with an Object unless his feeling of delight in it can be shared in communion with others" (*CJ*, sec. 41, p. 155). Kant explains how an interest in colorful adornments eventually yields to beautiful forms that convey no gratification at all and that serve only to confirm the principle of universal communication: "eventually, when civilization has reached its height it makes this work of communication almost the main business of refined inclination, and the entire value of sensations is placed in the degree to which they permit of

[53] Arendt, *L*, p. 73, citing Kant, "Conjectural Beginning of Human History," in *OH*, p. 54.

universal communication. At this stage . . . even where the pleasure which each one has in an object is but insignificant and possesses of itself no conspicuous interest, still the idea of its universal communicability almost indefinitely augments its value" (*CJ*, sec. 41, p. 156). In so saying, Kant not only suggests that claims of taste (which Arendt epitomizes as communicable) threaten to eclipse the experience of pleasure in the beautiful; he also reinforces the claim that pleasure in the beautiful should in principle be recoverable from claims of taste. The ideal of universal communicability is not just a substitute for but should also be an augmentation of the pleasures of the beautiful.

Though pleasure and pain do not figure prominently in her account of the aesthetic basis of politics, Arendt's writings nonetheless suggest that rationality and shareability are insufficient criteria for the judgments made in the public/political sphere. Indeed, Arendt's understanding of the dynamics of politics would suggest that she recognized a tension between the framework of rationality established by communication and the transformative ideals that transcend existing representations and help account for the acts of founding or constituting a state. This tension shows up in the way in which she treats the categories of exemplary validity and genius, which play a crucial role in the concluding pages of the 1970 *Lectures*. As in Kant, Arendt takes the genius as the one who establishes the rule and thereby makes an example of his or her unprecedented practice. For Arendt, the exemplar "is and remains a particular that in its very particularity reveals the generality that otherwise could not be defined" (*L*, p. 77). "If we say of somebody that he is good, we have in the back of our minds the example of Saint Francis or Jesus of Nazareth. The judgment has exemplary validity to the extent that the example is rightly chosen. Or to take another instance: in the context of French history I can talk about Napoleon Bonaparte as a particular man; but the moment I speak about Bonapartism I have made an example of him" (*L*, p. 84). In invoking the exemplar, Arendt nonetheless contravenes what Kant has to say (falsely, some would argue) about the immunity of the will to determination by examples; e.g.: "we cannot show with certainty by any example that the will is here determined by the law alone without any other incentives, even though this appears to be the case"; the freedom of the will is likewise something that Kant says cannot be exemplified: "since no example in accordance with any analogy can support it, it can never be comprehended or even imagined"; for Kant, it lies not so much beyond reason as before it, as a presupposition, namely, "the necessary presupposition of reason in a being that believes itself conscious of a will."[54] By contrast with a moral project that places the central concepts of "will" and "freedom" in principle out of the reach of representation, Arendt's "exemplar" and "genius" are empowered to establish not just a new law, or a new standard of lawfulness; they regularize or legitimize a form of creativity that can be assessed by its consequences. In other words, the "exemplary" work of the Arendtian genius proves valid insofar as it generates a succession of followers.[55] Indeed, it is clear that for Arendt everything the genius creates in new rules and in unprecedented examples seeks a more tangible, material, objective, and stable form in the public discourse of the state.[56] Two paradoxes follow from this claim. First, the regularization of the genius's example means the betrayal of the genius. Second, the example established by the genius allows for what Kant calls a "manner" (*modus*) but not a method of teaching (*CJ*, sec. 60, p. 226).

Not surprisingly in view of her interest in the *vita activa*, Arendt is drawn to the acts of founding and constituting a state, especially insofar as these "poetic" political acts serve to make substantive and representable (and, therefore, rational and regular) that which might otherwise stand beyond all powers of representa-

---

54 Kant, *Foundations of the Metaphysics of Morals*, trans. Lewis White Beck (Indianapolis, IN: Bobbs-Merrill, 1969), pp. 42, 89. Additionally, Kant says in the third *Critique* that while the work of the genius is to be followed and not imitated, the difference between these defies explanation: "the rule [must] be gathered from the performance, i.e. from the product, which others may use to put their own talent to the test, so as to let it serve as a model, not for *imitation*, but for *following*. The possibility of this is difficult to explain" (*CJ*, sec. 47, p. 171).

55 Cf. Kant's distinction between "following" (of which he approves) and "imitation" (of which he disapproves) in section 47 of the *Critique of Judgment* (p. 171). As Stanley Cavell remarked of Emerson in a passage that I believe has roots in Kant's third *Critique*, "the acceptance of an exemplar . . . is not grounded in the relation between the instance and a class of instances it stands for but in the relation between the instance and the individual other – for example, myself – for whom it does the standing, for whom it is a sign, upon whom I delegate something." "Aversive Thinking," in *Conditions Handsome and Unhandsome: The Constitution of Emersonian Perfectionism* (Chicago: University of Chicago Press, 1990), pp. 50–51.

56 In Kant, examples can simply help us verify the reality of concepts. Specifically, Kant says that "if the concepts are empirical the intuitions are called *examples*," (*CJ*, sec. 59, p. 221).

tion. Hence her clear admiration in *On Revolution* for the Constitution of the United States as the materialization of the power of law vested in a people.[57] Only in the United States, she notes, did a revolution issue in the act of "constituting" a republic (*OR*, p. 157). She views the Constitution as an enduring object that serves to materialize and make substantial a series of unpresentable beliefs held in principle by all. Similarly, she is drawn to the ways in which a documentary record makes that act rational precisely because it is the *materialization* of a set of principles or beliefs. To the founding fathers, she notes, "the seat of power . . . was the people, but the source of the law was to become the Constitution, a written document, an endurable objective thing, which, to be sure, one could approach from many different angles and upon which one could impose many different interpretations, which one could change and amend in accordance with circumstances, but which nevertheless was never a subjective state of mind, like the will" (*OR*, p. 156). In the context of politics, the reflective judgments incited by the "free particulars" that refuse the universal categories prepared for them in advance seek the objectivity and substantiality of the state as an *object* open for all to view, and, in that capacity, as the guarantors of rationality. In Arendt's own analysis, the problem with "discourse," "speech," and "action" is that they are not productive of any "thing." As she says in *The Human Condition*, "they do not themselves 'produce,' bring forth anything, they are as futile as life itself. In order to become worldly things, that is, deeds and facts and events and patterns of thoughts or ideas, they must first be seen, heard, and remembered and then transformed, reified as it were, into things – into sayings of poetry, the written page or the printed book, into paintings or sculpture, into all sorts of records, documents, and monuments" (*HC*, p. 95). Arendtian "action" needs a world, which incorporates labor and fabrication; likewise, politics needs an object, a polis or a state.

Arendt's analysis of the political act of "constitution" as a form of material making helps bring to light the Hegelian and Heideggerean (as opposed to the Kantian or Marxist) strains in her writing, and becomes evident in, among other places, her comment that the products of work are what go to make up a world:

[57] Hannah Arendt, *On Revolution* (New York: Viking, 1965). Henceforth cited as *OR*.

"Viewed as part of the world, the products of work – and not the products of labor – guarantee the permanence and durability without which a world would not be possible at all" (*HC*, p. 94). Recall that Hegel had described the activity of work as one way in which the negativity of desire can yield something that is permanent and enduring (but recall also that the dialectic of desire through which labor is externalized and passes into the condition of permanence was characteristic of the consciousness of the slave).[58] Drawing on Hegel, and on Kojève's reading of Hegel, Arendt emphasizes that action stands in need of an enduring world if it is to determine anything more than a sheerly negative relation to others. At the same time, and independent of Hegel and Kojève, her analysis of the nature of "constitution" reveals the fact that, in politics at least, the "made thing" (the constitution or the state) contains a tension that cannot easily be resolved. This is the tension between the creativity involved in founding or constituting a *political* world (which is meant to be a realm of free action but which relies on acts of making), and the expectation that any polis should conform to and ensure the standards of rationality embodied in "common sense." We might describe the twin poles of this tension as "genesis" and "normativity." As Arendt recognizes, every act of founding, every act of inauguration or of radical beginning, runs the risk of arbitrariness; what begins in an arbitrary way must be transformed into principle or rule if it is to be held in common by all. Indeed, she remains committed to the principle of politics grounded in an objectification of the *sensus communis* even if it requires her to take the risk of false prophecy described in Kant's essay on progress. For her, however, the problem is not so much how to avoid the false or self-fulfilling prophesy as how to preserve the creativity of the new beginning as it is transformed into the lawful rule which a democratic polis needs to presuppose. Her answer, given in *On Revolution*, is to treat as a potentially productive paradox what elsewhere is resolved or reduced in favor of "principle" or "rule":

What saves the act of beginning from its own arbitrariness is that it carries its own principle within itself, or, to be more precise, that beginning and principle, *principium* and principle, are not only related to each other, but

---

[58] See Hegel, *Phenomenology of Spirit*, trans. A. V. Miller (New York: Oxford University Press, 1975), sec. 195, pp. 117–18.

are coeval. The absolute from which the beginning is to derive its own validity and which must save it, as it were, from its inherent arbitrariness is the principle which, together with it, makes its appearance in the world. The way the beginner starts whatever he intends to do lays down the law of action for those who have joined him in order to partake in the enterprise and to bring about its accomplishment. As such, the principle inspires the deeds that are to follow and remains apparent as long as the action lasts. (*OR*, p. 214)

In *On Revolution*, it is the materiality of the Constitution that provides both the new beginning and the rule; in the *Lectures* of 1970, the *sensus communis* itself becomes the rule. Despite the differences between them, both works reveal Arendt's will to ensure the rationality of political life by grounding the state in the processes of representation and materialization, which action when divorced from world-making work cannot seem to do. As the criterion of rationality, representation is the way in which Arendt resolves the tensions in Kant between genesis and normativity, which we might also phrase as the tension between the creativity of the genius and claims of taste, or between the transformative (and potentially sublime) energies of revolution and the normativity of communicative reason. To understand the task of politics as ensuring normativity, either through representation or through communication, is to weaken its transformative potential and to render the act of founding unintelligible and impossible. By contrast, to view politics as "aesthetic" insofar as it depends upon the representation of ideals that are available only to the creative genius may well be to risk the legislative arbitrariness that Arendt so deeply feared. And yet the world-making that Arendt so highly prizes depends upon the powers of the genius she so deeply fears. (Glossing Kant's moral philosophy, Arendt sees the genius as a potentially arbitrary and tyrannical legislator; she reminds us that "man, insofar as he does anything at all, lays down the law; he is the legislator" [*L*, p. 50].) In light of the tensions between the legislative "genius" and the regularity of taste that appeals to our "common sense" it seems that the task ahead is to see the ways in which we can resist the temptation to resolve the aporia of reflective judgment or reduce the task of politics to the activities of cognition or production. We can instead look to Kant in order to understand how the problems broached in the third *Critique* can in turn provide the basis for a more fruitful conception of democracy than either Habermas or Arendt allows.[59]

In reading the *Critique of Judgment* as the "critique of political judgment" that Kant did not write, Arendt conceives the polis as an object-sphere governed by a faculty that, for Kant, had an ambiguous standing at best. By imagining the polis as a discursive social space or object-sphere, both Habermas and Arendt are forced to sacrifice some of the critical force that attaches to the indeterminacy of the aesthetic in Kant. What remains to be seen is whether a post-Enlightenment critique of politics that is more responsive to this indeterminacy can generate the transformative energies that Habermas and Arendt seem to lack without sacrificing the democratic desire to provide subjects with a space in which they can find recognition from one another. What becomes of the polis when the power of judgment is trained not upon some determinate object, but rather on what the determination of any object leaves out? As I want to suggest in the following chapter, poststructuralist political theory follows the lines of an aesthetic critique insofar as it attempts to think of the polis as something whose nature is essentially, constitutively incomplete. Such a conception of the polis leads to opportunities for more radical change than either Habermas or Arendt can allow. But, as we also shall see, poststructuralist political theory runs the risk of taking transformation as an end unto itself.

[59] David Ingram has an insightful discussion of these and related issues in his book *Reason, History, and Politics: The Communitarian Grounds of Legitimation in the Modern Age* (Albany: State University of New York Press, 1995), especially pp. 361–62. For Ingram, it is Derrida (against whom he poses Arendt) who most forcefully articulates the problem with any notion of politics or ethics founded on "indeterminacy." "Indeterminacy" is here aligned to radical transformation, which Ingram recognizes as potentially dangerous: "in Derrida's anarchistic universe, the rebellious reinvention of the constitution in every legislative and adjudicative act ensures the freedom of future generations. However, its fleeting legitimacy will be purchased at the expense of liberties that might otherwise have had the protection of standing law . . . Needless to say, the antipodes of permanent (legal) repetition and permanent (ethical) revolution do not leave much room for that historical progress so sought after by Derrida. Indeed, if Blumenberg is right, they do not leave much room for historical change as distinct from mere succession. In this dichotomous universe, progression of the past that progresses beyond the past remains essentially enigmatic" (p. 362). Ingram's understanding of the question of "progress" would nonetheless be enhanced by a consideration of the alternative vision that Nietzsche offers in the notion of "eternal return."

# 5

## The role of aesthetics in the radicalization of democracy

The history of the world cannot pass a last judgment. It is made out of judged judgments.                                    Jean-François Lyotard[1]

The work of Jürgen Habermas and Hannah Arendt is representative of some of the ways in which political theory in the aftermath of the Enlightenment remains linked to an "orthodox" interpretation of Kant's notion of reflective judgment. As far as Habermas is concerned, the theory of communicative action is meant to complete the Enlightenment project that Kant left unfinished, in part by invoking the ideal of a consensus or a convergence of opinions as the foundation of a peaceable state. In arguments that are meant to align this theoretical stance with a social and political progressivism, Habermas suggests in *The Philosophical Discourse of Modernity* that the possibility of "progress" was closed when the leading opponents of foundationalist metaphysics – Nietzsche, Heidegger, Bataille, and Derrida – chose to avoid the problem of reflective judgment in favor of a critique of subject-centered reason. Arendt's notion of judgment can be traced even more directly than Habermas's to Kant's aesthetic theory; the notion of "enlarged thinking" reflects her interpretation of the universality that is central to Kant's attempted resolution of the antinomy of taste. In both instances, appeal to notions said to be implicit in the theory of reflective judgment offers a source of hope in the face of the conditions diagnosed by Horkheimer and Adorno as funda-

[1] Jean-François Lyotard, *The Differend: Phrases in Dispute*, trans. Georges van den Abbeele (Minneapolis: University of Minnesota Press, 1968), p. 8.

175

mentally destructive of the modern Enlightenment and, indeed, of all forms of rationality in the West. Against the threat of the instrumentalization of reason and the reification of social relations, in which the concrete identities of individuals are effaced by the powers of abstract, universal reason, Habermas and Arendt invite us to imagine society as held together by the bonds of imaginative sympathy and common sense. As far as politics is concerned, Habermas and Arendt conceive of democracy as a mode of relationship in which the demands of reason and recognition can both be met. Recasting "reason" in terms of communication (Habermas) and judgment (Arendt) allows the reconciliation of cognition and recognition to take place.

At the same time, we have seen that Habermas's logic of consensus is based upon Kant's *sensus communis logicus* and that Arendt remains committed to a conception of the polis as an objectifiable space. They both show us how to imagine the polis as founded upon the resources of language or imagination through which particular preferences, desires, and feelings can be aligned with a universal capacity for reason, but they overlook the fact that life in the polis may depend upon affective relations that the logic of consensus does not admit: pleasure, antagonism, attraction, love. Admittedly, they have relatively little to say about transformation as a political goal. As I argue in relation to the more radical political theorists to be discussed in this chapter, a transformative politics requires reflective judgment precisely because the success or failure of radical transformation cannot be judged in accordance with a pre-established set of principles or rules; on the contrary, it is the goal of such politics to change the rules themselves. This is the insight that funds the awareness, shared by Žižek and Laclau, that the democratic polis has survived only because the ideal of a truly universal convergence of opinions proves impossible to achieve.[2]

To be sure, Arendt makes an effort to honor Kant's understanding of the difference between reflective and determinant judgments, and Habermas seeks to establish the theory of communicative action as a form of universal pragmatics rather than as a

---

[2] I would contrast this with Richard Rorty's neo-pragmatist advancement of irony as a critico-aesthetic posture insofar as Rorty's irony rejects the notion that democracy is made possible by its own limitations. See "The Continuity between the Enlightenment and 'Postmodernism,'" unpublished ms.

version of transcendental argument. Defending Arendt's notion of judgment, Martin Jay points out that by acknowledging the power of examples over the schematism of concepts, Arendt attempts to respond to one of Horkheimer and Adorno's central concerns: to respect particulars without reducing them to the status of mere instances of a general rule.[3] But Arendt's notion of the exemplar requires a theory of genius that seems to be at odds with her attachment to the rationality of political life. Perhaps in view of this fact, she subordinates the creative and legislative powers of the genius to what Kant calls the "discipline" of taste. Recall that Arendt rejects the idea that the genius might create anything radically new. Indeed, it would be a scandal to judgment if it were indeed within the power of genius to disclose an otherwise unavailable truth (as Heidegger claims is the authentic function of poetry in "The Origin of the Work of Art"). For Arendt, judgment must proceed by rule. Finally, by likening the formation of the polis to the production of enduring material objects and by emphasizing that material making endows human actions with the permanence they might not otherwise achieve, Arendt makes it clear that the polis must objectify (in her own terms, "reify") the very intersubjective relations that comprise it. Arendt's polis thus becomes a version of what Hegel described as "objective spirit." She situates the aesthetic critique of politics within the sphere of the *ergon*, i.e., of making oriented toward a determinate end. This in turn relieves her understanding of politics of the element of contingency or "purposive purposelessness" that characterizes action in the aesthetic domain. And for Kant at least that "purposive purposelessness" presents an opportunity for freedom. Consider for example the passage in which Kant describes how "flowers, free patterns, lines aimlessly intertwining – technically termed foliage – have no signification, depend upon no definite concept" but produce the free delight characteristic of the beautiful.[4] While there may well be a need to

---

[3] He also suggests that Arendt invokes the faculty of the imagination in order to explain how the participants in the polis can put themselves in the place of others without reducing others to versions of themselves. See Martin Jay, " 'The Aesthetic Ideology' as Ideology: Or What Does It Mean to Aestheticize Politics?" in *Force Fields: Between Intellectual History and Cultural Critique* (London: Routledge, 1993), p. 82.

[4] Immanuel Kant, *Critique of Judgment*, trans. James Creed Meredith (Oxford: Clarendon Press, 1986), sec. 4, p. 46.

recognize that the exigencies of political action require a more direct and immediate link to purposes than an aesthetically grounded notion of action can allow, a consequence of Arendt's interpretation of Kant is that she avoids thinking about the polis as a sphere that may not be fully determined by the concepts of production (causality) or perfection in relation to end.

Some of these same objections can be raised against Habermas, who takes the notion of communication as the basis for a theory of political relations in which the reflective aesthetic judgment is vested with the power to secure a stable *inter*subjective space. Though Habermas's communicative project is designed to be collective and reciprocal, this intersubjective space is controlled by the logic of determinant judgments. In Habermas, the notion of intersubjectivity serves to authorize and determine a place for the subject within a conceptual order of relations based upon the egalitarian pragmatism of language. Like Arendt, Habermas's notion of intersubjectivity brings to light the universalizing and identificatory moments of the "enlarged mentality" that binds subjects together in political life. But precisely because of its universalizing ambitions Habermas's theory of communicative action tends to reinforce sedimented social relations; it does little to help us imagine the polis as a space in which transformation can occur. Precisely at the moment where Kant's reflective aesthetic judgment discovers the gap between the empirical and transcendental positions of the subject to be both necessary and contingent, the Habermassian theory of communicative action insists upon bridging the gap. For Habermas, the breach between Kant's two worlds can be repaired insofar as intersubjective communication is possible.

Subordinating judgment and action to versions of the "concept" drawn from the fields of causality (production), finality (end), and intersubjectivity (communication) allows thinkers like Habermas and Arendt to endow the political sphere with a stability and a cohesion that it might not otherwise attain. Additionally, their appeal to the ideals of judgment and communication offers a way to pursue democratic politics in what might well seem inhospitable times. But in light of recent developments within the democratic cultures of the West, many of which reflect the emergence of elements that cannot be assimilated to the whole by appeal to the *sensus communis logicus*, the Habermassian and Arendtian positions are unlikely to carry much force. As we have already seen, Habermas and Arendt tend prematurely to foreclose the project of shaping universal agreement for claims that are based upon what Kant characterized a subjective moment of feeling. Accordingly, they tend not to recognize the ways in which democracy has been enhanced by the emergence of "particularisms" that undermine the notion of the polis as an integrated social whole.

In contrast to Habermas and Arendt, more recent radical rethinkings of democracy can be linked to versions of the theory of aesthetic judgment that stress modes of relation in which particulars are invested with the power to resist subsumption under universal principles or rules, or in which universals prove incomplete, hence incapable of subsuming every particular they might encounter. Given the limitations of projects like those of Habermas and Arendt, contemporary thinkers interested in radicalizing democracy have turned to the project of an aesthetically grounded critique as part of an effort to identify what the notions of communication and consensus seem to leave out: the ongoing desire of subjects to refashion the structures they inhabit, coupled with the desire to perpetuate democracy by recognizing that Enlightenment democratic universalism and its institutions were structurally, inherently incomplete. Theorists of radical democracy are thus drawn to the notions of "contingency," "dislocation," and "opacity" in order to explain how we can conceive the polis as something other than an all-encompassing object-domain or a space for affirming identities by virtue of their subsumption under some pre-existing universal rule. To judge from this perspective, thinkers like Habermas and Arendt adhere too closely to what Kant has to say about the universal validity of aesthetic judgments and overlook the way in which the indeterminacy of such judgments is crucial to the possibility of political transformation. Whereas Eagleton has argued that Kant's *ethics* are "incapable of generating any distinctive political theory of their own beyond a conventional liberalism,"[5] it seems that Kant's *aesthetics* have in fact played a significant role in a radical rethinking of democracy.

My aims in this chapter are severalfold: to make explicit the

---

[5] Terry Eagleton, *The Ideology of the Aesthetic* (Oxford: Blackwell, 1990), p. 97.

project of radical democracy as it relates to Kant's aesthetic critique; to explore the ways in which the critical categories of "contingency," "antagonism," and "dislocation" have taken the place of both romantic-revolutionary radicalism and modernist optimism as the basis for imagining political change; and finally to identify the ways in which an acceptance of the "failure" of democratic universalism remains an ineradicable, irreducible condition of "post-Enlightenment" political thought. To this end I want to comment on the work of theorists such as Roberto Unger, Jean-François Lyotard, Claude Lefort, Ernesto Laclau, and Slavoj Žižek, whose various efforts to reinvent democratic politics are indebted to a greater or lesser degree, directly or indirectly, to Kant's third *Critique*. Whereas it has been said both by Habermas and by Marxist literary critics (e.g., Fredric Jameson and Frank Lentricchia) that postmodern theory must forego any possibility of social or political change – indeed, that postmodernism places at risk the very notion of history upon which any possibility of change must rely – it seems that the opposite is closer to the truth, that "postmodern" political theory in fact demonstrates an unswerving commitment to the notion of change. In this it remains faithful to its modernist roots. The "difficulty" that we have seen to be characteristic of reflective judgment in Kant becomes the basis for a politics that adheres neither to the universalism of transcendental principles (e.g., "freedom," "equality") nor to a pragmatism that aspires merely to evaluate actions according to the principles of efficacy. In contrast to the emphasis that Arendt places on the role of the moral imagination in political life, and in contrast as well to the Habermassian grounding of politics in consensus, these thinkers stand in agreement that political subjectivity must be understood as resisting full articulation according to universal principles or rules, whether of essence, of cause, or of end. Democracy describes that form of politics suited to a subject that recognizes itself as having no essential nature, that refuses to understand itself as the effect of some external or underlying cause, and that regards change as inevitable insofar as closure is unattainable.

By virtue of the various forms of incompleteness just described, the democratic polis has been seen as an appropriate stage for what Laclau has described as the "revolution of our times." On Laclau's account, the groups responsible for this new "revolution" may appear to have taken up positions analogous to that of the "universal" Enlightenment subject, but their importance in determining the course of history in fact derives from what the notion of a "universal subject" leaves out – the contingency of the particular, understood as a function of the inability of such universal democratic ideals as "equality" and "autonomy" to embrace the whole.[6] Indeed, the emergence of a variety of relatively new social subjects with transformative potential – including student protesters, ecologists, feminists, and people of color – suggests that the founding principles of the liberal democratic state, including its most encompassing and global ideals, must themselves have been incomplete. But since, as Hegel saw, any theoretical awareness that might be adequate to such a fact inevitably arrives late on the scene, we must hasten to add that the challenge posed by these "new particularisms" is not to find a still more encompassing way to conceive the polis; it is rather to transform what is understood by politics in light of what the "original" conception of democracy is thus shown necessarily to have left out. Rather than a repudiation of the Enlightenment, the acknowledgment of this incompleteness represents a continuation of the Enlightenment's democratic politics, albeit in a new guise.

In contrast to Arendt's picture of the modern world, which

[6] By contrast, the neo-conservative response to the proliferation of new social movements represents a strengthening of hegemonic forms of power by reinvoking the principles of essentialism. Neo-conservatism seeks a total transformation of society based upon an insight into society's "true nature." It looks for a "profound transformation of the terms of political discourse and the creation of a new 'definition of reality,' which under the cover of the defense of 'individual liberty' would legitimize inequalities and restore the hierarchical relations which the struggles of the previous decades had destroyed" (Laclau and Mouffe, *Hegemony and Socialist Strategy* [London: Verso, 1985], p. 176; hereafter cited as *HSS*). Against "neo-conservatism" (which forms an unsuspecting alliance with liberalism in order to construct a new hegemonic articulation through a system of equivalences which would unify multiple subject-positions around an individualist definition of rights and a negative conception of liberty), the project of radical democracy aims at the construction of a different system of social relations. Rather than renounce the prevailing democratic ideologies, radical democracy is designed to deepen and expand democracy in the direction of a more radical plurality. Insofar as it can be shown that democracy is not definitively wed to the discourse of individual rights, it is possible to reimagine social relations on the basis of the antagonism between particulars and universals. What we are left with are neither the principles of "equality" and "universal rights" nor the anarchistic assertion of an essential particularism, but a vision of the polis that is able to embrace its own indeterminacy.

shares Horkheimer and Adorno's sense of the dangers of rationalization in contemporary life, a thinker like Laclau takes the antagonistic relations by which these "new particularisms" challenge
democratic universalism as providing concrete evidence for optimism about the fate of democracy in the (post)modern world:
"contrary to the assumptions of the thinkers of the Frankfurt
School, the decline of the 'major actors,' such as the working class
of classical socialism, has not led to a decrease in social struggles
or the predominance of a one-dimensional man, but to a proliferation of new antagonisms. The transformation of the contemporary social scene [under which Laclau includes the many movements that have sprung up since the mobilizations of 1968] clearly
bears this out . . . far from experiencing a process of depoliticiz-
ation and uniformization, what we are seeing now is a much
deeper politicization of social relations than ever before."[7] In so
saying, Laclau betrays his perhaps unwitting debts to the traditions of romantic and modernist revolutionary optimism. Indeed,
the project of radical democracy reflects its romantic/modernist
heritage in the two most basic requirements stipulated by Laclau.
The first is "to accept, in all their radical novelty, the transformations of the world in which we live – that is to say, neither to
ignore them nor to distort them in order to make them compatible
with outdated schemas so that we may continue inhabiting forms
of thought which repeat the old formulae." The second is "to start
from this full insertion in the present – in its struggles, its challenges, its dangers – to interrogate the past: to search within it for
the genealogy of the present situation . . . making the past a
transient and contingent reality rather than an absolute origin"
(*New Reflections*, p. 98). Such proposals attempt what would seem
to be an impossible feat: to marry the critical consciousness of
what Harold Bloom has dubbed the "school of resentment" (Althusser, Foucault) with an optimism that is fueled by the openness
of the present to the possibility of social and political change.

I will return to consider the aesthetic underpinnings of these
proposals in greater detail below. But first I want to retrace some
of the links between postmodern political theory and the Enlightenment by looking at the views expressed by Roberto Unger

[7] Ernesto Laclau, *New Reflections on the Revolution of Our Time* (London: Verso,
1990), p. 214.

in works like *Knowledge and Politics* (1975), *Passion: An Essay on Personality* (1984), and the volumes entitled *False Necessity* and *Plasticity into Power* (1987). According to Unger, contemporary political thought is obliged first and foremost to reckon with the "antinomies" inherited from the Enlightenment. The task for democratic political theory, he suggests, is to overcome the crippling antinomies of fact and value, reason and desire, value and rule, by drawing upon the resources of the modernist aesthetic tradition as exemplified in writers like Flaubert, Joyce, and Woolf. In Unger's view, modernism has its roots in the belief that all our patterns of action, including the institutional frameworks in which they are set, are artefactual creations, not essential features of the world. They are the contingent products of human intentions and aims, and can therefore be reshaped. Modernism's unfulfilled political task, Unger suggests, is to radicalize this insight into the nature of human action and thereby to open our social routines to the possibility of radical change. For Unger, the chief mystification about social and political life roots in the belief that the antinomies of Enlightenment thought represent the true configuration of subject and world, and likewise that our institutional frameworks represent something more than human creations. Whether this "something more" is thought to be a natural essence (which is a case Unger often cites) or something bureaucratic and institutional, the criticism is the same: both can and should be reduced to "politics." "The formative contexts of social life . . . or the procedural frameworks of problem solving and interest accommodation . . . [are] nothing but frozen politics: conflicts interrupted or contained."[8] Once this insight is reached, Unger argues, our circumstances will have been fundamentally transformed.[9]

But Unger's political modernism is not just the result of an attempt to break free from mystified beliefs about human nature; it is also a consequence of the need to resolve the contradictions

[8] Roberto Unger, *Social Theory: Its Situation and Its Task* (Cambridge: Cambridge University Press, 1987), p. 145.
[9] In "The Concept of Enlightenment" Horkheimer and Adorno had argued that revolutionary practice depends upon "the intransigence of theory in the face of the insensibility with which society allows thought to ossify." *Dialectic of Enlightenment*, trans. John Cumming (New York: Continuum, 1995), p. 41. The unanswered question is what "thought" would look like were we to free it from such ossification. For Unger, it seems that the tension between theory and practice is such that theory must ultimately be left behind.

with which particularities are rendered. The result is the creation of a new kind of universal, one that resides in (but is somehow not limited to) concrete expressions: "this something, the universal, cannot be reduced to abstract propositions. It is embodied in expressions. Nevertheless, the universal is not wholly confined to those expressions; it can be rediscovered elsewhere" (*Knowledge and Politics*, p. 144).

And yet it seems that none of these proposed "solutions" to the antinomies of Enlightenment thought in fact succeeds in resolving its difficulties. First, all these so-called solutions fail to deal with the propensity to form a symbolic order that goes beyond particulars. Consider Unger's concrete universal, which even by his own admission contains a necessary "surplus," something over and above the concrete, which renders it inexhaustible. Likewise, these "solutions" are all premised on a fulfillment of the promise made by the Kantian "as if": they depend upon a logic of belief that remains insufficiently aware of the degree to which belief remains alien and unjustifiable from the perspective of unbelief. Indeed, the upwelling of a rather anxious desire for belief at the conclusion of *Knowledge and Politics* confirms the fact that Unger's final and unsatisfied hope is for a theological solution to the antinomies of Enlightenment thought.[12] There, the indeterminacy of our position as subjects, as characterized by the Enlightenment antinomies of desire and reason, value and fact, begets an existentialist anxiety reminiscent of the fear and trembling of Kierkegaard and Pascal. This anxiety can only be quelled by a leap of faith, or by what Arendt regards as the dangerous secular version of that leap – by the creative but potentially irrational powers associated with the genius: "desirous of faith, touched by hope, and moved by love, men look unceasingly for God. Their search for Him continues even where thinking must stop and action fail.

---

[12] Žižek raises a question in the course of his analysis of Schelling that I think is entirely applicable to Unger's dilemma: what to do after one has "traversed the fantasy"? "How are we to avoid the painful conclusion that the nonexistence of the big Other, of the act *qua* real, is merely a fleeting 'vanishing mediator' between two Orders, an enthusiastic intermediate moment necessarily followed by a sobering relapse into the reign of the big Other? What corresponds to it in the domain of politics is the resigned conservative notion of revolution as a transitory moment of liberation, the suspension of social authority, which unavoidably gives rise to the backlash of an even more oppressive power." *The Indivisible Remainder: An Essay on Schelling and Related Matters* (London: Verso, 1996), p. 133.

And in their vision of Him they find the beginning and the end of their knowledge of the world and of their sympathy for others. So is man's meditation on God a final union of thought and love – love which is thought disembodied from language and restored to its source. But our days pass, and still we do not know you fully. Why then do you remain silent? Speak, God" (*Knowledge and Politics*, p. 295).

In his later work, Unger attempts to overcome these anxieties by limiting himself to the wholly secular, modernist insight that society is a man-made artefact with no "higher" rules, that none of our actions or routines is endowed with the force of necessity, that none can be aligned with a universal Truth. Basic to this insight is the principle of contextuality that emerges as a result of the elimination of one of Kant's "two worlds." Every action requires a selection from the range of all possible frameworks of those to be provisionally accepted as authoritative.[13] Insofar as all action is contextual, there is, on this account, no unconditional context, nor any comprehensive context of contexts, "no set of frameworks that can do justice to all our opportunities of insight and association – not even in the areas of experience where we might most expect to find such frameworks" (*Passion*, pp. 7–8). A second principle is related to this one and states that we can always break through the particular contexts of practical or conceptual activity in which we find ourselves engaged. All contexts, though enabling for action, can be reshaped. All action, though contextual, is potentially context-transforming. Together, these principles allow us to establish a contrast between "context-preserving routines" and "context-revising transformations" (*Passion*, pp. 7–8): "at any moment people may think or associate with one another in ways that overstep the boundaries of the conditional worlds in which they had moved till then . . . In the collision between the incongruous insight and the established structure, the structure may go under, and the proponents of the insight may discover retrospectively the terms that justify the forbidden idea" (*Passion*, p. 8).

The social and political insights that follow from these beliefs are consonant with what can be recognized as a modernist commitment to the "new." They ask us to build structures that are

---

[13] Unger, *Passion: An Essay on Personality* (New York: Free Press, 1984), p. 78.

more open to transformation because less rigid and less susceptible to entrenchment than the ones we inherited from the past:
"the more a structure of thought or relationship provides for the
occasions and instruments of its own revision, the less you must
choose between maintaining it and abandoning it for the sake of
the things it excludes. You can just remake or reimagine it"
(*Passion*, p. 10). To be sure, there is a potential for empowerment to
be derived by declaring that all action is contextual and by declaring that we are therefore free. To do so would "solve" a central
problem of the third *Critique*, for it would allow us to think that
the will can expect recognition from the world – indeed, that it can
gain that recognition *at will*. But the freedom we might thus
achieve would be inflated with a lingering romantic hope, for the
world in which we would be free would be one bereft of the
lawfulness or necessity that a thinker like Kant attributes to it.
Unger's insight into what the novelist Milan Kundera calls the
"lightness of being" thus dismisses the Kantian insight that the
lawfulness of nature represents an irreducible *external* force, not
itself a contingent product of desire or the will.[14]

By Unger's own account, there is another, unsurmountable
tension within the contextualist view of human personality that
proves to be its own self-limiting law. Unger asks: could not the
insight that all contexts are contingent itself be taken as a "universal" truth, itself subject to no further contextualization? If so, then
the thesis that all thought and action is contextual would be
falsified. Would this, the antithetical "truth" of contextualism,
result in its dialectical reversal? In order to avoid the fate in which
the very principle of contextualism unwittingly reverts to a universalism, but lacking a principle to explain how and when it does
occur, Unger simply concedes that context-breaking must be an
"exceptional and transitory" activity.[15] Furthermore, Unger offers
no account of the motives that would make context-breaking
attractive and says little about the desires by which it may be
driven, save for the overriding desire for change itself. It is clear
that Unger takes the goal of democratic society to be the creation

---

[14] There is a Nietzschean "solution" to this problem, which is to subjectivize force
or law (as "will to power") but to recognize that it necessarily contests and
opposes another, external will. This is Nietzsche's way of inheriting Hegel's
dialectic of master and slave. See chapter 7 below.
[15] Unger, *Social Theory*, p. 21.

of structures that are open to radical change. But can transformation be both its own justification and its own goal?

In order to probe these issues further, I want to return to the work of Ernesto Laclau. As we have already had occasion to glimpse, Laclau's commitment to social change, though decidedly post-Enlightenment in its theoretical orientation, is unmistakably romantic and modernist in its roots. Moreover, his understanding of the aesthetic mode of the political assumes that something like a political domain has in fact survived the devastations that Horkheimer and Adorno saw as a consequence of the Enlightenment. In response to their arguments, Laclau holds the belief that the Enlightenment did not turn out to be a dead end as far as politics is concerned. On the contrary, he argues that new political movements have been able to flourish because the foundations of Enlightenment democracy – located in the ideals of "equality," "autonomy," "legitimation," and "emancipation" – were structurally incomplete, not just historically unfinished projects, as Habermas would have it. If the discourse of democracy proved self-limiting theoretically, it was not because its goals went unrealized, but rather because its very formulation, which required a universal stance, made it impossible to credit the force of those particulars that turned out to be necessary for the achievement of its goals:

What we're seeing now . . . is not the entry into a world of repetition and vacancy, but the disintegration of that dimension of globality inherent to classical emancipatory discourses. It is not the specific demands of the emancipatory projects formulated since the Enlightenment which have gone into crisis; it is the idea that the whole of those demands constituted a unified whole and would be realized in a single foundational act by a privileged agent of historical change . . . it is not this or that "privileged agent" which is being questioned, but the category of "privileged agent" itself. (*New Reflections*, pp. 214–15)

In other words, democratic politics has survived as a realm of open contestation and struggle in part because the Enlightenment version of democracy failed to fully constitute the polis around the global ideals of "equality" and "autonomy." Indeed, Laclau argues that the weakening of the foundationalist ambitions of the Enlightenment's emancipatory discourses can in turn lead to a better understanding of democracy and to "freer" societies: "it is precisely this decline in the great myths of emancipation, universality and rationality which is leading to freer societies: where human beings see themselves as the builders and agents of change of their own world, and thus come to realize that they are not tied by the objective necessity of history to any institutions or ways of life – either in the present or in the future" (*New Reflections*, p. 216).

Laclau's position overlaps with Unger's anti-necessitarianism in that both seek to radicalize the contextualist principles inherent in the modernist tradition. Yet their solutions differ noticeably, in part because they begin from contrasting assumptions about the deep structure of democracy itself. Whereas Unger takes the classical antinomies of Enlightenment thought as the central point of reference for any analysis of democracy, Laclau locates the essential facts about modern democracy in an analysis of its "dislocated" symbolic social formation. Drawing principally on the work of the political theorist Claude Lefort, whose understanding of democracy combines a rereading of Hobbesian political theory with reflections on French revolutionary thought, Laclau suggests that the "democratic revolution" of the early modern period produced a profound shift within the symbolic structure of society. The result was the formation of a web of relations that was "essentially incomplete." Lefort's capsule summary of some of the differences between democratic and pre-democratic societies helps clarify this point. In pre-democratic societies, power was incorporated in the person of the king or prince, who was thought of as the representative of God. In democratic societies, by contrast, the central site of power is essentially empty. In attempting to displace authority from the sovereign to the people, power and law were divested of their transcendental guarantees:[16] "of all the regimes of which we know," writes Lefort, modern democracy is "the only one to have represented power in such a way as to show that power is an *empty place* and to have thereby maintained a gap between the symbolic and the real. It does so by virtue of a discourse which reveals that power belongs to no one; that those

[16] Commenting on Lefort, Laclau and Mouffe write that "every attempt to establish a definitive suture and to deny the radically open character of the social which the logic of democracy institutes, leads to what Lefort designates as 'totalitarianism': that is to say, to a logic of construction of the political which consists of establishing a point of departure from which society can be perfectly mastered and known" (*HSS*, p. 187).

who exercise power do not possess it; that they do not, indeed, embody it; that the exercise of power requires a periodic and repeated conquest; that the authority of those vested with power is created and re-created as a result of the manifestation of the will of the people."[17] Indeed, the constitution of a democratic society requires an evacuation of the site of power. The promise of emancipation is thus tied to the fact that democratic societies remain without any "positive determination." Behind the symbols of democratic power stands an "ought" grounded not in a transcendental authority – and certainly not in any materializable thing – but at best in another "ought." No doubt, this is the source of the primary passion that governs the Hobbesian state – fear, not as a positivity, but as the symptom of an essential lack. Lefort: "It is because the division of power does not, in a modern democracy, refer to an *outside* that can be assigned to the Gods, the city or holy ground; because it does not refer to an inside that can be assigned to the substance of the community. Or, to put it another way, it is because there is no materialization of the *Other* – which would allow power to function as a mediator, no matter how it were defined – that there is no materialization of the *One* – which would allow power to function as an incarnation" (*Democracy and Political Theory*, p. 226).[18]

There are consequences that follow from this view. First, the democratic construction of power as an "empty site" anchors a social logic in which appeals to community or calls for a restoration of the "wholeness" of the social order can only designate the force of a desire in search of an object that is "impossible" by virtue of the evacuation of its central site of power. This structural flaw in turn produces an unrepairable breach between the symbols of power and "real" power:

Modern democracy is . . . the only regime to indicate the gap between the symbolic and the real by using the notion of a power which no one – no prince and no minority – can seize. It has the virtue of relating society to the experience of its institution. When an empty place emerges, there can be no possible conjunction between power, law and knowledge, and their foundations cannot possibly be enunciated. The being of the social van-

[17] Claude Lefort, *Democracy and Political Theory*, trans. David Macey (Minneapolis: University of Minnesota Press, 1988), p. 225.
[18] The thrust of Lefort's argument has to do with the incomplete separation of the political from the theological.

ishes or, more accurately, presents itself in the shape of an endless series of questions . . . The ultimate markers of certainty are destroyed, and at the same time there is born a new awareness of the unknown element in history, of the gestation of humanity in all the variety of its figures.

(Lefort, *Democracy and Political Theory*, p. 228)

For a thinker like Habermas, such an analysis would raise fears that the democratic polis cannot possibly be the site of *legitimate* power. According to Laclau, there are two features of democracy that can make this indeterminacy worth the price: the hope of freedom and the promise of radical change.

Laclau's investment in notions like "dislocation" and "opacity" is meant to ensure that there will remain possibilities for political transformation in spite of the fact that "revolutionary action" as classically understood by thinkers on the Left (i.e. as action by a "universal subject of history") has been displaced by the contingencies of the new "particularisms" mentioned above. What is the source of these new particularisms and what is the nature of the agency associated with them? In approaching this issue, it is important to dissociate what Laclau means by "particularism" from the "individualism" of liberal democratic theory, if only because the rational "individual" as exemplified, e.g., in the Rawlsian theory of justice, in fact presupposes a theoretical position from which it could survey all possible choices and interests with a knowledge that any other individual might in principle also possess. The individual of the "original position" in Rawlsian liberalism is abstract and general, a consequence of the evacuation of particularity. As Žižek has pointed out, classical conceptions of democracy erase the particularities of race, gender, class, etc., so as to include everyone "without regard" to race, sex, religion, wealth, or social status.[19]

By contrast with the individualism of classical democratic theory, Laclau's "particularism" is informed by a conception of

[19] Žižek, *Looking Awry* (Cambridge, MA: MIT Press, 1991), p. 163. As Žižek elsewhere says, "the Rawlsian liberal-democratic idea of distributive justice ultimately relies on a 'rational' individual who is able to abstract a particular position of enunciation, to look upon himself or herself and all others from a neutral place of pure 'metalanguage' and thus to perceive all their 'true interests.' This individual is the supposed subject of the social contract that establishes the coordinates of justice. What is thereby *a priori* left out of consideration is the realm of fantasy in which a community organizes its way of life' (its mode of enjoyment)." Žižek, "Eastern European Liberalism and its Discontents," *New German Critique*, 57 (Fall, 1992), 44.

society as a set of internally mediated relations which admit neither of any "original position," nor of any "beyond" from which all options can be surveyed and an equilibrium of power assured. Every position is, in the Nietzschean sense, "perspectival." Any stance from which possible social choices could be surveyed, no matter how abstract, general, or seemingly universal, would itself be a social stance, hence not only particular in the empirical sense but also contingent. The result for Laclau is an understanding of the polis as a network of relations characterized by an irreducible set of antagonisms. Seen from the perspective of these antagonisms, the notion of an Archimedean "original position" is likely to appear as a purely fictional (not to say ideological) stance.[20]

As first articulated with Chantal Mouffe in the book *Hegemony and Socialist Strategy* (1985) and as later amplified in his *New Reflections on the Revolution of our Time* (1990), the theory of antagonism that forms the background for Laclau's understanding of "particularism" originates within the context of a rethinking of the Hegelian-bred notion of "contradiction" in light of Derrida's view of the "constitutive outside" or "necessary surplus" characteristic of all structures:

The Hegelian conception of contradiction subsumed within it both social antagonisms and the processes of natural change. This was possible insofar as contradiction was conceived as an internal moment of the concept; the rationality of the real was the rationality of the system, with any "outside" excluded by definition. In our conception of antagonism, on the other hand, we are faced with a "constitutive outside." It is an "outside" which blocks the identity of the "inside" (and is, nonetheless, the prerequisite for its constitution at the same time). With antagonism, denial does not originate from the "inside" of identity itself but, in its

[20] Laclau's position has an obvious resonance with Rorty's neo-pragmatist program of "contingency, irony, and solidarity." There is nonetheless an imperative at work in Rorty's project that is legible in terms of a modernist agenda that would privilege (or indeed, demand) the new. In spite of himself, Rorty's demand for "newer, more interesting" modes of self-description is symptomatic of a boredom with metaphysics. In Rorty, the pleasure of the aesthetic is coupled with a very particular sort of disinterest, namely, with a lack of interest in the transcendental position that sustains the Enlightenment notion of critique. At the same time, Rorty's refusal of any and all foundations represents a protracted development of Kant's effort to define a "sphere" (the aesthetic) in terms of its radical exclusion of all interest. Finally, Rorty's demand to present newer, more interesting phrases represents an outcome of the Enlightenment dialectic of boredom and genius.

most radical sense, *from outside*; it is thus pure facticity which cannot be referred back to any underlying rationality.     (*New Reflections*, p. 17)

This is the basis upon which Laclau proposes to refashion democracy so as to open the polis to the possibility of radical (revolutionary) change. The polis is contingent not just in the sense that the interests that comprise it cannot be derived from any conception of its essence; it is contingent in the more radical sense that its structure is inherently incomplete. What can be identified as the irreducible "difficulty" of a politics that insists upon the contingency of social relations nonetheless provides an imperative for democracy: "there is no radical and plural democracy without renouncing the discourse of the universal and its implicit assumption of a privileged point of access to 'the truth' which can be reached only by a limited number of subjects" (*HSS*, pp. 191–92). This in turn indicates what Laclau formulates as the "dislocation" of structures: "affirmation of a 'ground' which lives only by negating its fundamental character; of an 'order' which exists only as a partial limiting of disorder; of a 'meaning' which is constructed only as excess and paradox in the face of meaninglessness – in other words, the field of the political as the space for a game which is never 'zero-sum,' because the rules and the players are never fully explicit" (*HSS*, p. 193).

This conception of the polis in turn has implications for the ways in which we understand the role of agency in relation to historical change. As we have seen in connection with Kant's essay on progress, history in the classical Enlightenment view was linked to the notion of a universal subject. Even for Hegel and Marx history was tied to the actions of "essential" agents, whether individuals or a class. "Understanding history consists of an operation of recognition in which essential actors, whose fundamental identity is known in advance, are identified in the empirical actors personifying them . . . The *eidos* dominates exclusively and history is therefore a history without 'outside'" (*New Reflections*, pp. 21–22). For Laclau and Mouffe, by contrast, the task is to theorize a form of democracy in which there is no universal agent to serve as the essential agent in the drama of change. Rather than suggest, with Unger, that such change will occur as the result of the intermittent work of exceptional individuals, Laclau and Mouffe suggest that it will happen as a result of the antagonistic forces inherent within democratic structures, which by definition cannot be resolved.

*Pace* Horkheimer and Adorno, then, the consequences of Enlightenment rationality could not have been a foreclosure of the possibilities of democracy. Rather, a productive series of new antagonisms has emerged out of the reactions to the Enlightenment:

The fact that these "new antagonisms" are the expression of forms of resistance to the commodification, bureaucratization and increasing homogenization of social life itself explains why they should frequently manifest themselves through a proliferation of particularisms, and crystallize into a demand for autonomy itself. It is also for this reason that there is an identifiable tendency towards the valorization of "differences" and the creation of new identities which tend to privilege "cultural" criteria (clothes, music, language, regional traditions, and so on) . . . For this reason many of these forms of resistance are made manifest not in the form of collective struggles, but through an increasingly affirmed individualism.                                                        (*HSS*, p. 164)

The question in turn is how to radicalize democracy in light of what these changes reveal about its structure – that it is essentially "dislocated" or "incomplete."

Although Laclau's engagement with the philosophical tradition places him in the line of Hegel and Derrida, the crucial notions of "contingency" and "antagonism" can nonetheless be aligned with the difficulty of aesthetic reflective judgment as formulated in the third *Critique*. There is, to be sure, an orthodox reading of Kant that emphasizes the "radical contingency" of our natural existence relative to our moral being.[21] It is this contingency that makes it so surprising to find that nature does indeed contain the basis for assuming a "lawful harmony" between its products and our disinterested delight. But, as Paul Guyer rightly insists, there is no guarantee that we will in fact reach an accommodation with nature.[22] Among post-Kantian theorists of radical democracy such as Laclau, the subject formed as the result of contingency displaces the subject whose identity is determined in relation to some form of "universal judgment," especially the universal judgment of sovereignty or right. Its social context is that of a

[21] Paul Guyer, *Kant and the Experience of Freedom* (Cambridge: Cambridge University Press, 1993), p. 183.
[22] *Ibid.*, p. 183.

radical, Nietzschean heterogeneity, such as likewise obtains among Lyotard's various phrase-regimes, where no term can claim validity by seeking in a transcendent or underlying ground the rule of meaning ordering them all. Indeed, Laclau and Mouffe suggest that such heterogeneity involves a modification of the very notion of a "theoretical position":

The critique of the category of the unified subject, and the recognition of the discursive dispersion within which every subject position is constituted, therefore involve something more than the enunciation of a general theoretical position: they are the *sine qua non* for thinking the multiplicity out of which antagonisms emerge in societies in which the democratic revolution has crossed a certain threshold. This gives us a theoretical terrain on which the basis of the notion of *radical and plural democracy* . . . finds the first conditions under which it can be apprehended. Only if it is accepted that the subject positions cannot be led back to a positive and unitary founding principle – only then can pluralism be considered radical. Pluralism is *radical* only to the extent that *each term of this plurality of identities finds within itself the principle of its own validity, without this having to be sought in a transcendent or underlying positive ground for the hierarchy of meaning of them all and the source and guarantee of their legitimacy.* (*HSS*, pp. 167–68; last emphasis added)

This formulation, which represents a postmodern political version of reflective judgment, allows Laclau and Mouffe to overcome the logic in terms of which social struggles have traditionally been interpreted by critics on the Left. If one rejects the categorical status of the "working class," if one ceases to expect this class to assume the position of a universal subject-agent of history, then it becomes possible to recognize the irreducibility of the conflicts that are grouped under the heading of "workers' struggles." These conflicts cannot be described in terms of a single set of interests that is in any way privileged, central, or categorically distinct from all others. Laclau points to the ill-fated notion of "objective class interests" in support of this analysis. In order to fill the gap between the "universal" consciousness imputed to the working class and the "actual consciousness" of workers, the Communist Party set itself up as the representative of the interests of workers as a class. The result was what Laclau describes as "an enlightened despotism of intellectuals and bureaucrats" who attempted to speak in the name of the masses, who proposed to articulate their "true interests," but who in fact did nothing more than impose various forms of control upon them.[23] As Žižek points out in his essay on "Eastern European Liberalism and its Discontents," liberalism just as easily falls into a similar trap. Perhaps ironically, liberalism tends to secrete an attachment to "particularity" that turns out to be as "ideological" as the universalism it was meant to displace.

I will discuss Žižek's position in greater detail below. As far as Laclau and Mouffe are concerned, the essential fact of modern democracy lies in the realization that, since at least the 1960s, many movements on the Left, including ecologism, the student protest movements, and feminism, have found themselves in a position analogous to that of the working class in Marxism. While all these groups have from time to time adopted the rhetoric of romantic and modernist revolutionary optimism, none found it satisfying to occupy the position of a new, privileged agent of historical change. But Laclau and Mouffe go on to say that the condition of this impossibility is in fact necessary to the success of these movements. For if the fate of these groups is merely to reoccupy the place of a universal subject of history, then their efforts to reimagine democracy as a set of more radically contingent and transformable relations will have failed. On the contrary, these new social movements represent enhancements of the project of democracy only insofar as they recognize that they cannot occupy a position that will speak universally; in this they also remain faithful to the fundamental insight that all politics is local: "all struggles, whether those of workers or other political subjects, left to themselves, have a partial character, and can be articulated to [*sic*] very different discourses. It is this articulation which gives them their character, not the place from which they come. There is therefore no subject – nor, further, any 'necessity' – which is absolutely radical and irrecuperable by the dominant order, and which constitutes an absolutely guaranteed point of departure for a total transformation. (Equally, there is nothing which permanently assures the stability of an established order)" (*HSS*, p. 169).

In place of a subject with "an absolutely guaranteed point of departure for a total transformation" of society, Laclau and Mouffe think of the polis as the site of a series of partial and

[23] Laclau, *New Reflections*, pp. 91–92.

contingent struggles, with goals that can be mapped onto different and sometimes conflictive discourses, and which may in turn have a transformative effect upon them. The proliferation of new "particularisms" resistant to the original conception of democracy is in turn responsible for a shift in what we might understand "democracy" to involve.[24] For example, the democratic struggle for equality may be articulated through the discourse of feminism; but this articulation is likely to transform what we might expect the struggle for equality to produce. Likewise, the desire for community can be aligned with the interests of a global ecologism; but a commitment to ecologism would no doubt alter our notion of what we would expect a democratic community to include, or of how we regard those things it excludes. Each of these intersections revises our conception of what democracy might mean, but none of them alone nor all of them together represents democracy or the democratic subject as such. For Laclau in contrast to Unger, this suggests that the democratic polis is not merely a sum of the concrete interests comprising it, but is instead an "impossible object," one that is resistant to closure. Expanding on this same point, Žižek explains how the democratic subject (the "participant in the struggle for democracy") gradually learns that his or her position is an impossible one. The fact of this "impossibility" is a consequence of the familiar Hegelian dialectic of concept and experience, with the exception that the notion of democracy that results defies those cartoon versions of Hegel which portray the absolute as bereft of all contradiction:

insofar as the participant in the struggle for democracy "finds out by experience" that there is no real democracy without the emancipation of women, insofar as the participant in the ecological struggle "finds out by experience" that there is no real reconciliation with nature without abandoning the aggressive-masculinist attitude towards nature, insofar as the participant in the peace-movement "finds out by experience" that there is no real peace without radical democratization, etc., that is to say, insofar as the identity of each of the four above-mentioned positions is marked with the metaphoric surplus of the other three positions, we can say that something like a unified subject-position is being constructed: to be a democrat means at the same time to be a feminist, etc. What we must not overlook is, of course, that such a unity is always radically contingent, the result of symbolic condensation, and not an expression of some kind of

---

[24] Laclau and Mouffe, *HSS*, p. 164.

internal necessity according to which the interests of all the above-mentioned positions would in the long run "objectively convene."

("Beyond Discourse Analysis," in *New Reflections*, pp. 250–51)

There are several consequences that follow from these arguments. First, the romantic notion of revolution as bringing about a total or final transformation of society must be set aside. As Laclau and Mouffe argue, "if the various subject positions and the diverse antagonisms and points of rupture constitute a *diversity* and not a *diversification*, it is clear that they cannot be led back to a point from which they could all be embraced and explained by a single discourse" (*HSS*, p. 191). Laclau remains a (post)modernist, but one for whom discursive "discontinuity" rather than simple transformation or a commitment to the new is definitive of the political nature of social relations. The role of each "discontinuous" discourse is not just to contribute to the greater diversity of the whole but to comprehend itself in relation to a social "whole" that is understood as unattainable because dislocated, even fantasmatic. As we will see further below, Žižek takes the work of Laclau one step further: he argues that the points of "condensation" around which revolutionary action converges bear the traces of this discontinuity in the form of a visible split or gap between subject and symbolic structure. He offers the striking example of rebels in Romania after the fall of Ceaucescu waving the national flag with the Communist red star cut out, so that instead of the flag serving as a symbol of national unity, there was nothing but a hole in the center. As Žižek remarks, "it is difficult to imagine a more salient index of the 'open' character of a historical situation 'in its becoming.'"[25]

Second, the Marxist notion of ideology, traditionally founded upon a concept of "false consciousness" that understands itself against the ideal of transparent relations in the social whole must be substantially revised. Critics generally thought of as conservative, including Habermas, have often pointed out that poststructuralism would seem to present an insurmountable obstacle for the theory of ideology: if every social structure is decentered, the argument goes, if the search for identity reveals nothing but what Laclau describes as a "kaleidoscopic movement of differences,"

[25] Žižek, *Tarrying With the Negative: Kant, Hegel, and Critique of Ideology* (Durham, NC: Duke University Press, 1993), p. 1.

then what might it mean to say that subjects "misrecognize" themselves? Laclau proposes to "solve" this dilemma by redefining the notion of ideology in a way that reflects the antagonistic nature of the social order. Rather than think of ideology as that which obstructs subjects from coming to know their true essence, of reconciling their particular, historical being with the universal essence of mankind, he takes ideology as the prevailing form of the misrecognition of the dislocation of all structure. Accordingly, the most "ideological" position would be the one that dreams of a seamless suture: "the ideological would consist of those discursive forms through which a society tries to institute itself as such on the basis of closure, of the fixation of meaning, of the non-recognition of the infinite play of differences. The ideological would be the will to 'totality' of any totalizing discourse" (*New Reflections*, p. 92). So seen, the contrast is not between ideology and truth, but between the closure of a society modeled along the lines of a *Vernunftrepublik* and the potentially sublime, transformative discontinuities that a radical reconception of democracy promises for political life.

Laclau's theory of radical democracy remains indebted to Kant's third *Critique* insofar as notions like "contingency," "antagonism," and "dislocation" all represent postmodern versions of the difficulty that Kant identifies with the ambition of reflective aesthetic judgment to bridge the gap between the phenomenal and noumenal worlds. It is a theory that couples the modernist desire to embrace the new with a revolutionary optimism that bears traces of a political romanticism, all the while marking its sharp differences from romanticism and modernism.

In discussing Kant, Jean-François Lyotard adopts a premise that is nearly identical with the one we saw in Arendt, namely, that since Kant's "Critique of Political Reason" was never written, whatever politics one might wish from Kant must be sought in the theory of reflective aesthetic judgment. Lyotard's "aesthetic" understanding of justice in the theory of the differend is likewise indebted to Kant's third *Critique* – with the exception that Lyotard eliminates "pleasure" and "pain" so as to make judgment into a "political" version of the Nietzschean "yes and no of the palate": "I propose that we overlook that [the *Critique of Judgment*] is a critique of the feeling of pleasure and pain, and consider it exclusively as a critique of feeling, and I further propose to translate feeling by the simple assertion: *I am for, I am against, yes, no.* Assent granted or denied. I think that it is this sort of feeling that is put into play by any political judgment."[26] *Pace* Lyotard, I would suggest, first, that the affective subject must be acknowledged, and second that it must be imagined as acting within a symbolic domain if we are to speak of it as the "subject of justice" – a subject that not only chooses but also wills and wills, moreover, *as* a certain kind of person, with desires, passions, and attachments in addition to fears.[27] Moreover, Lyotard is concerned with the heterogeneity peculiar to the field of discourse rather than with the sympathetic identification that demands to be understood in terms of an aesthetic critique. This heterogeneity is vividly described in *The Differend*. Beginning from the notion that the Kantian faculties are capacities for cognition in the broad sense, but ultimately reading "faculties" as "genres of discourse," Lyotard goes on to say that

Each genre of discourse would be like an island; the faculty of judgment would be, at least in part, like an admiral or like a provisioner of ships who would launch expeditions from one island to the next, intended to present one island what was found (or invented, in the archaic sense of the word) in the other, and which might serve the former as "as-if intuition" with which to validate it. Whether war or commerce, this interventionist force has no object, and does not have its own island, but it requires a milieu – this would be the sea – the *Archipelago* or primary sea as the Aegean was once called.[28]

It is nonetheless important to recall the fact that the theory of reflective judgment as elaborated in Kant would seem to present a great difficulty for any theory of justice insofar as aesthetic judgment refuses to name its object-field. Whereas judgment in the legal sphere seems obliged to operate over a determinate territory if it is to claim legitimacy, Kantian aesthetic theory does not claim a domain of objects as properly its own; but neither is it a success-

---

[26] Jean-François Lyotard and Jean-Loup Thébaud, *Just Gaming*, trans. Wlad Godzich (Minneapolis: University of Minnesota Press, 1985), pp. 81–82.

[27] See Charles Altieri, "Judgment and Justice Under Postmodern Conditions," in Reed Way Dasenbrock, ed., *Redrawing the Lines: Analytic Philosophy, Deconstruction, and Literary Theory* (Minneapolis: University of Minnesota Press, 1989), p. 73.

[28] Lyotard, *The Differend: Phrases in Dispute*, trans. Georges van den Abbeele (Minneapolis: University of Minnesota Press, 1988), pp. 130–31.

ful "meta"-critique of all other object-spheres. As we have seen, it is defined negatively and by exclusion rather than by virtue of any positive identifications or claims. Indeed, even the feelings of "pleasure" and "pain" in Kant arise primarily in relation to what cognition and morality fail to embrace. Similarly, Kant defines aesthetic pleasure in terms of its refusal or rejection of interest, rather than in terms of the interests that positively constitute it. More conventional demands for justice, by contrast, are associated with a territorial delimitation of the powers of judgment. (Hence Kant's own recourse to the metaphors of "territory" and "realm" in defining the scope of the faculties of pure reason and practical reason, as if to claim for them the legitimacy of the legal sphere.) One of the most prominent features of Lyotard's theory of justice is that it allows him to respect the territorial indeterminacy of Kant's theory of aesthetics. At the same time, his notion of the differend represents an attempt to move from the aesthetic self-criticism of the Enlightenment to a more general statement of the situation and the task of reflective judgment in contemporary democratic societies.

In Lyotard, what is for Kant a crisis or impasse in Enlightenment thought – the inability to bring the system of critical thinking to a close – forms a context in which heterogeneous articulations vie contentiously with one another, but in which certain of those articulations are refused access to power. Lyotard replaces the demand for judgment in the form of an appeal to a higher tribunal with a notion of judgment as a way of recognizing claims that cannot be heard given the distribution of power of existing orders of discourse or "phrase regimes." Rather than think of judgment as the mechanism through which the claims of conflictive parties might be evaluated or ranked and the differences among them brought before some higher critical authority, Lyotard thinks of the differend as a means for registering the costs entailed in thinking of justice as a reconciliation of the differences among incommensurable standpoints. And rather than presuppose that the basis for judgment lies in the unity or shareability of experience, Lyotard invokes the incommensurability of phrase-regimes as a way to radicalize what Laclau and Lefort describe as the "essential vacancy" of the structure of democratic societies.

Especially in *The Differend*, but also in "Sensus Communis," *Just Gaming*, *Peregrinations*, and *Lessons on the Analytic of the Sublime*,

Lyotard uses Kant's theory of aesthetic judgment in order to rethink the relationship between the particular and the universal so as to reject both the "tyranny of concepts" that Horkheimer and Adorno feared as a consequence of the Enlightenment and the skeptical empiricism that would dispense with the possibility of judgment entirely. If questions of justice arise principally in cases where the relationship between particulars and universals is problematic, then neither rationalism (which grants a privilege to the universal over the particular) nor empiricism (which privileges particulars) is likely to be adequate to it. Neither one responds to cases in which a particular is brought into being as a consequence of its incommensurability with the universal. In an effort to address this issue, Lyotard attempts to make explicit the critical potential of Kant's de-territorialization of the aesthetic by identifying a form of judgment that would be immune to the pitfalls of both rationalism and empiricism.

In the ambit of the differend, the task of judgment is to deal with complaints that arise within the context of structures that preclude them from being recognized as such. A given appeal for justice may well originate in or incite pain, but it is not reducible to pain in the experiential sense. Rather, its status as a complaint and its alliance with what Adorno called "suffering" are functions of what cannot be said within the context of the social structures in force. Unlike what we think of as "litigation," in which the disputing parties recognize a common body of rules and acknowledge a common judge, the differend involves instances in which no covering law will apply to all the parties in a dispute; it is "a conflict between two parties that cannot be equitably resolved due to lack of a rule of judgment applicable to both arguments" (*The Differend*, p. xi). In Hegelian terms, the differend would constitute an instance of "infinite judgment."[29] Its very existence is a sign that the social whole is defined by an exclusionary violence, an indication that the very structure of society creates voices it cannot hear or must mis-recognize. "Differends" are created by the silent force of this necessary exclusion: "I would like to call a *differend* [*différend*] the case where the plaintiff is divested of the means to argue and becomes for that reason a victim. If the addressor, the addressee, and the sense of the testimony are neutralized, every-

---

[29] *Hegel's Logic*, trans. William Wallace (Oxford: Oxford University Press, 1975), p. 238.

thing takes place as if there were no damages" (*The Differend*, p. 9).

Lyotard's work thus provides a way of identifying the critical potential of reflective judgment by naming the force that prohibits certain domains of experience from entering the sphere of "legitimate" knowledge and thereby being brought under judgment. It attempts to radicalize the political consequences of the indeterminacy we find in Kant's third *Critique* by recognizing that judgment is neither a faculty with a "proper" (i.e. well-formed) object nor a means for adjudicating the competing claims of all the other faculties (e.g., morality and cognition). The judgment of the differend represents an effort to capture the force of this indeterminacy for a critique of the violence inherent in a conception of the polis as a domain in which discourse and action are assessed according to the principles of finality and/or cause.

Lyotard identifies the fundamental "gap" or "dislocation" of structures specifically with the position of those who are victimized by them. Consider in this regard Lyotard's remarks about the continuation of Marxism beyond what would seem to have been its end as a method of historical analysis. Marxism remains a viable mode of critique insofar as it is able to recognize those who are forced to suffer on account of capital's ambition to subsume every alternative mode of articulation: "The wrong [suffered by a class of bourgeois society] is expressed through the silence of feeling, through suffering. The wrong results from the fact that all phrase universes and all their linkages are or can be subordinated to the sole finality of capital . . . and judged accordingly. Because this finality seizes upon or can seize upon all phrases, it makes a claim to universality" (*The Differend*, p. 171). Just as Laclau and Mouffe think of social relations in terms of an irreducible antagonism, Lyotard conceives of structure as implicitly exclusionary and violent. Lyotard's theory of the differend projects a vision of the polis as a space in which victims struggle to gain a voice, only to find that they have restructured the polis such that others will in turn be victimized by it. Thus while Lyotard is able to demonstrate the ethical importance of identifying those who remain outside the system, the position of Lyotard's "victim" is unstable; indeed, the victim is in Hegelian terms dialectically identical with the criminal insofar as both call the universality of law into question. Žižek's remarks on a related subject in *For They Know Not What They Do* speak to this point: "in contrast to a legal conflict before the courts where both sides invoke particular laws one after another, yet both admit universal law (legality) as the obligatory medium, the criminal act calls into question the general sphere of law itself, law as such."[30] This analysis in turn follows Hegel's description of crime as an example of "negatively infinite judgment": "the person committing a crime, such as a theft, does not, as in a suit about civil rights, merely deny the particular right of another person to some one definite thing. He denies the right of that person in general, and therefore he is not merely forced to restore what he has stolen, but is punished in addition, because he has violated the law as law, i.e. law in general."[31]

Even on Lyotard's own account, the success of the differend depends upon a reduction of the dislocation among phrase regimes whereby the differend is transformed into litigation. The reduction of this dislocation in turn depends upon an understanding of the notion of "critique" that bears clear links to Enlightenment thought: "The analogy resulting from the als ob is an illusion when the differences are forgotten and the differend smothered. It succeeds in being critical, on the contrary, if the modes of forming and validating phrases are distinguished and if the fully disclosed differend can thereafter, following Kant's hope, be transformed into a litigation" (*The Differend*, p. 123). In other words, the Lyotardian differend understands its critical mission as dependent upon a "full articulation" of the differences among phrase-regimes. If "full articulation" is achieved, then otherwise unrecognizable complaints can be brought under the law as part of the process of litigation. The result is a confirmation of the universality of law – of legality as such – that is consonant with Enlightenment thought.

In concluding this discussion I want to consider the work of Slavoj Žižek, whose Lacanian readings of Hegel and Kant represent one

[30] Žižek, *For They Know Not What They Do: Enjoyment as a Political Factor* (London: Verso, 1991), p. 118. Cf. Lyotard himself, who writes that "The phrase of judgment still needs to be legitimated. That is the charge of normative discourse, of law in general, and of the law of the law (constitutional law)," *The Differend*, p. 149.

[31] *Hegel's Logic*, p. 238. Cf. Hegel's analysis of crime and punishment in *The Spirit of Christianity and its Fate*, in *Early Theological Writings*, trans. T. M. Knox (Philadelphia: University of Pennsylvania Press, 1975), p. 228. Jürgen Habermas takes up this subject in his essay on Hegel's Jena *Philosophy of Mind* in *Theory and Practice*, trans. John Viertel (Boston: Beacon Press, 1973), pp. 148–49.

of the most salient examples of the paradoxical fact that the postmodern opposition to the Enlightenment is in fact a continuation of it. As far as politics is concerned, Žižek offers an aesthetic interpretation of Enlightenment thought insofar as he attempts to reestablish the validity of pleasure (in Žižek's terms, "enjoyment") as a critical category for political analysis. While Žižek shares many of the presuppositions of the aesthetic critique of politics articulated by Unger, Lyotard, and especially Laclau, he is nonetheless cautious to avoid claiming victory for the notion of a "dislocated" structure if this involves a reductive understanding of the concept of "totality." Specifically, Žižek proposes to demonstrate the multifarious ways in which contradiction is not eliminated by but itself forms part of the Hegelian concept of the whole. In so doing, Žižek offers a dislocated concept of totality that bears striking resemblance to the Kantian notion of the irreducible "difficulty" that inhabits the project of reflective aesthetic judgment. The difference between Žižek and his philosophical predecessors, however, lies in the fact that the Slovenian understands the "indeterminacy" of structures as arising not just from the impossibility of synthesis or transcendence but rather from the ineluctibility of the very *desire for* transcendence. Inevitably, this desire meets with some impediment which, as a form of the Lacanian Real, gives rise to ever new symbolizations by means of which one may endeavor to "integrate," "domesticate," or otherwise reduce it, but which simultaneously consigns those efforts to failure (see *For They Know*, p. 100). This kernel of the Real, this impediment that provokes symbolic condensations, is on Žižek's account rigorously "non-historical." Indeed, history is itself for Žižek a consequence of the many failed attempts to grasp this strange kernel of the Real (*For They Know*, p. 101).

As Peter Dews has pointed out, Žižek's position is intelligible in relation to the historical circumstances out of which he writes: that of an Eastern European proponent of "Western Marxism" caught in between the moment of Tito's revolution and the breakup of the former Yugoslavia. But it is not reducible to those circumstances. Indeed, the issues revealed by that historical situation are best understood in terms of the much larger Enlightenment project and its reversals. This is to say that the general, structural problem facing Slovenian intellectuals in the early 1980s was not so different from that which Horkheimer and Adorno identified in "The

Concept of Enlightenment" – if not exactly the self-cancellation of the powers of critical reason and the exhaustion of democratic structures, then the transformation of those structures into the sources of political oppression *in the name of democracy*. The task for critical theory in such circumstances was to disclose the "oppressive and manipulative character of a system which was itself based upon the denunciation of bureaucratic manipulation":[32]

> not until the emergence of Yugoslav self-management did Stalinism effectively reach the level of deception in its strictly human dimension. In Stalinism, the deception is still basically a simple one: The power (Party-and-State bureaucracy) feigns to rule in the name of the people while everybody knows that it rules in its own interest . . . in Yugoslav self-management, however, the Party-and-State bureaucracy reigns, but it reigns in the name of an ideology whose basic thesis is that the greatest obstacle to the fulfillment of self-management consists in the "alienated" Party-and-State bureaucracy.[33]

Understood in a somewhat wider scope, this means that the only way to preserve the democratic ideals of "freedom" or "transparency" was to recognize and accept the irreducible element of opacity in all social relationships (*Limits of Disenchantment*, p. 237). Precisely on account of his refusal to reduce this opacity, Žižek regards Lacan as the true heir of Hegel, rather than as yet another post-foundationalist thinker committed to the project of overturning the Enlightenment; indeed, he takes Lacanian theory itself to be "the most radical contemporary version of Enlightenment" (*Sublime Object*, p. 7).

What then is the role of pleasure ("enjoyment") in the formation of political subjects and what is the place of pleasure among antagonisms that define relationships in the modern democratic state? For Žižek, the matter of pleasure is particularly important in relation to a series of issues concerning ethnicity and national identity in the revolutions of Eastern Europe. In spite of assumptions that a natural desire for democracy would flourish as soon as the strictures of totalitarianism were removed, what resulted were in fact a series of ethnic conflicts, where the "ethnos" was defined in relation to a series of unique pleasures and where the antagonists were characterized as posing threats to one's enjoyment. Why was this the case? Leaping from an empirical analysis to a

---

[32] Peter Dews, *The Limits of Disenchantment* (London: Verso, 1995), p. 237.
[33] Žižek, *The Sublime Object of Ideology* (London: Verso, 1989), p. 198.

psychoanalytic account of pleasure, Žižek's answer to this question sheds interesting light on the desire for transparency thought to be essential to democratic structures. Enjoyment reveals itself as a political factor, i.e., as the center of contested desires and fears, insofar as every reference to the "true interests" of agents must be referred to an investment in a fantasy space that is fiercely protected precisely because of the pleasures it provides. The polis is thus marked not so much as a site of conflictive interests (as might have been the case for classical liberalism), but rather as the site of a struggle between individuals' "true interests" on one level and the logic of envy or "theft of enjoyment" that on another level threatens the ideal of harmonious relations: what the "other" threatens is not myself but my fantasy space, along with the enjoyment it yields. The other is thus not merely an antagonist, but the agent of a much-feared "theft of enjoyment" whose very existence threatens to dissolve the space on which my fantasy rests.

Consider, for example, Žižek's interest in the question of nationalism. Why were those who predicted a flowering of democracy in Eastern Europe embarrassed by the eruption of interest in the national "thing"? In Žižek's terms, a nation exists only insofar as it is materialized in a set of social practices and transmitted through national myths that structure these practices. "The national Cause is ultimately nothing but the way subjects of a given ethnic community organize their enjoyment through national myths. What is therefore at stake in ethnic tensions is always the possession of the national Thing. We always impute to the 'other' an excessive enjoyment (by ruining our way of life) . . . what truly bothers me about the 'other' is the peculiar way he organizes his enjoyment, precisely the surplus, the 'excess' that pertains to this way: the smell of 'their' food, 'their' noisy songs and dances, 'their' strange manners, 'their' attitude to work."[34] Following this train of thought, Žižek argues that the element that holds a given community together cannot possibly be reduced to a point of symbolic identification. Much less can it be explained, as in Arendt, as a function of generalized imaginative sympathies. Rather, the bond linking the members of a community is supported by a shared relationship toward a "Thing" – in this case

[34] Žižek, *Tarrying with the Negative*, pp. 202–03.

toward the "Nation qua Thing," i.e., toward a fantasy space that provides a quotient of pleasure above and beyond what it may order or legislate. The Nation-Thing resists description as an object whose features comprise a "specific way of life." There is, as Žižek says, always "something more" in it; *pace* Arendt, this "something more" is the very element that resists materialization, as in the case of the collective but oftentimes unspoken "beliefs" that bind the members of a community: "members of a community who partake in a given 'way of life' *believe in their thing*, where this belief has a reflexive structure proper to the intersubjective space: 'I believe in the (national) Thing' equals 'I believe that others (members of my community) believe in the Thing.' The tautological character of the Thing – its semantic void which limits what we can say about the Thing . . . is founded precisely in this paradoxical reflexive structure. The national Thing exists as long as members of the community believe in it; it is literally an effect of this belief in itself" (*Tarrying*, pp. 201–02).

Insofar as the relationship toward the Thing is structured as a fantasy, it remains the site of irreducible contradictions. Foremost among these is that the Thing is considered both as inaccessible to others and also as threatened by them (*Tarrying*, p. 203). What we conceal by imputing the theft of enjoyment to others is the traumatic fact that we never possessed what was allegedly stolen from us. As in Lacanian psychoanalysis, the lack is not only irreducible but also constitutive. Political circumstances in the former Yugoslavia provide Žižek with a "case study" of precisely such a paradox, riddled as they were with numerous alleged "thefts of enjoyment":

Every nationality has built its own mythology narrating how other nations deprive it of the vital part of enjoyment the possession of which would allow it to live fully . . . Slovenes are being deprived of their enjoyment by "Southerners" (Serbians, Bosnians . . . ) because of their proverbial laziness, Balkan corruption, dirty and noisy enjoyment, and because they demand bottomless economic support, stealing from Slovenes their precious accumulation of wealth by means of which Slovenia would otherwise have already caught up with Western Europe. The Slovenes themselves, on the other hand, allegedly rob the Serbs because of Slovenian unnatural diligence, stiffness, and selfish calculation. Instead of yielding to life's simple pleasures, the Slovenes perversely enjoy constantly devising means of depriving Serbs of the results of their hard labor by commercial profiteering, by reselling what they bought cheaply in Serbia.                                              (*Tarrying*, p. 204)

The theoretical consequences of the transformation of a constitutive lack into the ideologically driven fear of having one's pleasures stolen nonetheless reach well beyond this particular case. One reaction to the discovery of this constitutive lack might well be to invent some form of idealism for the "new particularisms" of which Laclau writes, e.g., to cast ecologism in the form of "New Age Consciousness," with a commitment to the balanced circuit of nature as a "metaphysical" ideal, or, contrastingly, to advocate the dismantling of affirmative action policies in the name of the political ideal of "equality." In opposition to such views, Žižek suggests that we must instead dare to accept the constitutive "lack of identity" characteristic of democratic societies – to risk, in his words, "tarrying with the negative." We must be willing to encounter negativity without asking for the safety that is provided by Kant's account of the sublime. The viability of this recommendation, the value of this risk, is predicated upon the possibility of transforming what is perceived as a purely negative moment or "constitutive lack" into a political virtue, not to say into a moment of enjoyment; it relies not only on the principle of courage that sustains Enlightenment reason, but on the derivation of pleasure from what would seem to be the Enlightenment's unhappiest moment.

Insofar as this is possible at all, we must, on Žižek's account, accept that the functions of democratic institutions are to guarantee the "lack" (non-closure) of the polis, to protect the emptiness of the locus of power, and to insure social cohesion by reinforcing this emptiness. This may nonetheless result in a strengthening of the alienation between subjects and the state;[35] indeed, the democratic state would be a positivization not of anything objective and real, as would be the case for Arendt, but rather of "the *distance* separating the locus of Power from those who exert it" (*For They Know*, p. 269). "Pure" democracy would be possible on the basis of these conditions, which define it as impossible; that impossibility is an enabling defect ("its limit, the irreducible 'pathological'

---

[35] Such is the case with the Hegelian monarch, whom Žižek characterizes as "an empty, formal agency whose task is simply to prevent the current performer of Power (executive) from 'glueing' onto the locus of power – that is, from identifying immediately with it" (*For They Know*, p. 269).

remainder, is its positive contradiction," according to Žižek in *Looking Awry*, p. 166). In contrast to Arendt, who insists upon viewing the state in its ideal form as the locus of non-alienated labor working within a space that is open for all to view, Žižek leaves us to ponder the paradoxical view that the success of democracy depends upon the alienation of those subjects whom the state would most wish to certify as free.

Because the distance between the locus of "Power" and those who exert it can neither vanish nor remain intact, Žižek proposes an accommodation that transforms the "as if" of Kantian thought into a symptom: though we know full well that democracy-in-itself is impossible to attain, we nonetheless act as if it were. Rather than eliminate ideology, this version of the "as if" depends upon what Žižek calls a "fetishistic split" that in turn reduces the impossibility of democracy, makes it once again possible. Far from indicating democracy's fatal flaw, this split becomes democracy's source of strength. It makes modern democracy's empty center, its "nothing," into "something." Whereas totalitarianism was forced to conjure up enemies external to itself (in just the way that the Reagan administration conjured up images of an "Evil Empire"), contemporary democracy must face the fact that, since there is no external enemy, its limit must lie within itself – in the very emptiness of the site of power and in the internal antagonisms that result from this fact. With the assistance of Lacan, Žižek thus adds a new twist to the thesis of the "dialectic of enlightenment" advanced by Horkheimer and Adorno: that the political consequences of the Enlightenment are neither the collapse of democratic structures nor their fulfillment, but a political transformation in which the survival of democracy is enabled by that which limits it most. In theoretical terms, Žižek's analysis of the "loss of the loss" – the recognition that the center is empty, that we never in fact possessed what was lost – yields (de)constructive politics: "when we are faced with a breakdown of the hitherto stable social order, 'loss of loss' names the experience of how this preceding stability was itself false, masking internal strife."[36] It goes nearly without saying that Žižek thereby revokes the presupposition of the unity of experience governing Kant's third *Critique*. But this, Žižek suggests in a further turn of the screw, is precisely

---

[36] *Ibid.*, p. 169.

what the process of judgment reveals: the acknowledgment that all is not in fact "rational," the recognition that antagonism is irreducible, and the discovery that the laws of necessity are valid only in retrospect.

The contingency of structures theorized by Laclau and Mouffe, Unger's contextualist critique of "false necessity," Lyotard's notion of the differend, and Žižek's analysis of enjoyment as a political factor all represent protracted developments of the indeterminacy that Kant attributes to aesthetic reflective judgment in the third *Critique*. In stressing the contextuality of structures and the contingency of contexts, theories of radical democracy sustain a vision of the polis that explains and enables transformation by means of a structural flaw. If the Enlightenment was committed to the superiority of necessity over contingency, then reflective judgment is called upon to account for the primacy of contingency in the world. As Kant had already explained, aesthetic reflection involves a form of potentially infinite judgment where the particular is given first, and the corresponding universal must be found. Postmodern political theory adds to this the recognition that "finding" the universal involves recognizing that it is always already lost. That fact is itself an incitement to come to grips with the role of the affects in shaping political life.

# 6

❖❖❖❖❖❖❖❖❖❖❖❖❖❖❖❖❖❖❖❖❖❖❖❖❖❖❖❖❖❖❖❖❖❖❖❖❖❖❖❖❖❖

# Infinite reflection and
# the shape of praxis

❖❖❖❖❖❖❖❖❖❖❖❖❖❖❖❖❖❖❖❖❖❖❖❖❖❖❖❖❖❖❖❖❖❖❖❖❖❖❖❖❖❖

Žižek's Lacanian analysis of pleasure ("enjoyment") as a political factor represents one of the most ingenious attempts to rethink some of the practical questions that originate in the theory of aesthetic reflective judgment associated with Kant's third *Critique*. Beginning from the familiar deconstructive notion that structures are shaped by a constitutive absence or lack, and then specifying the ways in which the object-substitutes for that lack tend to produce an irrevocable distortion of desire, Žižek transforms the question of reflective judgment into a theory of ideology that bears striking resemblances to a symptomatology of cultural forms.[1] Given the particular "difficulty" associated with aesthetic judgment and its dissociation in Kant from any determinate object-sphere, the linkage between the aporetic "object" of aesthetic reflection and Žižek's Lacanian notion of the symptom is not

[1] For Žižek, as for Lacan, symptoms are in themselves "meaningless" traces; their meaning is constructed retroactively. Žižek's engagement with Hegel on this point is in evidence in, among other places, *Tarrying with the Negative: Kant, Hegel, and the Critique of Ideology* (Durham, NC: Duke University Press, 1993), pp. 143–44. As far as the notion of "symptom" is concerned, Wittgenstein introduces the following caution, which can help us shift from the domain of psychoanalysis to that of judgment: "The fluctuation in grammar between criteria and symptoms makes it look as if there were nothing at all but symptoms. We say, for example: 'Experience teaches that there is rain when the barometer falls, but it also teaches that there is rain when we have certain sensations of wet and cold, or such-and-such visual impressions.' In defense of this one says that these sense-impressions can deceive us. But here one fails to reflect that the fact that the false appearance is precisely one of rain is founded on a definition." Ludwig Wittgenstein, *Philosophical Investigations*, trans. G. E. M. Anscombe (New York: Macmillan, 1953), sec. 354, pp. 112–13. Henceforth cited as *PI*. (I cite the *Philosophical Investigations*, part 1, according to section number and page; I cite part 2 by referencing part and page.)

altogether surprising. Since nothing positive, no substantive "beauty," can be found underlying the passions of pleasure and pain, the aesthetic domain may well appear to be like a realm of symptoms: both are effects ungroundable in any determinate cause. In Kant's language, beauty may be the symbol of morality (*CJ*, sec. 59), but it is in no sense the cause of pleasure.[2] Likewise, Žižek's analysis of ideology is consistent with Kant's account of the peculiar "purposelessness" of art. As Kant explains in his discussion of finality in the *Critique of Judgment* (sec. 10), we find ourselves in the realm of the aesthetic when the representation of an effect precedes, "takes the lead," over its cause (p. 61). As we have already seen, Kant's arguments about the universal validity of aesthetic judgment appeal to the notion of a "common thing" in order to endow the realm of effects with the purposiveness and necessity that we are accustomed to expect of the natural world. But Kant finds that what is held in common is above all a form of feeling or an affect (*sensus communis*), not a thing.[3] Moreover, the aesthetic common sense that Kant invokes in order to establish the validity of the claims made on the basis of these feelings is something that must be both presupposed and (re)created in the very process of making such claims. Because the community to which judgment refers is never fully formed, aesthetic reflection is, in principle at least, infinite in scope.

To see aesthetic judgment in this way requires a distinction between judgments that are ungroundable because infinitely reflective and judgments that are arbitrary or capricious. Whereas the former register subjectivity as a consequence of the contingency of the world, the latter are grounded in assertions of the subjective will. Reflective judgments represent the subject's impli-

---

[2] As Kant also explains, we are not in aesthetic judgments concerned with the "real existence of the thing." *Critique of Judgment*, trans. James Creed Meredith (Oxford: Clarendon Press, 1986), sec. 2, p. 43. (Henceforth cited as *CJ*.) In this respect, Kant is a Nietzschean.

[3] It is worth clarifying that feeling does not occupy a causal link in the chain of aesthetic reflection; one is not entitled to say "the flower is beautiful *because* it gives me pleasure." Kant remarks: "the beautiful and the sublime agree on the point of pleasing on their own account. Further they agree in not presupposing either a judgment of sense or one logically determinant, but one of reflection. Hence it follows that the delight does not depend upon a sensation, as with the agreeable, nor upon a definite concept, as does the delight in the good, although it has, for all that, an indeterminate reference to concepts. Consequently the delight is connected with the mere presentation or faculty of presentation" (*CJ*, sec. 23, p. 90).

cation in what Žižek describes as a "crack" in the Kantian universal, whereas willful or arbitrary judgments represent a form of
subjective self-assertiveness wherein contingency-bred affect has
been replaced by the force of sheer will. As we have seen above, it
is the conflation of these two forms of judgment that leads Habermas to raise fears that a legitimation crisis may result from the
introduction of aesthetic principles into the realm of politics. By
contrast, a politics that is responsive to the contingency of the
world asks us to imagine a form of praxis for which neither an
ideal form of understanding, nor an absolute certainty of judgment, would be enough, but which would instead reckon with the
passions of pleasure and pain as traces of our imbrication in that
very contingency. As we shall see in what follows, a recognition of
the potentially infinite nature of reflection can likewise provide
the basis for a critique of ideology as a sedimented form of
judgment wherein the process of reflection is prematurely, even
forcibly, foreclosed.[4] If traditional accounts of ideology depend
upon a notion of "false consciousness" that in turn takes clear
perception, absolute certainty, and transparent social relations as
ideal norms, then this rethinking of ideology would direct us
toward a critique of those forms of praxis that claim to have
achieved absolute certainty by eliminating any gap between epi-
stemologically certain knowledge and "mere belief." In the process, we can see "ideology" not as an abnormality or a distortion,
but rather as something customary and normal, as part of the
fabric of the "everyday."[5]

Žižek is hardly the first to have noticed the ways in which ideology suppresses the difficulty of judgment. The ideological under-
pinning of social relations that seek to ground themselves in

[4] In thinking of ideology in this way, one could appeal once again to Kant's
suggestion that a certain pleasure and even a wonder accompanied the very first
cognitive judgments, but that this pleasure was subsequently lost as those
judgments became routine. See *CJ*, Introduction, pp. 27–28.

[5] In Žižek's terms, "I know that there is no God, but I respect religious ritual and
take part in it because this ritual supports ethical values and encourages brother-
hood and love among people," or, still more generally, "'I know that there is no
God, but nevertheless, I operate as if (I believe that) he exists." *For They Know Not
What They Do: Enjoyment as a Political Factor* (London: Verso, 1991), pp. 242–43.
Žižek's formulation is from Octave Mannoni, "Je sais bien, mais quand même . . ."
in *Clefs pour l'imaginaire* (Paris: Editions du Seuil, 1968). Cf. Wittgenstein: "When I
talk about language . . . I must speak the language of every day." (*PI*, sec. 120, p.
48.)

absolute certainties is the subject of Roland Barthes's early critique of mythmaking, a critique that takes myth as the fruit of an anthropomorphizing desire for social relations that would appear as grounded in nature itself – for a world that would, ideally, speak itself.[6] In Barthes's early work, "semiology" is meant to provide a methodological resistance to the interpretation of signs as the natural "prose of the world" rather than as the consequences of purely contingent social and historical arrangements. (Cf. Wittgenstein: "Every sign *by itself* seems dead. *What* gives it life? – In use it is *alive*. Is life breathed into it there? Or is the use its life?"[7]) First, Barthes identifies the narrative structures (*mythoi*) by means of which the purposiveness we attribute to nature is reproduced within the world of culture. Second, Barthes identifies "mythical speech" with a depoliticized form of speech that eliminates contradictions and reduces the complexity of human actions. "In passing from history to nature, myth . . . abolishes the complexity of human acts, it gives them the simplicity of essences, it does away with dialectics, with any going back beyond what is immediately visible, it organizes a world which is without contradictions because it is without depth, a world wide open and wallowing in the evident, it establishes a blissful clarity: things appear to mean something by themselves" (*Mythologies*, p. 143). Finally, Barthes's critique of myth confronts the ways in which the bourgeoisie has refused to accept its own contingency as a class by representing itself as naturally justified: "the bourgeoisie has obliterated its name in passing from reality to representation . . . it makes its status undergo an *ex-nominating* operation: the bourgeoisie is defined as *the social class which does not want to be named*" (p. 138); "the bourgeoisie hides the fact that it is the bourgeoisie and thereby produces myth" (p. 146).[8]

---

[6] Ronald Barthes, "Myth Today," in *Mythologies*, trans. Annette Lavers (New York: Hill and Wang, 1972), p. 137.

[7] Wittgenstein, *PI*, sec. 432, p. 128.

[8] Perhaps not surprisingly, Adorno locates the resources for this same "bourgeois" illusion within the aesthetic sphere. On Adorno's account, it was the autonomization of the senses that fueled the naturalistic illusion of the bourgeoisie: "as the principle of replication was eliminated from painting and sculpture and as the use of flourishes in music receded, it became all but inevitable that the elements thus set free (colours, sounds, configurations of words) began to act as though they were able to express something in themselves. This is an illusion, of course, for these elements gain the ability to speak only when placed in some context." *Aesthetic Theory*, ed. Gretel Adorno and Rolf Tiedemann, trans. C. Lenhardt (New York: Routledge and Kegan Paul, 1984), p. 134.

The demythologizing ambition of *Mythologies* leads Barthes to distinguish two kinds of speech. One, described as a "metalanguage," is destined to produce endless repetition and periphrasis. It involves a "speaking about" that attempts to displace the contingency of the world by a system of false necessities and second-order coherences. The other type of speech is described as a "language-object." This mode of speech is imagined as a form of action, a veritable form of world-making not at all unlike the "world disclosure" that Heidegger associates with art. In Barthes's analysis, this is the language of "man the producer," and according to the early Barthes it is only in reclaiming the language of production from a world saturated by myth that one can hope to restore a sense of the complex contingencies of human action. This in turn is the source of Barthes's post-romantic desire to link poetry (*poiēsis*) and revolution:

There is therefore one language which is not mythical, it is the language of man as a producer: wherever man speaks in order to transform reality and no longer to preserve it as an image, wherever he links his language to the making of things, metalanguage is referred to a language-object, and myth is impossible. This is why revolutionary language proper cannot be mythical. Revolution is defined as a cathartic act meant to reveal the political load of the world: it *makes* the world; and its language, all of it, is functionally absorbed in this making. It is because it generates speech which is *fully*, that is to say initially and finally, political, and not, like myth, speech which is initially political and finally natural, that Revolution excludes myth. (*Mythologies*, p. 146)

As this passage clearly demonstrates, however, the convergence of poetry and revolution risks reintroducing the same naturalistic fallacy that Barthes so desperately wants to exclude. It does so because it takes "production" as mode of discourse in which human beings can work directly upon the world – "speaking the world" itself and not merely speaking "about" it. By contrast, Barthes's later work, especially *Camera Lucida*, ascribes significance to human action by invoking a notion of "concrete particularity" that reflects Kant's own emphasis on the difficulty of reflection. Here, Barthes's analysis of the relationship between the *punctum* (the detail or "particular") and the *studium* (the universal subject or social truth) represents a way of recognizing the power of the concrete particular to disrupt the homogeneous social codings in which it is embedded. The *punctum* is not in any sense "created" by the photographer-artist. Rather, photography shows that this irreducible particular, this "it," is the consequence of a passive, unguided relationship between the photograph and the viewer. The *punctum* is not at all unlike "thought" in Nietzsche, which comes not when the ego wants it to but when "it" wants. As such, "it" becomes an objective index of the subjective particular that resists subsumption under principles of universal knowledge or normative social codings (the *studium*). In contrast to the *studium*, the *punctum* establishes the rule of contingency and chance. (Cf. Wittgenstein: *"This is how it strikes me.* When I obey a rule, I do not choose. I obey the rule blindly" [*PI*, 1, 219].)

   *Camera Lucida* begins, like Kant's third *Critique*, with an account of the contingency of the aesthetic domain as encountered in the difficulties of taxonomy that photography presents:

from the first step, that of classification (we must surely classify, verify by samples, if we want to constitute a corpus), Photography evades us. The various distributions we impose upon it are in fact either empirical (Professionals/Amateurs), or rhetorical (Landscapes/Objects/Portraits/Nudes), or else aesthetic (Realism/Pictorialism), in any case external to the object, without relation to its essence, which can only be (if it exists at all) the New of which it has been the advent; for these classifications might very well be applied to other, older forms of representation. We might say that Photography is unclassifiable. Then I wondered what the source of this disorder might be.[9]

The source of photography's taxonomic indeterminacy lies in what Kant described as the "subjective" element associated with the beautiful and the sublime: the "pleasure" and/or the "pain" that accompanies a given representation. Barthes writes: "among those [photographs] which had been selected, evaluated, approved, collected in albums or magazines and which had thereby passed through the filter of culture, I realized that some provoked tiny jubilations, as if they referred to a stilled center, an erotic or lacerating value buried in myself (however harmless the subject may have appeared)" (*Camera Lucida*, p. 16). Likewise, Barthes speaks of the affects as having an "ontological" truth; in photography, he says, there are moments "where affect (love, compassion, grief, enthusiasm, desire) is a *guarantee of Being*" (*Camera*

---

[9] Barthes, *Camera Lucida*, trans. Richard Howard (New York: Hill and Wang, 1981), p. 4.

*Lucida*, p. 113; emphasis added.)[10]

Not surprisingly, *Camera Lucida* moves from the difficulty of classifying the aesthetic object to an account of the particular, irreducible, pleasure and pain that the object may call forth. Indeed, Barthes's own account of photography is so subjective and "particular" that the object most important to it (the Winter Garden photograph of his deceased mother) is never itself reproduced in the text. The opacity that underlies this image in *Camera Lucida*, attributable to the death of his mother, triggers the memory of ontological and psychological loss. Anticipating Derrida's work on mourning, *Camera Lucida* concentrates on the traumatic kernel of subjectivity that cannot find an equivalent in any objective representation. And, since the photograph in question is one of his mother as a child, *Camera Lucida* is the narrative of a "double loss."

In reflecting upon this already doubled loss, Barthes seeks to arrest the dialectic of desire whose all too familiar alternatives are a profitless nostalgia and a romantic wish for the re-enchantment of the world (here, no doubt, under the aegis of the benevolent Mother). Whereas the condition of the aesthetic in Kant is one of communication, of discourse, of talk, Barthes attempts to record a death that would provoke no further discourse – a "flat death" (p. 92): "nothing to say about the death of one whom I love most, nothing to say about her photograph, which I contemplate without ever being able to get to the heart of it, to transform it" (p. 93).[11] But recognizing that even the predication of mortality can generate an anthropomorphic desire, Barthes looks to the photograph as a way to renounce the myth of "active memory" and

[10] Barthes's *punctum* is the visual equivalent of what Aristotle described as a function of the affects (*pathē*) of being.

[11] Barthes is dealing with what Jean-Luc Nancy later describes as the impossibility of encountering death. "Since Leibnitz there has been no death in our universe," writes Nancy; "in one way or another an absolute circulation of meaning (of values, of ends, of History) fills or reabsorbs all finite negativity, draws from each finite singular destiny a surplus value of humanity or an infinite superhumanity . . . Generations of citizens and militants, or workers and servants of the States have imagined their death reabsorbed or sublated in a community, yet to come, that would attain immanence. But by now we have nothing more than the bitter consciousness of the increasing remoteness of such a community, be it the people, the nation, or the society of producers. However, this consciousness, like that of the 'loss' of community, is superficial. In truth, death is not sublated." *The Inoperative Community*, trans. Peter Connor et al. (Minneapolis: University of Minnesota Press, 1991), p. 13.

with it the desire for spiritual communion with the dead. Barthes's photograph strives to be resolutely singular, untranscendent, non-dialectical, and "mortal":

like a living organism, [the photograph] is born on the level of the sprouting silver grains, it flourishes a moment, then ages . . . Attacked by light, by humidity, it fades, weakens, vanishes; there is nothing left to do but throw it away. Earlier societies managed so that memory, the substitute for life, was eternal and that at least the thing which spoke Death should itself be immortal: this was the Monument. But by making the (mortal) photograph into the general and somehow natural witness of "what has been," modern society has renounced the Monument. A paradox: the same century invented History and Photography. But History is a memory fabricated according to positive formulas, a pure intellectual discourse which abolishes mythic Time; and the photograph is a certain but fugitive testimony; so that everything, today, prepares our race for this impotence: to be no longer able to conceive *duration*, affectively or symbolically: the age of the Photograph is also the age of revolutions, contestations, assassinations, explosions, in short, of impatiences, of everything which denies ripening.

*(Camera Lucida*, pp. 93–94)

By so saying, Barthes also places photography at the very crux of modernity, where modernity is understood, in the manner of Baudelaire, as having a fundamentally aesthetic and non-transcendent basis. Modernity names the epoch of the "transitory" and the "fugitive" (Baudelaire), of "revolutions, contestations, assassinations, explosions, and impatiences" (Barthes).[12] It is the space of the politics of antagonism, of the unsuturable whole, of a fundamental contingency – all of which require the work of infinite, reflective judgment that ideology tends to suppress.

---

[12] In so saying, Barthes marries a Kantian problematic to a modernist aesthetic whose origins lie in Baudelaire's essay "The Painter of Modern Life." In this tradition, the "modern" does not stand opposed to "ancient"; rather, it indicates "the ephemeral, the fugitive, the contingent, the half of art whose other half is the eternal and the immutable." Baudelaire describes "modernity" as that moment when truth became epitomized in the aesthetics of the contingent particular: "this transitory, fugitive element, whose metamorphoses are so rapid, must on no account be despised or dispensed with. By neglecting it, you cannot fail to tumble into the abyss of an abstract and indeterminate beauty, like that of the first woman before the fall of man." Charles Baudelaire, "The Painter of Modern Life," in *The Painter of Modern Life and Other Essays*, trans. Jonathan Mayne (New York: Da Capo Press, 1986), p. 13. Together with Barthes, Baudelaire suggests that modernity is fundamentally aesthetic insofar as it was the moment when the non-universalizable particular was brought to light.

If there is a link between the aesthetic critique of ideology that we see in Barthes and a psychoanalytic interest in the "deep structures" of consciousness, it is because both reveal our tendency to treat as "necessary" those very practices and beliefs whose existence cannot be conclusively demonstrated (e.g., the normative codings in Barthes's *studium*, Heidegger's notion of the "background," or Lacan's "big Other"). Psychoanalysis, ideology-critique, and aesthetic reflection all strive to uncover the sedimented judgments upon which such practices depend. Pascal's famous wager about the existence of God makes a related point about the "ideological" nature of belief. Indeed, the famous wager begins from an "ideological" investment in the existence of God for pragmatic and, one might add, conservative reasons – as a way to avoid disrupting the established forms of life that such belief makes possible. The first part of the fragment on the wager in the *Pensées* aims to show why it is in fact rational to bet on the existence of God. But the second part of Pascal's fragment undermines the first by presenting the objections of an imaginary interlocutor who exposes that belief as *nothing more than* a "form of life," i.e., as an accommodation engendered by force of habit: "you want to be cured of unbelief and you ask for the remedy," says the interlocutor, then "learn from those who were once bound like you and who now wager all they have. These are people who know the road you wish to follow, who have been cured of the affliction of which you wish to be cured: follow the way by which they began. They behaved just as if they did believe, taking holy water, having masses said, and so on. That will make you believe quite naturally."[13] The freedom to participate "authentically" in practices – to participate without ideological compulsion or constraint – thus depends on recognizing that while there may be nothing *essentially* good or meaningful about practices, they may be accepted as "good" and "meaningful" nonetheless. The refusal to reconcile the two faces of Pascal's wager stands behind Kierkegaard's renowned "leap of faith." What is interesting about Kierkegaard's "leap" from an aesthetic point of view is the way in which it rejects ideological foreclosure in order to register the discontinuity between the worlds of belief

---

[13] Blaise Pascal, *Pensées*, trans. A. J. Krailsheimer (Harmondsworth: Penguin Books, 1966), no. 418, p. 152. Žižek offers a related discussion of Pascal in *For They Know Not What They Do*.

and unbelief. If Pascal's analysis of the wager shows that belief is both rational and irrational (i.e., ideological), then Kierkegaard reflects the affective consequences of such a contradictory and undecidable stance – in "fear and trembling" and other forms of *angst*. (Wittgenstein, as we shall see, takes the instance of belief as an example of the logical impossibility of certain kinds of doubt, hence as an indication both of what counts as reliable "knowledge" and of the limits of reason: "One can mistrust one's own senses, but not one's own belief" [*PI*, p. 190].)[14]

For the larger part of its history, however, philosophy has attempted to limit the task of reflective judgment by accepting ideology as an evil necessary to any practical purpose. Consider as one prominent example of this fact Descartes's description of the provisional moral code ("morale provisoire") in the *Discourse on the Method*. The "morale provisoire" provides a support for praxis while the question of "absolute truth" remains outstanding. The philosopher's commitment to the principle of "clear and distinct ideas" is thus preserved by a set of operative (read: ideological) beliefs which conceal the fact that such a measure of certainty may never be obtained:

before starting to rebuild your house, it is not enough simply to pull it down, to make provisions for materials and architects (or else train yourself in architecture), and to have carefully drawn up the plans; you must also provide yourself with some other place where you can live comfortably while building is in progress. Likewise, lest I should remain indecisive in my actions while reason obliged me to be so in my judgments, and in order to live as happily as I could during this time, I formed for myself a provisional moral code consisting of just three or four maxims.[15]

Descartes's maxims say: obey the laws and the customs of your country; be decisive in your actions; master your desires; and

---

[14] Cf. Wittgenstein's claim that "'mathematical certainty' is not a psychological concept," *PI*, p. 224.

[15] René Descartes, *Discourse on the Method*, III. In *The Philosophical Works of Descartes*, vol. I, trans. John Cottingham, Robert Stoothoff, and Dugald Murdoch (Cambridge: Cambridge University Press, 1985), p. 122. In an interesting comment on Descartes's "morale provisoire," Žižek suggests that "the real aim of ideology is the attitude demanded by it, the consistency of the ideological form, the fact that we 'continue to walk as straight as we can in one direction'; the positive reasons given by ideology to justify this request – to make us obey ideological form – are there only to conceal this fact: in other words, to conceal the surplus-enjoyment proper to the ideological form as such.'" *The Sublime Object of Ideology* (London: Verso, 1989), p. 83.

choose the best occupation you can find. By invocation of this provisional moral program, the not-yet-attainable ideal of a genuinely universal truth is saved from defeat by the empirically contingent facts that may prevent it from being reached. Descartes's "absolute truth" is saved, moreover, by what Horkheimer and Adorno would call a form of instrumental reason. This is a mode of "practical rationalism" (Weber's term) that is, at best, meliorist in its aspirations. The thoroughgoing pragmatism of Descartes's provisional moral maxims requires a compromise with the same contingent, empirical, and "pathological" reality that Descartes had hoped to escape. Indeed, the Cartesian maxims suggest that the neo-pragmatist revolt *against* Cartesian thought among contemporary philosopher-critics like Richard Rorty and Stanley Fish is in fact based upon a repetition of this ideology, minus the "as if" posture by which Descartes attempts to hold apart the provisionality of his "morale provisoire" and absolute truth.

For neo-pragmatist thinkers, effective (*wirklich*) beliefs are not contingent upon the inaccessibility or the withdrawal of absolute truth. This is because neo-pragmatists are firmly convinced that "absolute truth" is nothing more than a vaporous idea, one of the "metaphysical comforts" or accommodations that Nietzsche so deeply despised. Hence Fish's modifications of what is in essence a form of the Cartesian "morale provisoire" in the following commentary on the relationship between "force" and "law." Fish's hope is to preserve the possibility of making distinctions between (normative) "law" and (ideological) "force" in the short run, while arguing that no such distinctions can be made in anything like absolute terms:

> Legal actors, like everyone else, live within the temporary ascendencies they at once affirm and undo (by endlessly modifying the givens that make action possible), and no analysis of their situation, even the analysis offered here, will remove them from it. That is to say, the acknowledgment that from the long-run point of view law is inseparable from force is itself without force, since no one inhabits the long-run point of view, and in the succession of short runs that make up our lives, the distinction between law and force is unassailable, although one can always assail the form it has presently assumed.[16]

---

[16] Stanley Fish, "Force," in *Doing What Comes Naturally: Change, Rhetoric, and the Practice of Theory in Literary and Legal Studies* (Durham, NC: Duke University Press, 1989), p. 523. The essay is largely an engagement with H. L. A. Hart's influential study, *The Concept of Law* (1962).

For his part, Rorty argues that the only distinctions a neo-pragmatist should find worth making are the immediate ones between some "actual" state of affairs and some other possible state of affairs, whether better or worse:

From a pragmatist point of view, to say that what is rational for us now to believe may not be true, is simply to say that somebody may come up with a better idea. It is to say that there is always room for improved belief, since new evidence, or new hypotheses, or a whole new vocabulary, may come along. For pragmatists, the desire for objectivity is not the desire to escape the limitations of one's community, but simply the desire for as much intersubjective agreement as possible, the desire to extend the reference of "us" as far as we can. Insofar as pragmatists make a distinction between knowledge and opinion, it is simply the distinction between topics on which such agreement is relatively easy to get and topics on which agreement is relatively hard to get.[17]

Let us set aside the political and ethical questions raised by Rorty's desire to "extend the reference of 'us' as far as we can" and concentrate instead on the rejection of the deep-structure theories that Rorty tends to group under the heading of "metaphysics." Rorty's stance is particularly relevant to the present discussion because in *Contingency, Irony, and Solidarity* the turn away from deep structures is explicitly aligned with an "aesthetic" stance. As far as Rorty is concerned, poets and novelists (especially modernist ones) know something that philosophers apparently do not: that the world is a web of contingencies, and that we are consequently unable to discover any universal truth that binds us all from origin to end. In response, Rorty invites us to become skeptical ironists, eternally negating the desire to regard any stance as founded upon something permanent or universal (Spirit, Being, Truth). The ironist instead confronts an array of "authority figures" whose power and influence are revocable

---

[17] Richard Rorty, "Solidarity or Objectivity?" in *Objectivity, Relativism, and Truth: Philosophical Papers Volume* I (Cambridge: Cambridge University Press, 1991), p. 23. There are numerous passages from Fish's work that could be used to complement this one. To take but one example, consider Fish on what Horkheimer and Adorno called "emancipation": "what the critical theorists call liberation or emancipation is nothing more (or less) than the passing from one structure of constraint to another, a passing that will always be attended by the 'discovery of new possibilities,' but of possibilities that will be no less (or more) constrained than those that have been left behind." "Critical Self-Consciousness or Can We Know What We're Doing?" in *Doing What Comes Naturally*, pp. 459–60.

precisely because they are deemed contingent. (By the same token, Rorty limits the force of contingency almost entirely to the task of making authority revocable.) The ironist's principal goal is to debunk authority by showing that there is no objective "ground," nothing essential in the realm of the real, to which any authority can possibly refer. The pragmatist can appropriate the freedom afforded by this ironic stance in order to show that there may be better beliefs, if not a better authority, to put in their place. Consider Rorty's account of Proust and Nietzsche in this regard:

> Proust temporalized and finitized the authority figures he had met by seeing them as creatures of contingent circumstance. Like Nietzsche, he rid himself of the fear that there was an antecedent truth about himself, a real essence which others might have detected. But Proust was able to do so without claiming to know a truth which was hidden from the authority figures of his earlier years. He managed to debunk authority without setting himself up as authority, to debunk the ambitions of the powerful without sharing them. He finitized authority figures not by detecting what they "really" were but by watching them become different than they had been, and by seeing how they looked when redescribed in terms offered by still other authority figures, whom he played off against the first . . . Proust has no problem of how to avoid being *aufgehoben*. Beauty, depending as it does on giving shape to a multiplicity, is notoriously transitory, because it is likely to be destroyed when new elements are added to that multiplicity.[18]

In chapters above I have already suggested why I believe Rorty's position is, if not ideological, then at the very least insufficiently reflective insofar as Rorty fails to recognize himself as a descendant of the same Enlightenment he proposes to reject. If Habermas attempted to "save" Horkheimer and Adorno from the destructive consequences of their own critique by claiming that

---

[18] Rorty, *Contingency, Irony, and Solidarity* (Cambridge: Cambridge University Press, 1989), pp. 103–05. Rorty's stance in this passage is remarkably similar to Lukács's description of the process of form-making in the novel, where irony likewise prevails: "the composition of the novel is the paradoxical fusion of heterogeneous and discrete components into an organic whole which is then abolished over and over again . . . Irony is the objectivity of the novel." *Theory of the Novel*, trans. Anna Bostock (Cambridge, MA: MIT Press, 1973), pp. 84, 90. Rorty regards novels as a "safer" medium than theory for expressing the contingency of authority because the novel (literature) rejects the drive for a perspective that might finally overcome contingency in an ultimate *aufhebung*. The links between Lukács and Rorty can nonetheless be explained in terms of their relationship to Kant – specifically, in terms of their relationship to the Kantian view that the subject constructs the world.

*Dialectic of Enlightenment* was, in the end, a text seeking to illuminate its readers, then Rorty remains, by the same logic, a purveyor of Enlightenment beliefs, albeit in a somewhat diminished form. Works like *Philosophy and the Mirror of Nature* and *Contingency, Irony, and Solidarity* are linked to the Enlightenment insofar as they claim to have seen one final, ironic, truth: that there is no final truth. The result is a therapeutic philosophical effort that nonetheless represses the agonistic relations between the (neo)pragmatist present and the "metaphysical" or "foundationalist" past and simply announces its own success. In place of the more complex process of reflection associated with Nietzsche's "eternal return of the same" or Hegel's "causality of fate" Rorty's neo-pragmatism offers a form of self-perficient therapy.[19] Rorty thus may recognize, with Hegel and Wittgenstein, that the only "solution" to a philosophical problem lies in its self-displacement, but he remains unaware of the fact that any attempt willfully to produce that displacement is bound to represent an external and ineffective effort at philosophical "success."[20] Philosophical truths may well be "nothing more than" beliefs, but the will cannot force itself either to believe or to stop believing.

When faced with such questions, Rorty happily accepts the Enlightenment's practical agenda while eviscerating its theoretical grounds. Faithful to his pragmatist roots, Rorty attempts to "solve" the problem of the division of theory and practice by rejecting theory *tout court*. Thus in relatively recent writings on this subject Rorty has recommended that we abandon the Enlightenment's intellectual ambitions while conserving its liberal

[19] Compare also what I take to be the richer implications of Stanley Cavell's assessment: "Innovation in philosophy has characteristically gone together with a repudiation of the past – of most of the history of the subject. But in the later Wittgenstein (and, I would now add, in Heidegger's *Being and Time*) the repudiation of the past has a transformed significance, as though containing the consciousness that history will not go away, except through our perfect acknowledgment of it (in particular, our acknowledgment that it is not past), and that one's own practice and ambition can be identified only against the continuous experience of the past.) *Must We Mean What We Say?* (Cambridge: Cambridge University Press, 1969), p. xix.

[20] Wittgenstein writes: "The philosopher's treatment of a question is like the treatment of an illness" (*PI*, sec. 254, p. 91). Cf. Žižek, who argues that a philosophical problem disappears only when, as in Hegel, we attempt to take into account its context of enunciation – i.e., when we "stage" it. What Žižek asks for is not an illustration of philosophical problems but, much like Hegel and Wittgenstein, a "scenic representation" that would bring to light the unspoken presuppositions behind them.

political stance.[21] If the Enlightenment dream was indeed composed of two distinct parts – one theoretical and the other practical-political – and if the problem taken up in Kant's third *Critique* was to reconcile these two, then Rorty effectively claims to have solved the problem of reflective judgment by having decided which of the two was true, which an illusion.

To be sure, Rorty's position represents a noble attempt to respect the contingency of the world of appearances by enlisting the work of poets and novelists in a campaign of aesthetic resistance against the universalizing tendencies of "metaphysics." If "metaphysics" is Rorty's name for what Kant calls determinant judgment, then such a position offers the means by which we might potentially win the particulars back. But even as it may redeem the contingency of appearances, this incarnation of the neo-pragmatist project remains insufficiently self-conscious and needlessly ideological. As far as literature is concerned, Rorty's analysis depends upon the very genre distinction he would urge us to forget. Specifically, Rorty assumes as part of his "morale provisoire" that the ironic insights of poems and novels are preferable to philosophy's preoccupation with "absolute truth." But, not unlike Descartes, Rorty sustains a long-range commitment that contravenes his provisional moral code – a commitment to the ultimate contingency of things, hence to a withering away of the distinction between the contingent and the absolute, between "literary" and "philosophical" modes of discourse. In place of Kant's account of judgments that take their bearings by pleasure and pain, Rorty offers purely pragmatic pronouncements upon the nature of truth as a function of "what works." Indeed, the neo-pragmatist appeal to aesthetics requires a suppression of affect, as signaled both by the "therapeutic" nature of its aims and by the fact that Rorty's interest in art is not driven by pleasure but rather by a pragmatic interest in reducing pain.

To be sure, when Kant looked to aesthetic reflective judgment, his hope was to bind the worlds of theory and practice as one. In Kant's terms, this meant reconciling "freedom" and "nature" – to recall once again the words of the third *Critique*, showing both that "the concept of freedom is meant to actualize in the sensible world the end proposed by its laws" and that "nature must

---

[21] Rorty has developed this position in an as yet unpublished essay entitled "The Continuity Between the Enlightenment and 'Postmodernism.'"

consequently also be capable of being regarded in such a way that in the conformity to law of its form it at least harmonizes with the possibility of the ends to be effectuated in it according to the laws of freedom" (*CJ*, Introduction, p. 14.) But, as we have had occasion to remark numerous times above, what Kant in fact discovered was that reflective judgment could not bridge this gap, or could not bridge it to the satisfaction of reason. Consequently, Kant's reflective judgment appears to have no place of its own among the faculties of cognition and morality (*CJ*, Introduction, p. 15). Rather, Kant takes pleasure and pain as the points at which the subject's openness to infinite reflection, its self-consciousness, begins to grasp the contingency of the real. In claims about beauty, that contingency is revealed in the need to presuppose the very form of agreement or "common sense" that aesthetic judgments are said to produce. In the sublime, reason is itself shown to be contingent insofar as it fails to find a rule for that which is "absolutely great" (*CJ*, sec. 25, p. 94).

To think that aesthetic judgment is linked as much to contingency as to universality or to necessity is to suggest the ways in which the project of infinite reflection can resist a premature, ideological foreclosure of our relationship to the real. At several points in his writings, Rorty appeals to Wittgenstein in order to make a similar point, albeit within the context of a neo-pragmatist agenda. For example, Rorty invokes Wittgenstein's analogy between "vocabularies" and "tools" to help illustrate the contingency of language – namely, that all vocabularies, even the ones most essential to our self-descriptions, are "human creations, tools for the creation of such other human artefacts as poems, utopian societies, scientific theories, and future generations."[22] To accept the contingency of language requires abandoning the notion that there may be a final justification for our beliefs. Hence Rorty's link between contingent vocabularies and those "poeticized" cultures in which the primacy of "fiction" is placed in service of a (post)modernist commitment to the new – to new justifications as well as to new creations: "a poeticized culture would be one which would not insist we find the real wall behind the painted ones, the real touchstones of truth as opposed to touchstones which are merely cultural artefacts. It would be a

---

[22] Rorty, *Contingency, Irony, and Solidarity*, p. 53.

culture which, precisely by appreciating that all touchstones are such artefacts, would take as its goal the creation of ever more various and multicolored artefacts" (*Contingency*, pp. 53–54). Yet Rorty's desire to align the "contingency" of language with a (post)modernist political and aesthetic agenda is powerless to resist the collapse of Kant's empirical and transcendental worlds; rather, it becomes a vehicle for a politically driven recovery of the world of appearances. Otherwise put, Rorty's "various and multi-colored artefacts" are not aesthetic effects in search of a rule; rather, such artefacts are *themselves* taken to provide the criterion, norm, or rule for praxis.

If the neo-pragmatist *morale provisoire* represents an ideological prop that provides a ground for action in the absence of necessary or absolute truths, then what might a praxis of infinite reflection look like? What position might such a mode of reflection assume with respect to the idealized picture of a perfect correspondence between mental representations (philosophy's "clear and distinct ideas") and a world of objective facts? Especially when set beside Rorty's neo-pragmatism, the analysis of "language-games," "rule-following behavior," and "forms of life" sketched out by Wittgenstein in the *Philosophical Investigations* provides an illuminating attempt to avoid explaining praxis by a series of underlying rules. Whereas it is sometimes said (by, among others, Rorty himself) that Wittgenstein's later philosophy involves a repudiation of Kantian thought (especially insofar as Kant is linked to the "metaphysical" tradition of Plato and Descartes) the *Philosophical Investigations* and other texts of the "later" Wittgenstein in fact represent a continuation, in the realm of a philosophy of praxis, of the consequences of reflective judgment mapped out by Kant. Seen in the light of Kant's third *Critique*, the point of Wittgenstein's analysis of language-games goes considerably beyond the liberal aestheticism evidenced in Rorty's interest in difference and diversity (the "creation of ever more various and multi-colored artefacts" referred to in the passage cited above). Wittgenstein may be interested in such variety, but primarily insofar as any one practice is irreducible to any other. More important is that what Wittgenstein understands as "knowing the meaning" of a word or phrase involves a performance rather than the knowledge of a rule. Moreover, it involves the ability to extend a practice to situations that are not covered by existing rules. How can this be?

On a skeptical reading of Wittgenstein, of course, there can be no such thing as meaning anything whatsoever by any word. "Knowing the meaning" of a phrase would seem to embed reflection not only upon cognate phrases but upon all future performances of that phrase as well.[23] Each new instance of "meaning," each new application, would seem to involve a leap in the dark. ("'What you are saying, then, comes to this: a new insight – intuition – is needed at every step to carry out the order "+n" correctly'" [*PI*, sec. 186, p. 75].) Likewise, any intention could be interpreted so as to accord with anything we might choose to do.[24] But this skeptical view can be refuted if one rejects the foundationalist presuppositions that underlie it. This argument is not produced theoretically (e.g., through the presentation of a more comprehensive view) but rather involves *showing* the difference between those positions that are inside language-games and those positions that are outside such games. Indeed, Wittgenstein's later work represents a classic case in which the "staging" of thought can demonstrate the degree to which the content of an enunciation is in fact carried by the context of its articulation – including, in this case, by language itself:[25] "when a sentence is called senseless, it is not as if it were its sense that is senseless. But a combination of words is being excluded from the language, withdrawn from circulation" (*PI*, sec. 500, p. 139); "to understand a sentence is to understand a language" (*PI*, sec. 199, p. 81). Wittgenstein's interest in the power of enunciation leads to the following claim about the advancement of

---

[23] Robert Steiner offers the following observation: "To play chess, writes Wittgenstein, is to have all the rules in your head though you may not engage them. And though you may not use all the possible moves, you must know them – they must be hypothetical – in order to play the game. Out of the hypothetical, therefore, the actual emerges, meaning that the trace of a different use of a rule is contained as a necessary hypothesis of any one use." *Toward a Grammar of Abstraction: Modernity, Wittgenstein, and the Paintings of Jackson Pollock* (University Park: Pennsylvania State University Press, 1992), p. 17.

[24] Saul Kripke, *Wittgenstein on Rules and Private Language* (Oxford: Oxford University Press, 1982), p. 55. Kripke cites sec. 202 of the *Philosophical Investigations* as evidence, though there is reason to doubt whether it actually supports his claim: "'obeying a rule' is a practice. And to think one is obeying a rule is not to obey a rule. Hence is it not possible to obey a rule 'privately': otherwise thinking one was obeying a rule would be the same thing as obeying it." (*PI*, sec. 202, p. 81.)

[25] As far as the "staging" of thought is concerned, recall Wittgenstein's remark: "What *can* be shown *cannot* be said." *Tractatus Logico-Philosophicus*, trans. D.F. Pears and B. F. McGuinness (London: Routledge and Kegan Paul, 1974), 4.1212.

"theses" in philosophy: "If one tried to advance theses in philosophy, it would never be possible to debate them, because everyone would agree to them" (*PI*, sec. 128, p. 50). Philosophy, as Wittgenstein regards it, is the realm of reflective rather than determinant judgments, and in language-games that reflection takes the form of praxis. Moreover, this reflective praxis is situated within a framework of shared assumptions that, much like Kant's "common sense," must be both proved and presupposed.

Wittgenstein's displacement of "objectivism" by such contextualist pronouncements suggests that there must indeed be some unspoken assumptions or other forms of agreement (e.g., shared beliefs, "common sense") binding us within language-games or "forms of life." When Wittgenstein suggests, e.g., that learning is based on believing or when he says that "knowledge is in the end based on acknowledgment," he allows us to make a link between these unspoken presuppositions and the "common sense" of Kant's aesthetic judgment.[26] Specifically, Wittgenstein argues that "if language is to be a means of communication there must be agreement not only in definitions but also . . . in judgments" (*PI*, sec. 242, p. 88). Wittgenstein's "unspoken presuppositions" (beliefs) are like the ideas which Kant says we surely must have but remain nonetheless unaware of[27] – with the exception that for Wittgenstein there is no expectation that these presuppositions constitute the rules according to which the moves within language could be determined. On the contrary, they represent purely tacit knowledge. Hence Wittgenstein's fascination with Saint Augustine's remark about the nature of time: "if no one asks me about it, I know what it is; if I am asked for an explanation, I do not know" (*PI*, sec. 1, p. 3). As far as Wittgenstein is concerned, we can never distance ourselves enough to gain a "theoretical" grasp of the unspoken agreements at work in language-games while still remaining within such games, whereas those same agreements are bound to appear arbitrary or meaningless when seen from any

[26] Wittgenstein, *On Certainty*, ed. G. E. M. Anscombe and G. H. von Wright, trans. Denis Paul and G. E. M. Anscombe (New York: Harper and Row, 1969), paras. 170, 378.
[27] Kant, *Anthropology from a Pragmatic Point of View*, trans. Victor Lyle Dowdell (Carbondale: Southern Illinois University Press, 1978), p. 18. Kant's discussion makes it apparent that such ideas are the products of various types of confusion or obscurity; hence their great distance from the unspoken assumptions at work in Wittgenstein's language-games.

stance outside language-games. This becomes strikingly apparent in Wittgenstein's lectures on religious belief. Just as the "unspoken presuppositions" at work in language-games seem to be immune to negation, there seems to be no "opposite" to a belief, only positions that are external to it: "Suppose that someone believed in the Last Judgment, and I don't," writes Wittgenstein; "does this mean that I believe the opposite to him, just that there won't be such a thing? I would say: 'not at all, or not always.'"[28] In the *Philosophical Investigations* Wittgenstein thus remarks that "what has to be accepted, the given, is – so one could say – forms of life" (*PI*, p. 226). Not surprisingly, then, a critic like Albrecht Wellmer finds that Wittgenstein's views cannot be assimilated either to the position he calls "structuralist objectivism" or to what he dubs poststructuralist skepticism.[29] Language-games and the life-forms they model are grounded at best in (shared) practices that in turn establish distinctions between what is rational or true and what is not: "It is possible to interpret this prior commonality of a world disclosed through language as a prior 'accord,' provided that we do not conceive this in terms of 'conventions,' or of 'consensuses,' which might be either rational or irrational. It is much rather an accord which is constitutive of the possibility of distinguishing between true and false, between reasonable and unreasonable" (*The Persistence of Modernity*, p. 67). But the commonalities in question are likewise dependent for their coherence upon distinctions that they themselves establish (including the distinctions between "true" and "false," "reasonable" and "unreasonable").

Thus rather than say that Wittgenstein's analysis of meaning and language-games represents a new form of skepticism,[30] it

[28] Wittgenstein, *Lectures and Conversations on Aesthetics, Psychology and Religious Belief*, ed. Cyril Barrett (Berkeley: University of California Press, n.d.), p. 53.

[29] Albrecht Wellmer, *The Persistence of Modernity*, trans. David Midgley (Cambridge, MA: MIT Press, 1993). "The former [structuralist objectivism] fails because it ignores the pragmatic dimension of a significative relation that is essentially open and not objectifiable; the latter [neo-structuralist skepticism] because it relates the openness and non-objectifiability of linguistic meanings to the uncontrollable non-identity of each individual use of a sign" (pp. 67–68).

[30] Cf. Wellmer: "Wittgenstein's way of doing philosophy incorporates a new form of skepticism which even casts doubt on the certainties of Hume or Descartes. His skeptical question runs, 'How can I know what I am talking about? How can I know what I mean?' What is destroyed by the critique conducted by the philosophy of language is the subject as author and ultimate arbiter of its own intentions" (*ibid.*, p. 65).

makes more sense to say that in the *Philosophical Investigations* Wittgenstein invites a form of reflection that we may find strange in a world where knowledge has come to mean the subsumption of free particulars under universal categories and rules. In this respect, the *Philosophical Investigations* carries forward the project of aesthetic reflection initiated by Kant. As for the possibility of linking the "metaphysical" Kant with the "post-metaphysical" Wittgenstein, I have already suggested why it would be wrong to place the *Critique of Judgment* entirely within the tradition of "Western metaphysics" and, likewise, why such an omnibus term is likely to limit the possibility of finding an alternative form of rationality within the tradition so described. Consider as further evidence Kant's analysis of the "symbolic" linkage between beauty and morality in section 59 of the third *Critique*, which hardly represents the thinking of a philosopher undyingly committed to the primacy of the "thing in itself" over and above the contingencies of language or to what Rorty describes as the "correspondence" theory of the truth. In fact, it anticipates Wittgenstein in some rather striking ways.

Under the rubric of "hypotyposis" – a form of substitution that presents something under another aspect ("presentation, *subjectio sub adspectum*") – Kant draws a distinction between two modes of figurality directly relevant to Wittgenstein's conception of language-games.[31] The first, less problematic, kind of figuration is dubbed "schematic." In "schematic hypotyposes," as in cases of determinant judgment, Kant imagines a direct correspondence between an intuition and a concept. Here, concept and intuition are associated with one another on an *a priori* basis. Interestingly enough, Kant does not give any examples of this kind of hypotyposis. He only seems to suppose, as a point of reference, that there must be something like a natural or spontaneous affinity between intuition and concept. In the "schematic" hypotyposis it is as if the intuition "speaks itself" through concepts. The other, more problematic and interesting kind of hypotyposis, described as "symbolic," draws substantially more attention from Kant. Symbolic hypotyposes express concepts for which no underlying intuition is available (*CJ*, sec. 59, p. 223).

[31] These correspond roughly to what Hegel would later call "sign" and "symbol." See chapter 3 above, and also Paul de Man's essay, "Sign and Symbol in Hegel's Aesthetics," *Critical Inquiry*, 8 (1982).

They work instead by *analogy* with direct intuition. Just as with metaphor, Kant's symbolic hypotyposes depend upon a "transfer" of some sort. Specifically, they "transfer reflection upon an object of intuition to quite a new concept." As examples, Kant offers the notions of *ground* (understood as "support" or "basis"), *to depend* (to be held up from above), and to *flow from* (meaning to follow). We are already familiar with Kant's most famous examples from a previous chapter: the representation of a monarchical state as a "living body" and of an absolutist state as a "hand-mill." Insofar as each of these substitutions requires a novel association of intuition and concept, each one represents the work of genius in miniature, and each one requires an act of aesthetic judgment for its comprehension.

This is confirmed by Kant's explanation of how such "substitutions" are apprehended. First, we undertake the "application" of the concept to the object of a sensible intuition (though how and why this "application" occurs Kant never says). Second, we apply the "rule" of reflection at work in that intuition to a new and unrelated object, of which the former then serves as the model or "symbol." But this application cannot be predicted in advance, and certainly does not operate in conformity with a rule. Symbolic hypotyposes thus go to demonstrate, if not why beauty *must be* a symbol of morality, then why it *can only be* such: "even common understanding is wont to pay regard to this analogy; and we frequently apply to beautiful objects of nature or of art names that seem to rely upon the basis of a moral estimate. We call buildings or trees majestic and stately, or plains laughing and gay; even colors are called innocent, modest, soft, because they excite sensations containing something analogous to the consciousness of the state of mind produced by moral judgments" (*CJ*, sec. 59, p. 225). Hypotyposes thus also demonstrate why it is left to taste to move us from aesthetic reflection to praxis, for in treating the linkage of beauty and morality as presupposed, it makes that transition possible "without too violent a leap, for it represents the imagination, even in its freedom, as amenable to a final determination for understanding, and teaches us to find, even in sensuous objects, a free delight apart from any charm of sense" (*CJ*, sec. 59, p. 225). In other words, taste produces the affinities that all modes of figurality, including hypotyposis, require. In making possible the "leap" from one realm to another (and in spite of Kant's insistence on the difference between the two) taste is a form of genius, albeit genius in a diminished form.

As far as Wittgenstein is concerned, the analysis of rule-following behavior in the *Philosophical Investigations* provides an engagement with the practical implications of the process of infinite reflection that can be associated with the theory of aesthetic judgment articulated in Kant's third *Critique*. Wittgenstein's presentation of the problem of rule-following behavior begins from the following paradox. In section 201 of the *Philosophical Investigations*, Wittgenstein says that "no course of action could be determined by a rule, because every course of action can be made to accord with the rule . . . if everything can be made out to accord with the rule, then it can also be made out to conflict with it" (p. 81). In *Wittgenstein on Rules and Private Language* Saul Kripke in fact takes this as the "central problem" of the *Philosophical Investigations*. Because he is so circumspect about the validity of covering laws – because covering laws can always seem to be *ad hoc* – Wittgenstein prefers to see *all* claims of knowledge as bounded by tacit agreements about what it makes sense (or not) to say or do. Indeed, Wittgenstein assimilates cognition directly to praxis (i.e., to forms of life): "The grammar of the word 'knows' is evidently closely related to that of 'can,' 'is able to'" (*PI*, sec. 150, p. 59).[32] Likewise, "'obeying a rule' is a practice" (*PI*, sec. 202, p. 81). Questions about mathematical rules stand on the same footing as questions about sensory perception. The one is no more or less open to doubt than the other. Hence in the *Remarks on the Foundations of Mathematics* Wittgenstein asks: "How do I know that in working out the series +2 I must write '20,004, 20,006' and not '20,004, 20,008'? – (The question: 'How do I know that this color is "red"?' is similar.")[33] As Žižek remarks, it is relatively easy to accept *momentarily* the absence of the "big Other" who might answer such questions – "to suspend the big Other by means of the act *qua* real."[34] But Wittgenstein's analysis of rule-following behavior aims at something substantially less transitory. Wittgenstein assimilates determinant and reflective judgments by reference to a form of praxis in which

[32] Cf. "Try not to think of understanding as a 'mental process' at all" (*PI*, sec. 154, p. 61).

[33] Wittgenstein, *Remarks on the Foundations of Mathematics*, ed. G. H. von Wright et al. (New York: Macmillan, 1956), I, sec. 3.

[34] Žižek, *The Indivisible Remainder: An Essay on Schelling and Related Matters* (London: Verso, 1996), p. 133.

rationality is determined by the ability to "go on." This means, first, that following a rule makes reference to – invokes but also helps sustain – a set of shared beliefs. Wittgenstein's answer to the problem of "subjectivism" is thus to make the claims of judgment public and shareable (if not universal) and to recognize that what enables the public validation of judgment is nothing more than similar practices, themselves in need of validation, carried out by others: "to think one is obeying a rule is not to obey a rule. Hence it is not possible to obey a rule 'privately': otherwise thinking one was obeying a rule would be the same thing as obeying it" (*PI*, sec. 202, p. 81).[35]

The desire for an irreducible example that would define the application of a rule for all future cases is less easily put to rest than skeptical doubts about rule-following behavior. Recognizing the temptation to seek out an example or fundamental measure that would stand outside language-games altogether, Wittgenstein works to re-weave the desire for an absolute determination of the real into the fabric of language-games, wherein such examples are revealed as contingent upon all other moves in the game. An example that sets a rule may play a "peculiar role" in language-games, but it is not categorically different from other examples: "There is *one* thing of which one can say neither that it is one meter long, nor that it is not one meter long, and that is the standard meter in Paris. – But this, of course, is not to describe any extraordinary property to it, but only to mark its peculiar role in the language-game of measuring with a meter rule. We define: 'sepia' means the color of the standard sepia which is there kept hermetically sealed . . . This sample is an instrument of the language used in ascriptions of color. In this language-game it is

---

[35] In sec. 199 Wittgenstein had asked: "Is what we call 'obeying a rule' something that it would be possible for only one man to do, and to do only once in his life?" (*PI*, p. 80). Cf. Kant, who argues that "a person who is without a sense of smell cannot have a sensation of this kind communicated to him, and, even if he does not suffer from this kind of deficiency, we still cannot be certain that he gets precisely the same sensation from a flower that we get from it" (*CJ*, sec. 39, pp. 148–49). If this leaves the question of taste within the realm of the empirical, then consider sec. 44, where Kant argues that "the universal communicability of a pleasure involves in its very concept that the pleasure is not one of enjoyment arising out of mere sensation, but must be one of reflection" (p. 166). Kripke makes the not unrelated argument that Wittgenstein regards the fundamental problems of the philosophy of mathematics and of the so-called "private language argument" as at root identical. See especially chapter 2 of *Wittgenstein on Rules and Private Language*.

not something that is represented, but is a means of representation" (*PI*, sec. 50, p. 25). Or, in a similar vein: "Imagine someone saying 'But I know how tall I am!' and laying his hand on top of his head to prove it" (*PI*, sec. 179, p. 96).

The question nonetheless remains: to what extent does a rule define a practice, limit or delimit it? (Likewise, to what extent does a practice establish, or fix, a rule?) Take the case of a machine – in Wittgenstein's example, a physical or symbolic machine – whose action seems to leave no room for doubt about how it will proceed in any given case. Such a machine would represent the fantasy of a fully determined protocol for following rules, to the extent that we might be tempted to imagine the entire range of its actions or outcomes as somehow present within the machine itself: "The machine's action seems to be in it from the start . . . But when we reflect that the machine could also have moved differently it may look as if the way it moves must be contained in the machine-as-symbol far more determinately than in the actual machine. As if it were not enough for the movements in question to be empirically determined in advance, but they had to be really – in a mysterious sense – already present. And it is quite true: the movement of the machine-as-symbol is predetermined in a different sense from that in which the movement of any given actual machine is predetermined" (*PI*, sec. 193, p. 78). So too with signs: "How does it come about that this arrow → points? Doesn't it seem to carry in it something besides itself? – 'No, not the dead line on paper; only the psychical thing, the meaning, can do that.' – That is both true and false. The arrow points only in the application that a living being makes of it. This pointing is not a hocus-pocus which can be performed only by the soul" (*PI*, sec. 454, p. 132).

As far as rules are concerned, we imagine that a rule itself is somehow guiding behavior when we follow it: "Let us imagine a rule intimating to me which way I am to obey it" (*PI*, sec. 232, p. 87); "following a rule is analogous to obeying an order" (*PI*, sec. 206, p. 82); "when I obey a rule, I do not choose. I obey the rule blindly" (*PI*, sec. 219, p. 85). Still, there remains the sense that following a rule reaches "beyond all the examples" (*PI*, sec. 209, p. 83). A rule stands like a "sign-post," but, Wittgenstein asks, "does the sign-post leave no doubt open about the way I have to go? Does it shew which direction I am to take when I have passed it?"

(*PI*, sec. 85, p. 39.) (Likewise, "the application of a word is not everywhere bounded by rules" [*PI*, sec. 84, p. 39]). One passage in particular from *The Blue and Brown Books* illustrates just how a rule can never fully determine the cases it is meant to govern, in part because the process of following a rule requires a reliance on prior knowledge about how to follow rules that is not in turn provided by the rule itself. The process is the equivalent, in the domain of praxis, of the very difficulty that Kant attributed to reflective judgment in his discussion of a "sifting principle" in the Preface to the first edition of the third *Critique* (p. 3).[36] Wittgenstein writes: "We introduce different ways of reading tables. Each table consists of two columns of words and pictures . . . In some cases they are to be read horizontally from left to right, i.e. according to the scheme:

In others according to such schemes as:

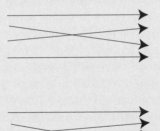

or:

etc.

Schemes of this kind can be adjoined to our tables, as rules for reading them. Could not these rules again be explained by further

---

[36] So too with philosophical reflection upon "philosophy," which Wittgenstein rapidly deflates: "One might think: if philosophy speaks of the use of the word 'philosophy' there must be a second-order philosophy. But it is not so: it is, rather, like the case of orthography, which deals with the word 'orthography' among others without then being second-order" (*PI*, sec. 121, p. 49).

rules? Certainly. On the other hand, is a rule incompletely explained if no rule for its usage has been given?"[37] At some point reasons come to an end; and that, for Wittgenstein, is the point at which action proceeds in full light of its own contingency: "How can [someone] know he is to continue a pattern by himself – whatever instruction you give him? – Well, how do I know? – If that means 'Have I reasons?' the answer is: 'my reasons will soon give out. And then I shall act, without reasons'" (*PI*, sec. 211, p. 84). This acknowledgment of the limits of reasons is Wittgenstein's insight into the fundamentally ideological equation, "I know that there is no God but nevertheless I act as if there were." (Cf. Kant, who theorized that apprehension of the sublime required prior education into culture.[38])

What marks Wittgenstein's "acting without reasons" as a form of praxis distinct from arbitrary or irrational behavior is his commitment to the common ground on which our practices rest; this commitment remains firm even in the face of his refusal to fetishize the notion of "reason" or "ground." Moreover, when language is seen as a repository of reflective judgments, all of which have the potential to be enacted, it becomes clear that there is nothing special or mysterious about the "arbitrary" nature of signs, and likewise nothing extraordinary about the "ideological" character of belief. In this respect, Rorty's interpretation of Wittgenstein is right. What a Kantian reading of Wittgenstein nonetheless shows is that language embeds a practical form of reflection based on the contingency of life-forms that cannot be legitimized by anything other than their internal coherence. Our moves within language-games register nothing more or less than the depth of the commitments that we make. Wittgenstein writes: "the difficulty is to realize the groundlessness of our believing."[39] So too with acting, speaking, and other forms of

[37] Wittgenstein, *The Brown Book*, in *The Blue and Brown Books: Preliminary Studies for the Philosophical Investigations* (New York: Harper and Row, 1965), pp. 90–91.
[38] Kant writes: "without the development of moral ideas, that which, thanks to preparatory culture, we call sublime, merely strikes the untutored man as terrifying." Kant goes on to defend the notion of a natural sublime with a grounding in human nature: "the fact that culture is requisite for the judgment upon the sublime in nature . . . does not involve its being an original product of culture and something introduced in a more or less conventional way into society. Rather is it in human nature that its foundations are laid" (*CJ*, sec. 29, p. 116).
[39] Wittgenstein, *On Certainty*, sec.166, p. 24.

praxis. It is precisely this groundlessness – better put, this contingency – that allows subjects to "be themselves," to participate in language-games, and to have a form of life.

Finally, it should be said that one of the self-imposed goals of modernism in philosophy and the arts was precisely this: to refuse everything that artificially or extraneously supports our inherited "forms of life" – including the notions of "support" and "art" and "philosophy" themselves. Not unlike Wittgenstein's later writings, modernism in philosophy and the arts endeavored to reactivate judgments that had become a sedimented part of the "prose of the world." (The critics of modernism might well respond that the contemporary arts accomplish this rejuvenation of judgment at the *expense* of the world.) For the moment, though, it may be enough to see that Wittgenstein's treatment of language-games represents a philosophy of praxis that bears significant debts to the reflective judgment of Kant's third *Critique*. In contrast to orthodox forms of ideology-critique, which are supported by a deep-structure understanding of action and belief, Wittgenstein's analysis makes it clear that we are in no position to determine which elements would constitute the deep-structure "causes" of action and which their superstructure "effects." What philosophy on a Wittgensteinian account can provide – beyond a consciousness of its own limits – is a model of agency in which a cause and its effects stand on a par. Psychologically, Wittgenstein's version of aesthetic reflection yields a form of intentionality that does not rely on a deeper interiority for support.[40]

[40] Charles Altieri makes a related point in *Subjective Agency* (Oxford: Blackwell, 1994).

# 7

❖❖❖❖❖❖❖❖❖❖❖❖❖❖❖❖❖❖❖❖❖❖❖❖❖❖❖❖❖❖❖❖❖❖❖❖❖❖❖❖❖❖❖❖

# Feeling and/as force

❖❖❖❖❖❖❖❖❖❖❖❖❖❖❖❖❖❖❖❖❖❖❖❖❖❖❖❖❖❖❖❖❖❖❖❖❖❖❖❖❖❖❖❖

Passion: the lucidly gathering grip on being.            Martin Heidegger[1]

Throughout the preceding chapters, I have emphasized the need to dissociate the issues raised by Kant's theory of aesthetic reflection from what we have come to recognize as autonomous works of art. That dissociation is necessary in view of the fact that what lies at stake in Kant's third *Critique* is not just the fate of artworks as a class but a particular mode of judgment and its responsiveness to sensuous particulars – to feelings of pleasure and pain – that cannot be reduced to any underlying cause or conceptual scheme. When Nietzsche railed against the logic of causality and similar modes of deep-structure thinking in the sketches that comprise *The Will to Power* (see, e.g., sec. 545 ff.), he was extending a theme from Kant's *Critique of Judgment*, albeit within the context of an attack on the philosophical culture of which Kant was believed to be a part: "cause is a capacity to produce effects that has been super-added to the events," Nietzsche wrote; "interpretation by causality a deception."[2] The process of aesthetic reflection as I have described it so far does not require us to track the causes of aesthetic effects; indeed, it banks on the hope that the very indeterminacy of pleasure and pain with respect to the

---

[1] Martin Heidegger, *Nietzsche I: The Will to Power as Art*, trans. David Farrell Krell (New York and San Francisco: Harper and Row, 1979), p. 48.
[2] Friedrich Nietzsche, *The Will to Power*, ed. Walter Kaufmann, trans. Walter Kaufmann and R. J. Hollingdale (New York: Vintage, 1968), sec. 551, p. 296. (Henceforth cited as *WP*.)

fact-world of cognition and the value-world of morality may deflect our fascination with the notion of cause and that this, in turn, may help reveal something that the apportionment of the world into "facts" and "values" fails to grasp – the force of the feelings that accompany our representations of values and facts.[3] Rather than accept cognition as normative for knowledge and causality as normative for action, aesthetic reflection seeks to model both knowing and acting on affect. What remains to be seen is how affect can indeed count as a form of knowing the world or acting in it, how it can lend validity to the kinds of judgment that Kant called "reflective." How can affect be taken to epitomize judgments that proceed without the benefit of objective measures or external criteria? Nietzsche's "will to power" is nothing if not sure of itself; but how can that certainty be asserted as universally binding? How might it lay claim to the kind of validity for which we would ordinarily require a third-person point of view? To recognize Kant's understanding of affect as a valid form of cognition faces further challenges from competing theories of desire. For many contemporary thinkers, "affect" names either the non-cognitive positivity of the drives that impel human striving or the complex network of negations associated with desire; it is subsumed under either the "negative ontology" of what Lacan names the subject's constitutive "lack" or under the sheer positivity that Kant himself describes as the subject's vital force or "feeling of life."[4] Around these divergent conceptions of affect stand correspondingly contested visions of subjectivity, in which Kant's own notion of desire – generally thought of as idealist and optimistic in its attachment to the principle of freedom – is customarily pitted against psychoanalytic and materialist conceptions of the psyche that raise serious questions about the status of the will as an autonomous and self-determining center of value. While I think it can be shown that Kant's account of feeling and force in the third *Critique* anticipates and even incorporates el-

---

3 See Martin Heidegger, "The Age of the World Picture," in *The Question Concerning Technology and Other Essays*, trans. William Lovitt (New York: Harper and Row, 1977), on representation as an effort to place objects within a fixed "frame" (*Gestell*).

4 Immanuel Kant, *Critique of Judgment*, trans. James Creed Meredith (Oxford: Clarendon Press, 1986), sec. 1, p. 42. (Henceforth cited as *CJ*.) This contrast is taken up in relation to Nietzsche and Lacan by Slavoj Žižek in *The Indivisible Remainder: An Essay on Schelling and Related Matters* (London: Verso, 1996), pp. 132–33.

ements of both these conceptions, my more pressing aim is to suggest that Kant works from a rather different problematic toward a rather different set of concerns. Kant is sympathetic with the "romantic" project to find a place for the subject within the world of experience as a whole; his (romantic) wish is to re-enchant the world, to discover that nature in fact answers to our concerns. (Cf. Eagleton: "The sense that the object makes consists entirely in the sense that it makes for us. This theoretical insight, however, cannot undo our imaginary projections . . . The aesthetic is thus the wan hope, in an increasingly rationalized, secularized, demythologized environment, that ultimate purpose and meaning may not entirely be lost."[5]) But to do so Kant must also regard the subject as more than merely natural. He must reconcile the principles of a materialist psychology with an understanding of purpose that is not reducible to its physiological roots. Kant's "taste of reflection" thus begins in the body but is at constant pains to distinguish itself from the bodily "taste of sense," or from what Nietzsche called the "yes and no of the palate." Kant thus accepts the premise that judgments of taste involve feelings that begin in the body – in the case of pleasure, in a "feeling of life" that seems remarkably close to Nietzsche's "will to power." But he remains nonetheless committed to the idea that beauty can and does point beyond itself, toward moral goodness. Phrased in what are by now familiar terms, Kant hopes that the theory of reflective judgment will bridge the gap between the sensible and supersensible worlds, that it will show that the world of experience is, in the end, one. But as we have already had ample occasion to see, Kant's analysis of aesthetic reflection succeeds only in discovering that the unity of experience cannot be proved. Hence the reliance upon analogy in explaining the linkage of beauty and morality, as in Kant's treatment of hypotyposis in section 59 of the *Critique of Judgment*. (Recall that for Kant "symbolic hypotyposes . . . express concepts without employing a direct intuition for the purpose, but only drawing upon an analogy with one" [*CJ*, sec. 59, p. 223].) But if hypotyposes are not "mere marks" but the expression of relations that do indeed make sense, then the question remains: what kind of sense do they make? Unlike Terry Eagleton, who has seen Kant's reliance upon analogy as standing at the heart of whatever

[5] Terry Eagleton, *The Ideology of the Aesthetic* (Oxford: Blackwell, 1990), p. 88.

is ideological about the third *Critique*,[6] I would suggest that the problem of sense in the third *Critique* reveals Kant's genuine concern to bridge a "romantic" interest in the subject as a center of feeling and force, as capable of recognizing itself in a world that is affectively charged with meaning, with a modernist and even postmodern awareness of the utter contingency of that same world.

There are, no doubt, political consequences that follow from Kant's efforts, though they are not the ones that Eagleton detects. If the transcendental claims Kant makes for judgment support the democratic ambitions that a thinker like Arendt associated with taste,[7] the romantic elements in Kant's account of affect would seem to link him to the antidemocratic tendencies that are generally associated with the Nietzschean will to power – to the idea of a "superman," or of a "rank ordering" in society, or to the notion of a lawgiver-genius who creates nothing less than a world.[8] Similarly, if the appeal to a *sensus communis* made in the

[6] Eagleton: "If the aesthetic yields us no knowledge . . . it proffers us something arguably deeper: the consciousness, beyond all theoretical demonstration, that we are at home in the world because the world is somehow mysteriously designed to suit our capacities. Whether this is actually true or not we cannot say, since we can know nothing of what reality is like in itself. That things are conveniently fashioned for our purposes must remain a hypothesis; but it is the kind of heuristic fiction which permits us a sense of purposiveness, centeredness and significance, and thus one which is of the very essence of the ideological." *Ibid.*, p. 85.

[7] Specifically, in the discussion of taste in Rousseau's *Emile*. See Susan Meld Shell, *The Embodiment of Reason* (Chicago: University of Chicago Press, 1996), pp. 81–87.

[8] For one of Nietzsche's several statements about rank ordering, see *Beyond Good and Evil*, trans. Walter Kaufmann (New York: Vintage, 1989), p. 71. Charles Altieri raises a closely related set of questions about the social consequences of Nietzsche's commitment to the affects in *Subjective Agency* (Oxford: Blackwell, 1994); see especially ch. 4, p. 133. But the matter should not be limited to the antidemocratic implications of Nietzsche's thought. The Nietzschean implications of the social theories of Weber and Scheler are significant. See, for instance, Scheler on the "order of ranks" among value modalities, in "The Sphere of Values," reprinted in *Max Scheler on Feeling, Knowing, and Valuing*, ed. Harold J. Bershady (Chicago: University of Chicago Press, 1992), p. 229. At the same time, Scheler undertakes a substantial critique of Spinoza's conatus that underlies Nietzsche's thought and makes substantial modifications of Nietzsche's theory of resentment. See especially "Negative Feelings and the Destruction of Values: Ressentiment," pp. 116–43. Not at all surprisingly, Kant struggles with the Nietzschean implications of the question of genius. While he respects the "exemplary originality of talent" he also worries about our exposure to mere "apes of genius"; this danger is real insofar as one cannot tell the "true" genius from the fake: "This type, like that of the quack and the charlatan, is very detrimental to progress in scientific and ethical education when he, like the professional or dictator, dogmatizes from the chair of wisdom in the tone of

image of the beautiful reflects an interest in democratic principles of justice, the more powerful feelings associated with the sublime would seem to suggest a mode of self-assertion with little regard for procedural justice or democratic institutions. Whatever the outcome of this dilemma, I want to hold open the possibility for future investigation that the unresolved tensions visible within Kant's third *Critique* have a bearing, directly or indirectly, on the efforts of thinkers from Ralph Waldo Emerson to John Rawls and Stanley Cavell to imagine a specifically *American* form of democracy, i.e., one that would make an accommodation for the "self-reliant" individual within the world of the everyday. Here, the question is: can one reconcile a personal power that would arrogate the force of judgment wholly unto itself with an affinity for the humble, the low, the ordinary, as Emerson suggests?

Before proceeding ahead, however, it is worthwhile to remark that while Nietzsche and Kant both name aesthetics as the field in which judgments based on affect can be attested as true, neither of them limits questions of aesthetics to what we ordinarily think of as works of art. To be sure, Kant's own reflection on the separation of experience into two distinct domains, the phenomenal and the noumenal, introduces the desire for reconciliation by means of a "third term" which one may reasonably associate with works of art.[9] (Recall Kant's claim that while philosophy is divisible into only two parts – the theoretical and the practical – the critical system must have three prongs.[10]) The belief that "beauty" is a feature of autonomous works of art – that artworks are the bearers of such a property – has often been read as a consequence of the Enlightenment's separation of the theoretical and practical domains of experience. But, as Adorno's *Aesthetic Theory* suggests, this does not mean that the problems posed by the theory of reflective judgment are irrelevant to art. On the contrary, some of the most influential strains of "modernist" art (e.g., abstract expressionism in painting) took it as their task to demonstrate that affect is precisely what an adherence to cognitive representations

conviction on matters of religion, politics, and morals, and thus knows how to conceal the paltriness of his mind." Kant, *Anthropology from a Pragmatic Point of View*, trans. Victor Lyle Dowdell (Carbondale: Southern Illinois University Press, 1978), pp. 125–26.
[9] For Habermas, this is the "symbolic" domain.
[10] Kant, *CJ*, Introduction, p. 17.

of the world was bound to suppress.[11] Likewise, they offer models of action that deflect our interest in product and cause – or transform that interest – in order to concentrate instead on the act's style and mode. As but one example, think of the line in Jackson Pollock not as the trace of an intention but as raising the question of the difference between an accidental and a determinate force. If one is tempted to read the line in Pollock as an element of "non-sense," this is indeed because it refuses to trace an intention. Rather than invest in cognitive and moral models that are controlled by representations, hence subservient to "third-person" points of view, the modernist arts tend to concentrate on what Charles Altieri has called the subject's expressive qualities, or perhaps more accurately, the qualities of expressive agency; they attempt to derive their validity from the intensity of these expressions rather than from any external supports. Unlike descriptions or representations, expressions link the "what" of a given articulation with the mode – the "how" – of that articulation, so that, in Altieri's words, "the agent's way of participating in the description becomes the focal concern."[12] The style or mode in which the action is performed thus becomes the principal source of its validity, its "truth."[13] Particularly in their expressivist dimension, the modernist arts confirm Kant's commitment to aesthetic reflection as a mode of judgment whose orientation is subjective rather than objective but which nonetheless claims to be universally valid.

To interpret modernism's ambitions as Kantian at heart is not inconsistent with Adorno's understanding of the "difficulty" that

[11] As Stanley Cavell remarked of Beckett's *Endgame*, modernist works of art feel obliged to dismantle the world they face – not because the world is empty of meaning but rather because it is too full. Cavell, "Ending the Waiting Game: A Reading of Beckett's *Endgame*," in *Must We Mean What We Say?* (Cambridge: Cambridge University Press, 1969), pp. 115–62.
[12] Altieri, *Subjective Agency*, p. 91.
[13] As but one example of the incipient modernism of the third *Critique*, recall Kant's distinction between "beautiful objects" and "beautiful views of objects": "In the latter case taste appears to fasten, not so much on what the imagination grasps in this field, as on the peculiar fancies with which the mind entertains itself as it is being continually stirred by the variety that strikes the eye. It is just as when we watch the changing shapes of the fire or of a rippling brook: neither of which are things of beauty, but they convey a charm to the imagination, because they sustain its free play" (Kant, *CJ*, "General Remark," p. 89.) Insofar as even modernist expressions have a public and material shape, modernism runs a continual risk – that it may impart a misplaced concreteness to what is without a form of its own.

challenges modern art in *Aesthetic Theory*. In modernism, Adorno says, art views its very existence as the central issue, as something that can no longer be taken for granted. Recall Adorno's words from the opening of *Aesthetic Theory*, which we have already had occasion to cite: "Everything about art has become problematic: its inner life, its relation to society, even its right to exist."[14] Modernist works are built around the awareness that there is no general set of criteria that "art" is obliged to meet; as Kant already saw, the essence of art cannot be gathered from rules but must be disclosed in performance and practice. Art, Kant says, must itself furnish the rule in the process of its enactment ("the rule must be gathered from the performance" [*CJ*, sec. 47, p. 171]). Modernist works temper this romantic notion with the awareness that nothing whatsoever stands behind them, that they, as surfaces, have renounced the illusionism of depth. This is one reason why modernist works of art stand in such a precarious relationship with what we ordinarily think of as the "world," and especially with the representational (and ideological) frames through which the world is known.[15] For Adorno, however, modernism involves something still more complex than the brute rejection of "frame," "support," or "apparatus." Adorno proposes that modernism's relationship to "world," hence to "truth," is better described in terms of a logic of identity and difference according to which art both *is* and *is not* a part of the rational-real; art *is* and *is not* a participant in the structures of ideology that mediate our relationship to the world of objects, if only because art both *is* and *is not* a (mere) thing: "what art does is revoke the violence done by rationality by emancipating rationality from its confinement in empirical life where it is apparently chained to a given material, i.e. nature" (*AT*, p. 201). On the one hand, Adorno agrees that the task of art is to set itself apart from everything that exists in the world: "there is nothing in art that does not derive from the world; and yet all that thus enters art is transformed. Therefore

---

[14] Theodor Adorno, *Aesthetic Theory*, ed. Gretel Adorno and Rolf Tiedemann, trans. C. Lenhardt (London: Routledge and Kegan Paul, 1984), p. 1. (Henceforth cited as *AT*.)

[15] Jay M. Bernstein suggests that the critical power associated with modernist works of art stems from an awareness of what they are unable to disclose: "their failure to reveal a world, or to reveal only what is already known, their lack of cognitive power, their exclusion from questions of truth, is the source of their power, their negative cognition." *The Fate of Art* (University Park: Pennsylvania State University Press, 1992), p. 134.

ment" to the romantic ideology from which the later Nietzsche struggled – some would say unsuccessfully – to clear free.

To think of art as the source of a vital connection to the "living thing" in a world of dead letters and inert signs was an understandably alluring attraction in the aftermath of the Enlightenment's fascination with cognitive models that presented knowing as a form of representing.[21] The romantic commitment to knowledge as force and feeling is, of course, consistent with the desire for an "organic" form of creativity that critics since at least Kant have identified with the powers of the genius. Indeed, at least one recent thinker has made the case – not implausibly – that the closely related problem of generation, of the emergence of a rational, spiritual existence out of dead matter, is in fact a central issue in the third *Critique*: "The question of the possibility of generation, or the apparent, and apparently absurd, emergence of life and reason out of 'dead matter' or 'unreason' is a seminal expression of the problem raised by our contingency as individuals and as a species, and of our consequently ineluctable concern to discover how it is we come to find ourselves in the world . . . The overall strategy of the third *Critique* is to accept the ineluctability of this concern (with what threatens to dissolve the mind/ matter boundary) as itself defining."[22] For those inclined to emphasize Kant's romantic side, the genius is nothing less than the subject's appropriation of nature's creative force; if nature is defined in terms of its fundamental "conformity to law," then genius is nature subjectivized, or humanized, insofar as it is itself the source of laws. Endowed with a secular form of "grace," Kant's genius is, like Shelley's poet, a potential lawgiver or "unacknowledged legislator of the world."[23] In the language of Coleridge's *Statesman's Manual*, the genius yields precisely what Kant expected beauty to provide, or what Emerson hoped the circles of nature might show: "the translucence of the special in the individual, or of the general in the special, or of the universal in the

---

[21] The literature on this topic is now massive. Among the most important are Heidegger's essay "The Age of the World Picture" and Richard Rorty's *Philosophy and the Mirror of Nature* (Princeton: Princeton University Press, 1979).

[22] Shell, *The Embodiment of Reason*, p. 190. Cf. Cavell on genius and generation in *Conditions Handsome and Unhandsome* (Chicago: University of Chicago Press, 1990).

[23] Percy Bysshe Shelley, "The Defence of Poetry," in Donald Reiman and Sharon Powers, eds., *Shelley's Poetry and Prose* (New York: Norton, 1977).

general; above all . . . the translucence of the eternal in and through the temporal."[24]

Contemporary critical theory itself stands in a surprisingly ambivalent relationship to the notion of creative force that informs the romantic myth. On the one hand, most recent criticism has been quite suspicious of any effort to represent creative activity as fueled by nature's own originary force. Indeed, key figures of contemporary criticism like Paul de Man and Harold Bloom struggled to define their critical positions against romantic attachments to the power of the creatively inspired genius. Hence de Man's insistence that his fascination with the blindness that underlies every moment of creative insight was indeed part of a project of ideology critique;[25] hence Bloom's various accounts of the modern writer's agonistic relations with his forebears. And yet contemporary criticism, no less than contemporary art, seems unable or unwilling to divest itself of the notion of a self-acting and -authenticating force. As Richard Rorty pointed out, the titans of modern thought, Nietzsche above all, continued to stage themselves in more or less Kantian-romantic terms, as powerful enough to establish the criteria by which they would themselves be judged. (Cf. Jackson Pollock's famous remark: "I am nature."[26]) Hence the unexpected affinities between the Kantian "genius," the Rortian "ironist," and, not least, the Bloomean "strong poet/artist." (Nietzsche once again shows the antidemocratic implications of such views: "A people is nature's detour to arrive at six or seven great men – and then to get around them."[27]) The result is a substantial blurring of the line between the "naive" and "ironic" versions of romanticism, which contemporary criticism wishes otherwise to keep apart.[28] Says Rorty, "the generic task of the ironist is the one Coleridge recommended to the great and original poet: to create the taste by which he will himself be

[24] Samuel Taylor Coleridge, *The Statesman's Manual* (New York: Harper and Bros., 1875), p. 438, as cited in Paul de Man, *Blindness and Insight*, 2nd edn. (Minneapolis: University of Minnesota Press, 1983), p. 192.

[25] Michael Sprinker, *Imaginary Relations* (London: Verso: 1987).

[26] Pollock is reported to have made this assertion in a conversation with Lee Krasner.

[27] Nietzsche, *Beyond Good and Evil*, sec. 126, in *The Portable Nietzsche*, trans. and ed. Walter Kaufmann (Harmondsworth: Penguin Books, 1976), p. 444.

[28] Cf. Jean-Luc Nancy and Philippe Lacoue-Labarthe's pregnant remark: "Romanticism is our naiveté." *The Literary Absolute*, trans. Philip Barnard and Cheryl Lester (New York: State University of New York Press, 1988), p. 17.

judged. But the judge the ironist has in mind is himself. He wants to be able to sum up his life in his own terms. The perfect life will be one which closes in the assurance that the last of his final vocabularies, at least, really was wholly *his*."[29]

To be sure, modernism is not inconsistent with a Nietzschean valorization of force. This is because "will to power" is not the name of anything that inherently structures the self, but is instead what "deep-structure" theories about the self seem unable to grasp – the subject as constituted by the intensity of its expressions, as the consequence of an ongoing pleasure generated by the very drives and desires that impel it, including the desires that would impel it to reject the kind of self-consciousness associated with the project of a philosophical "critique." But the modernist preoccupations that have their roots in Kant's third *Critique* were at the same time part of an effort to gain a reflective claim over the language of passion, purpose, and power that the Bloomean band of "strong poets" claimed as a discovery of their own. Indeed, philosophy's increasing self-consciousness about the limitations of its own powers and scope as witnessed, e.g., in the writings of Wittgenstein, Heidegger, and Derrida, would seem to demand an alternative both to relatively unreflective versions of what Nietzsche understood the "will to power" to mean and to the refusals of Nietzsche that thinkers like Habermas and MacIntyre have proposed as part of their respective critiques of Enlightenment thought. My aim here is to suggest that while Kant's theory of aesthetic reflection may not have solved these problems – indeed, that the very idea of a "solution" might well force the will to submit to external controls – Kant's interest in feeling as the basis of judgment nonetheless provides a compelling point of departure for just such an alternative. If Nietzsche's "will to power" can help remind us that Kant's theory of judgment is an attempt to regain confidence in the truth of the affects, Kant can help us understand Nietzsche's "will to power" as needing a grammar of reflection in order to lay full claim to the title of truth. For even Nietzsche was forced to recognize that the will must pit itself against the force of another will if it is to validate itself as true.[30] This much follows from Nietzsche's understanding of

---

[29] Rorty, *Contingency, Irony, and Solidarity* (Cambridge: Cambridge University Press, 1989), p. 97.
[30] See Altieri's discussion of Nietzsche in *Subjective Agency*, p. 133.

force itself. In Heidegger's words, "what lives is exposed to other forces, but in such a way that, striving against them, it deals with them according to their form and rhythm, in order to estimate them in relation to possible incorporation or elimination" (*Nietzsche I: The Will to Power as Art*, p. 212).

I want to pursue the question of the validity of feeling and force, ultimately with an eye to investigating their claims to judgment, by recalling the Nietzschean moments in Kant's discussion of the "feeling of life" (*Lebensgefühl*) that stands at the root of the analysis of pleasure in the third *Critique*, and move from there to suggest why Kant's analysis of affect in the analytic of the beautiful found itself obliged to enter the more complex territory of the sublime. To begin, recall that Kant identifies the "feeling of life" as the physiological basis of the affective apprehensions that accompany our cognitive and moral representations of the world. Indeed, this "feeling of life" is identified as early as section 1 of the *Critique of Judgment* as the "determining ground" for claims of taste; it is the very basis of our feelings of pleasure and, by contrast, of pain. Pleasure, for its part, derives from the continuation of a healthy physiological state; displeasure (pain) results from the conversion of such a state into its opposite.[31] Accordingly the "free play" of sensations is a source of pleasure because, on Kant's account, it promotes a "feeling of health" (*CJ*, sec. 54, p. 197). If we should linger over the beautiful in extended contemplation, this is because such contemplation is itself a force that enhances life, a power that "strengthens and reproduces itself" (*CJ*, sec. 12, p. 64). Heidegger's volume on Nietzsche, *The Will to Power as Art*, seeks to correct the misunderstanding – allegedly precipitated by Kant – that aesthetics is a matter of pure, disinterested pleasure and argues instead that art is epitomized by the force of enthusiasm or "rapture" (*Rauch*).[32] As far as the beautiful is concerned, Kant may indeed strive to exclude all interested modes of pleasure, but he remains unswervingly committed to the idea that feeling is anchored in the organism,

---

[31] *CJ*, sec. 10, p. 61. Pleasure is not only a form of self-preservation but of the enhancement of life. For Aristotle this would be called "flourishing."

[32] This excess of feeling no doubt belongs to the Kantian sublime, but cf. Kant's remark that enthusiasm is the idea of the good to which affection has been superadded (*CJ*, "General Remark," p. 124).

that it begins in its attachment to the body, and is bent on the furtherance of life.[33] Aesthetic pleasure is thus linked to the purposiveness of life itself, which seeks at bottom to perpetuate itself.

Although Kant ultimately aims to distinguish his account of reflective judgment as resting on "transcendental" principles from the physiological understanding of taste advanced by his predecessor, Edmund Burke, the basis of Kant's aesthetics remains far more closely wedded to physiology than is generally supposed. Consider the numerous instances in which Kant appeals to Epicurus to argue that the sensuously grounded *Lebensgefühl* forms the basis for judgments of taste. Citing Epicurus, Kant approvingly notes that while gratification and pain may proceed from the imagination or even from representations of the understanding, these are always in the last resort corporeal, "since apart from any feeling of the bodily organ life would be merely a consciousness of one's existence, and could not include any feeling of well-being or the reverse, i.e. of the hindrance of the vital forces" (*CJ*, "General Remark," p. 131). As Kant goes on to say in a passage with strong debts to empirical psychology, "the mind is all life (the life-principle itself), and hindrance or furtherance has to be sought outside it, and yet in the man himself, consequently in the connection with his body" (*CJ*, "General Remark," p. 131).

At the same time, Kant admits that physiology can only explain how we *do* in fact judge, not how we *ought* to judge (*CJ*, "General Remark," p. 132).[34] For this Kant needs to explain the generation of transcendental principles (mind) from physiology

---

[33] Eagleton's *The Ideology of the Aesthetic* sustains this view, though with a suspicious eye toward the political uses of the discourse on the body.

[34] Indeed, one of the central tasks of the third *Critique* is to establish that claims of taste originating in the body can indeed be asserted as valid – that they can have the force of certainty that would make them necessary for others to accept, thus command universal assent. Kant: "In this modality of aesthetic judgments, namely their assumed necessity, lies what is for the *Critique of Judgment* a moment of capital importance. For this is exactly what makes *a priori* principle apparent in their case, and lifts them out of the sphere of empirical psychology, in which otherwise they would remain buried amid the feelings of gratification and pain (only with the senseless epithet of finer feeling), so as to place them, and, thanks to them, to place the faculty of judgment itself, in the class of judgments of which the basis of an *a priori* principle is the distinguishing feature and, thus distinguished, to introduce them into transcendental philosophy" (*CJ*, sec. 29, p. 117).

(nature); he must find a way to shift from empirical psychology to the *a priori* principles of reflection: "were taste not in possession of *a priori* principles," he writes, "it could not possibly sit in judgment upon the judgments of others, and pass sentence of commendation or condemnation upon them, with even the least semblance of authority" (*CJ*, "General Remark," p. 132).[35] But in part because Kant admits that he cannot provide a derivation for these a priori principles, his arguments in the third *Critique* resort to analogy in order to make a transition between the two realms of experience possible. The unity of experience turns on analogy, which performs the work of judgment. Analogy is Kant's "solution" to the problem of reflective judgment; it functions as judgment, allowing Kant to link the otherwise separate domains of feeling and thought. Consider Kant's somewhat extended analysis of the pleasure that is associated with laughter as but one example of the primacy of analogy in this mode of thought. Suggesting that there must be a "sympathetic association" between the bodily organs and thoughts in the mind, Kant describes the pleasure we feel when we laugh in the following terms:

it is readily intelligible how the sudden act . . . of shifting the mind now to one standpoint and now to the other, to enable it to contemplate its object, may involve a corresponding and reciprocal straining and slackening of the elastic parts of our intestines, which communicates itself to the diaphragm (and resembles that felt by ticklish people), in the course of which the lungs expel the air with rapidly succeeding interruptions, resulting in a movement conducive to health. This alone, and not what goes on in the mind, is the proper cause of the gratification in a thought that at bottom represents nothing. (*CJ*, sec. 54, p. 201)[36]

If laughter describes the pleasure that is associated with a thought that "represents nothing," i.e. which does not depend upon the existence of the object of our attention, then what can be said of pleasures that are conditional or contingent, as in the case of pleasures that are consequent upon a prior moment of suffering

[35] Likewise, Kant concedes to Epicurus that gratification is animal but goes on to say that the spiritual feeling of respect for moral ideas does not suffer as a consequence (*CJ*, sec. 54, p. 202).
[36] Consider also Kant's remarks about the verbal analogies that treat states of mind as if they were themselves affective modes of being – e.g., thoughts *"that split the head"* or *"that break your neck"* or feelings *"that harrow the heart"* (*CJ*, sec. 54, pp. 201–02).

or pain?[37] Do such pleasures respond to physiological experiences or to prior reflections? What, moreover, would the validity of such feelings be? Since Kant's account of the beautiful does not quite say that the affects are themselves forms of judgment, he finds himself obliged to make some crucial modifications to his theory of reflection in his analysis of the sublime. In the "Analytic of the Sublime" Kant concedes that emotion originates in physiological motion, and suggests that we welcome such motion "in the interests of good health" (*CJ*, "General Remark," p. 126). We can thus assume that the sublime aspires to whatever certainty the emotions themselves would entitle us to claim. But since the feeling of health associated with the beautiful is essentially unreflective, much in the way a drive is unreflective in seeking to perpetuate itself, he goes on to explain how the sublime is substantially more complex and self-conscious, how it involves more than mere emotion. The question is how the more complex sublime can claim universal validity: "Beautiful nature contains countless things as to which we at once take every one as in their judgment concurring with our own, and as to which we may further expect this concurrence without facts finding us far astray. But in respect of our judgment upon the sublime in nature we cannot so easily vouch for ready acceptance by others."[38] Unlike the beautiful, which is driven by the refusal or renunciation of interest, the sublime seems to *contravene* the interest of sense. The sublime springs from opposing forces. Citing Burke's account (and significantly anticipating Hegel's description of the play of opposing forces in the analysis of "force and understanding" in the *Phenomenology of Spirit*), Kant suggests that the sublime results not from a blend of pleasure and pain but from the dynamic interplay of these opposing forces (*CJ*, sec. 27, p. 106): "'the feeling of the sublime is grounded on the impulse towards self-preservation and fear, i.e. on a pain, which, since it does not go the length of disordering the bodily parts, calls forth movements which, as they

---

[37] For Nietzsche, this is not a special case: "Why is all activity, even that of a sense, associated with pleasure? Because before it is an obstacle, a burden existed? Or rather because all doing is an overcoming, a becoming master, and increases the feeling of power?" (*WP*, sec. 661, p. 349).

[38] *CJ*, sec. 29, p. 115. Kant's own answer to the question is that "a far higher degree of culture, not merely of the aesthetic judgment, but also of the faculties of cognition which lie at its basis, seems to be requisite to enable us to lay down a judgment upon this high distinction of natural objects" (*ibid.*).

clear the vessels, whether fine or gross, of a dangerous and troublesome encumbrance, are capable of producing delight; not pleasure but a sort of delightful horror, a sort of tranquility tinged with terror'" (Burke, *Philosophical Investigations as to the Origins of the Beautiful and the Sublime*, as cited by Kant, *CJ*, "General Remark," pp. 130–31). Unlike the beautiful, the sublime is a "strenuous" affect (*animus strenuus*), which is to say that its purpose is to overcome forces of great resistance (*CJ*, "General Remark," p. 125). Moreover, the sublime involves something like an internal judgment upon or immanent critique of feelings that in the beautiful would go uncontested or unchecked. Kant says that the pleasure of the sublime results from "the feeling of a momentary check to the vital forces followed at once by a discharge all the more powerful" (*CJ*, sec. 23, p. 91).

If Kant's initial definition of the sublime is that which is "absolutely great" (*CJ*, sec. 25, p. 94), hence not measurable in terms of pre-existing criteria, he goes on to qualify the sublime in nature as a response to "might," where "might" names a power that is superior to great hindrances (*CJ*, sec. 28, p. 109).[39] Moreover, Kant's linkage of the sublime to the categories of dominion and might can help suggest why this feeling can exact adherence to laws that are not physical, i.e., why it can oblige the subject to act "in accordance with a law *other* than that of its empirical determination" ("General Remark," p. 120; emphasis mine). Since no object of nature can be "absolutely great," the sublime must be found outside nature. It refers us to the ideals of reason, the greatest of which for Kant is the moral law.[40] Thus the sublime is not just about superiority but a distinctively *moral* superiority: "that, too, which we call sublime in external nature, or even in internal nature (e.g. certain affections) is only represented as a might of the mind enabling it to overcome this or that hindrance of sensibility by means of moral principles, and it is from this that it derives its interest" (*CJ*, "General Remark," p. 124).

In the sublime, Kant moves from a theory of the subject as lying at the crux of the phenomenal and noumenal worlds to an understanding of subjectivity as constructed in fearful response to a law that is imagined as standing beyond empirical terms. What is the

[39] Kant adds that it is termed "dominion" if it is also superior to the resistance of that which itself possesses might (*CJ*, sec. 28, p. 109).
[40] See Bernstein, *The Fate of Art*, p. 38, on this subject.

subject's relationship to such a law? In the sublime, Kant says, the subject "feels the sacrifice or deprivation, as well as its cause, to which it is subjected" (CJ, "General Remark," p. 120). The experience of the sublime is one of a pleasurable privation insofar as in it the imagination willingly deprives itself of its freedom:

delight in the sublime in nature is only *negative* (whereas that in the beautiful is *positive*): that is to say it is a feeling of imagination by its own act depriving itself of its freedom by receiving a final determination in accordance with a law other than that of its empirical employment. In this way it gains an extension and a might greater than that which it sacrifices. But the ground of this is concealed from it, and in its place it *feels* the sacrifice or deprivation, as well as its cause, to which it is subjected.

(CJ, "General Remark," p. 120)

Indeed, Kant's account of the sublime elevates this moment of sacrifice to the level of a moral achievement, arguing that it is through such a feeling that one best gains a sense of respect for the (moral) law as such: "the feeling of our incapacity to attain to an idea *that is a law for us*, is respect" (CJ sec. 27, p. 105).[41] Since the experience of the sublime provokes reason to feel temporarily inadequate, Kant suggests that the moral law is made known to us in the sublime through the experience of insufficiency and, moreover, that moral goodness *must* be represented as sublime:

The object of a pure and unconditioned delight is the moral law in the might which it exerts in us over all antecedent motives of the mind. Now, since it is only through sacrifices that this might makes itself known to us aesthetically . . . it follows that the delight, looked at from the aesthetic side (in reference to sensibility) is negative, i.e. opposed to this interest, but from the intellectual side, positive and bound up with an interest. Hence it follows that the intellectual and intrinsically final (moral) good, estimated aesthetically, instead of being represented as beautiful, must rather be represented as sublime, with the result that it arouses more a feeling of respect (which disdains charm) than of love or of the heart being drawn towards it.      (CJ, "General Remark," pp. 123–24)

The question nonetheless remains how it is that the subject derives pleasure (and not unadulterated suffering or pain) from this experience. Recall that for Kant even humility can be counted as potentially sublime insofar as it involves the voluntary submission to pain: "even humility . . . is a sublime temper of the

---

[41] Note that in the *Critique of Practical Reason* Kant attempts an a priori derivation of the feeling of respect from universal moral concepts.

mind voluntarily to undergo the pain of remorse as a means of more and more effectually eradicating its cause" (*CJ*, sec. 28, p. 114). But what specifically is the pleasure that attaches to feelings that Nietzsche would identify as part of the "slave morality"? What is the pleasure that allows for and even rewards our submission to the (moral) law? One answer, which also helps locate the Kantian sublime within the more encompassing drama of self-conscious reflection, is that this pain is tolerated because it is not in fact real pain, its fear not real fear, or not the fear of anything real.[42] The experience of the sublime is in fact premised upon the underlying belief that we will be held safe, on a tacit agreement that underlies our willing suspension of disbelief. Indeed, Kant himself says that we agree to submit ourselves to the terrifying experience of the sublime only because we know in advance that we will be protected from any physical harm. Remember, the fear of the sublime is a false fear; its risk is buffered by the prior knowledge that all will be well:

The astonishment amounting almost to terror, the awe and thrill of devout feeling, that takes hold of one when gazing upon the prospect of mountains ascending to heaven, deep ravines and torrents raging there, deep-shadowed solitudes that invite to brooding melancholy, and the like – all this, when we are assured of our own safety, is not actual fear. Rather is it an attempt to gain access to it through imagination, for the purpose of feeling the might of this faculty in combining the movement of the mind thereby aroused with its serenity, and of thus being superior to internal and, therefore, to external, nature, so far as the latter can have any bearing upon our feeling of well-being.

(*CJ*, "General Remark," p. 121)

What confidence justifies such risk? Kant's answer to this question, which refers centrally to the role of "culture," suggests nothing less than the existence of a set of background beliefs akin to what Marxism would count as "ideology," where ideology functions as the all but transparent screen that allows us to suspend disbelief:

without the development of moral ideas, that which, thanks to preparatory culture, we call sublime, merely strikes the untutored man as terrifying. He will see in the evidences which the ravages of nature give of her

---

[42] For a discussion of Nietzsche, Foucault, and Althusser (among others) on subjection, see Judith Butler, *The Psychic Life of Power* (Stanford, CA: Stanford University Press, 1997).

dominion, and in the vast scale of her might, compared with which his own is diminished to insignificance, only the misery, peril, and distress that would compass the man who was thrown to its mercy. So the simple-minded, and, for the most part, intelligent, Savoyard peasant . . . unhesitatingly called all lovers of snow-mountains fools . . . Culture is requisite for the judgment upon the sublime (more than for that upon the beautiful).[43]

Indeed, Kant's reliance on "culture" is no doubt the reason why some Marxist critics (e.g. Terry Eagleton) have detected an element of "bad faith" in his account of the sublime. But even readers substantially more sympathetic to Kant's third *Critique* like Jay Bernstein have suspected that the dynamic of the sublime is that of a struggle for recognition whose ultimate purpose is to confirm the mastery of the Master: "Kant's account of the sublime is the *parergon* of the life and death battle for pure recognition . . . is the Master's moment, the moment when self-consciousness is affirmed in its transcendence of sensible being while the heteronomy of reason, the other *in* self-consciousness, reason as the voice of the other in the subject, is refused . . . This play of recognition and non-recognition exactly duplicates the master's recognition and non-recognition of the slave. The experience of the sublime is that of the approach of the other, where the framing of the scene and the interplay between reason and imagination in it reveal that other to be the human other" (*The Fate of Art*, p. 176). To rephrase this matter in different terms: while the sublime is a "strenuous affect" that proves the greatness of human beings as moral agents, it risks sacrificing that greatness to another (e.g., Lacan's "big Other"), such that the drama of recognition may be foreclosed. The experience of the sublime thus stands as potential confirmation of Horkheimer and Adorno's reading of Sadean morality in *Dialectic of Enlightenment* no less than of Lacan's rapprochement of Kant and Sade.

If the sublime suggests that subjectivity, even in its strongest affective moments, may be constructed through subjection, then it is not surprising to find that some of the most interesting efforts in philosophy after Kant have attempted to preserve the experi-

---

[43] *CJ*, sec. 29, pp. 115–16. Kant reasons that culture is thus what saves us from utter humiliation, "even though as mortal men we have to submit to external violence" (p. 111).

ence of alterity that is transmitted in the sublime – the strangeness
that incites reflective judgment – while reducing its alliance with
the play of mastery. It is with precisely such a project that the
work of Heidegger and Wittgenstein can be aligned. The question
is whether a reduction of the sublime is not also doomed to bar
affect from playing any role at all in the construction of the world.
In *Being and Time*, for instance, Heidegger associates "everydayness" with "that state of mind which consists of a pallid lack of
mood."[44] Heidegger nonetheless clarifies that neither "everydayness" nor "lack of mood" are affectless states. On the contrary, he
explains that their effect is rather one of an expenditure of affect,
its dispersion in the world: "in everydayness *Dasein* can undergo
dull suffering, sink away in the dullness of it, and evade it by
seeking new ways in which its dispersion in its affairs may be
further dispersed" (*Being and Time*, p. 422.). This drama of affect is
no longer "metaphysical" in that it does not acknowledge the
judgment or authority of a superior force; it recognizes that the
forces of avoidance and resistance are functions of the subject
itself, forces by which the subject paradoxically consents to be
bound.[45] So too with Wittgenstein's appeal to a range of concepts
laden with everydayness, such as "language-game," "practice,"
and "form of life." In reading the later Wittgenstein, it can be
tempting to think that "practice" is designed to settle the difference between the phenomenal and noumenal worlds; but Wittgenstein's understanding of language as a form of practice can
better be read as a trace of that irreparable division, hence as
occupying the very realm that Kant understood to be held by
affect. Wittgensteinian "practice" may be aligned conceptually
with action but it is strictly non-teleological (end-less), just as
Kant conceptualizes aesthetic production to be. "Practice" is,

---

[44] Heidegger, *Being and Time*, trans. John Macquarrie and Edward Robinson (New
York: Harper and Row, 1962), p. 422.

[45] Eagleton likewise reads this as part of a Marxist allegory: "The subject for Kant,
then, is everywhere free and everywhere in chains; and it is not difficult to
decipher the social logic of this contradiction. In class society, the subject's
exercise of freedom is not only characteristically at the expense of others'
oppression, but is gathered up into an anonymous, subjectless process of cause
and effect which will finally come to confront the subject itself with all the dread
weight of a fatality or 'second nature' ... In such conditions, freedom is bound to
appear at once as the essence of subjectivity and as utterly unfathomable as the
dynamic of history which is nowhere locatable in the material world" (*Ideology
of the Aesthetic*, pp. 79–80).

moreover, uniquely responsive to what limits action, to what the subject undergoes, hence to passion. Wittgenstein: "What has to be accepted, the given, is – so one could say – forms of life."[46] Likewise it is tempting to read Wittgenstein's *Tractatus* as pointing to a range of experiences that are "mystical" insofar as they are beyond language, or are ineffable, as measuring something great, perhaps even sublime. But what the Wittgenstein of the *Tractatus* insists must remain in "silence" can be better understood as a region of non-sense that points to the limits of sense (meaning) – i.e. points to sense as constructed by an encounter with its limit. (Wittgenstein: "What we cannot speak about we must pass over in silence."[47]) If one is inclined to read the *Philosophical Investigations* as reconciling us with the everyday, or as returning us to an everyday world that is reconciled with itself, then perhaps the most important caveat to add is that the *Investigations* also show us everything that is strange and contingent about the everyday. A Wittgensteinian example: "when I say that the orders 'Bring me sugar' and 'Bring me milk' make sense, but not the combination 'Milk me sugar,' that does not mean that the utterance of this combination of words has no effect."

Wittgenstein's *Philosophical Investigations* are relentless in their insistence on a matter that was central to Kant's aesthetics: the negotiation that takes place between the experiential and rational meanings of "sense." Wittgenstein insists that "the meaning of a word is not the experience one has in hearing or saying it" (*PI*, II, p. 181), and likewise that "'seeing as . . . ' is not a part of perception" (*PI*, II, p. 197). This process of negotiation between the two senses of "sense" takes place within the range of practices that Wittgenstein characterizes as "forms of life." What these practices share is their solicitation from us of a grammar – a set of interlocking correspondences or linkages – rather than a hermeneutics that would pretend to answer questions about what a given locution would *mean*. In part what Wittgenstein wants to say is that the "meaning" of a move within a language-game can

46 Ludwig Wittgenstein, *Philosophical Investigations*, trans. G. E. M. Anscombe (New York: Macmillan, 1953), sec. 498, p. 138. Henceforth cited as *PI*. (I cite the *Philosophical Investigations*, part 1, according to section number and page; I cite part 2 by referencing part and page.)
47 Wittgenstein, *Tractatus Logico-Philosophicus*, trans. D. F. Pears and B. F. McGuinness (London: Routledge, 1961).

only be told by its consequences, certainly not by its causes; meaning can be understood as a matter of "performative effects."

But rather than conclude by looking further at the question of meaning in Wittgenstein as a matter of performance (a topic that has been amply discussed in studies that address Wittgenstein's relationship to "ordinary language philosophy," and especially to J. L. Austin[48]), I want instead to comment on Nietzsche's role in the development of a grammar of judgment based on affective force. In order to do so I turn back to Nietzsche's effort to displace "truth" by "force" and to incorporate "force" within the larger critique of the concept of "cause," the better to grasp Nietzsche's desire to rescue the appearing world. Insofar as Nietzsche's overarching concern was indeed to save the appearing world, to provide instruction in "yea-saying," I take it that his valorization of force can be located as an affirmative moment in the project of an aesthetic critique.

The notes that comprise *The Will to Power* are supremely conscious of the claims of force as valid representations of truth. Where truth is measured by force, validity is a question of the intensity of effects: "'True' from the standpoint of feeling – : that which excites the feeling most strongly" (*WP*, sec. 533, p. 280). But this means that Nietzsche must dissociate the notion of force qua *Lebensgefühl* from that of cause. Consider his response to skeptical claims: "'No matter how strongly a thing may be believed, strength of belief is no criterion of truth.' But what is truth? Perhaps a kind of belief that has become a condition of life? In that case, to be sure, strength would be a criterion; e.g., in regard to causality" (*WP*, sec. 532, p. 289). Consider as well his deconstruction of "cause" as the effect of a compulsion that is added to the notion of force:

When we do something there arises a feeling of force [*Kraftgefühl*], often even before the deed, occasioned by the idea of what is to be done (as at the sight of an enemy or an obstacle to which we feel ourselves equal): it is always an accompanying feeling. We instinctively think that this feeling of force is the cause of the action, that it is "the force." Our belief in causality is belief in force and its effect; a transference from our experience; and we identify force and the feeling of force. – Force, however,

---

[48] See, for example, Cavell, "Austin at Criticism," in *Must We Mean What We Say?*, pp. 97–114.

never moves things; the force we feel "does not set the muscles in motion" . . . Causality is created only by thinking compulsion into the process. (*WP*, sec. 664, p. 350)

Nietzsche's project remains in many ways the same as Kant's, namely, to "complete" the physical notion of a force, to preserve intentionality without a corresponding commitment to interiority.[49] In Nietzsche's case, this meant associating "force" with what he perhaps inaptly described as an "inner will" (the will to power) – inapt because Nietzsche's force never loses its association with the processes of physiological expression that mark the organism's striving: "The victorious concept of force, by means of which our physicists have created God and the world, still needs to be completed: an inner will must be ascribed to it, which I designate as 'will to power'" (*WP*, sec. 619, pp. 332–33). Not unlike Kant's sublime, the will to power is obliged to try and test itself against forces of great magnitudes. Yet Nietzsche's force not only enacts but also suffers a judgment that makes no higher appeal than to the body, which is to say, to itself: "to start from the body and employ it as a guide. It is the much richer phenomenon, which allows of clearer observation" (*WP*, sec. 532, p. 289).

In so saying Nietzsche anticipates the aesthetic criteria that the more heroic strains of modernism would impose upon themselves. His condemnation of everything that is mannered or false is likewise pregnant with modernist ambitions: "overabundant development of intermediary forms; atrophy of tropes; traditions break off, schools [*sic*]; the overlordship of the instincts (prepared philosophically: the unconscious *worth more*) affect the will power, the willing of end *and* means, has been weakened" (*WP*, sec. 74, p. 48). What Nietzsche could not wholly shed was the romanticism to which these heroic views remained attached – the privileging of the language of tone as "purer" than that of words (see *WP*, sec. 809), the fascination with intoxication as an enhanced state of mind, the revulsion against imitation, and the corresponding hope for a re-enchantment of the world, for the making of it new, to be achieved ideally by art: "Compared with music all communication by words is shameless; words dilute and brutalize; words depersonalize; words make the uncommon common" (*WP*, sec. 810, p. 428).

[49] See Altieri, *Subjective Agency*.

By seeing Nietzsche as the inheritor of such concerns it may also become clear why the alternatives facing criticism today are falsely understood as involving a choice between faith in the validity of "transcendental judgment" that is said to characterize Kant and what Habermas has described as the "irrationalism" of Nietzsche's aesthetic critique. On the contrary, the Nietzsche of the *Will to Power* is heir to Kant of the third *Critique*. Both are drawn equally to a romantic hope in the power of human passion to fill the world with a purposiveness it has lost and to the modernist awareness that the world is ultimately no more determinate than our passionate investments in it. In spite of what Horkheimer and Adorno are taken to have said in "The Concept of Enlightenment," both Nietzsche and Kant represent consequences of Enlightenment thought.

# Index